2614

The Once & Future Church

CONTRIBUTORS:

William W. Bassett
Paul M. Boyle, C.P.
Francis Dvornik
James Hennesey, S.J.
William K. Leahy
John E. Lynch, C.S.P.
Richard P. McBrien
Frederick R. McManus
Robert E. McNally, S.J.

alba house alba house - DIVISION OF THE SOCIETY OF ST. PAUL STATEN ISLAND, N.Y. 10314

The Once & Future Church

: A Communion of Freedom

BX
1802
.O5

Studies on Unity & Collegiality in the Church

Editor

James A. Coriden

Nihil Obstat:
    Austin B. Vaughan, S.T.D.
    Censor Librorum

Imprimatur:
    Joseph P. O'Brien, S.T.D.
    Vicar General, Archdiocese of New York
    February 16, 1971

The nihil obstat and imprimatur are official declarations that a book or pamphlet is free of doctrinal or moral error. No implication is contained therein that those who have granted the nihil obstat and imprimatur agree with the contents, opinions or statements expressed.

ISBN: 0-8189-0203-5

Library of Congress Catalog Card Number 73-158568

Designed, printed and bound in the U.S.A. by the Pauline Fathers and Brothers of the Society of St. Paul, 2187 Victory Blvd., Staten Island, N.Y. 10314 as part of their communications apostolate.

Copyright 1971 by the Society of St. Paul, 2187 Victory Blvd., Staten Island, N.Y. 10314.

TABLE OF CONTENTS

INTRODUCTION

The Second Vatican Council was a pastoral event. Perhaps none of its principles will have more of a pastoral impact than the concept of collegiality. This doctrine can refashion the countenance of the Church.

When the Second Vatican Council spoke of collegiality, the Fathers referred only to the bishops of the world. Together with their head, the Bishop of Rome, the Episcopal College has a genuine responsibility for the Church throughout the world. Collegiality is the name given to this common episcopal responsibility and the correlative group authority of the bishops.

In a different sense but equally real manner the principle of shared responsibility applies to all organs and individuals in the Church. Together they *are* the Church, the People of God, and they have a genuine shared responsibility for the Church throughout the world.

One clear correlative of collegiality is the principle of subsidiarity. Decentralization is a common human desire. All peoples wish to make decisions on those things which affect them. The principle of subsidiarity simply recognizes as policy the responsibility for decisions being made, by individuals or groups, at the lowest possible level consistent with the welfare of the entire organization.

We readily assume that what we know has always been that way. Children, for example, can hardly visualize a society without electricity, telephone or radio. This tendency is particularly apparent in matters connected with the sacred.

In the Church, authority has known a variety of forms and functions. Authority is subsidiary to the intrinsic purpose of Christian self-determination and the freedom of sons of God. Christian leadership is to be pastoral and ministerial.

This book does not discuss decentralization on a pragmatic level. It is not a study of the desirability of implementing collegiality. Rather the chapters analyze the theological and historical foundations for the doctrine. The Church is collegial in its nature, and hence, its manner of governing must be collegial. This book is a call to collegiality, to a restoration of responsibilities.

The historical papers are impressive in their concatenation of citations of collegial action in the early Church. Some of the examples of due process in the early Church point curious fingers at our current procedure of one person being legislator, administrator and judge.

Frequently discussions about collegiality or subsidiarity are overlaid with a rhetoric which gives the impression that this is the key to the parousia. Proponents or practitioners of subsidiarity can sound as though they advocate absolute autonomy and complete independence.

The process of decentralization is not merely difficult, it contains the seeds of many dangers. Unity can be weakened and thus endangered. Unity in any organization or organism implies some degree of centrality.

The interrelation between unity and collegiality is impressively highlighted in this book. Attitudes and unwritten conventions are as integral an element in organizational cohesiveness as are formal structures. Structures of collegiality and forms of subsidiarity must be accompanied by an informed awareness of unity and by conventions of Christian collaboration.

Because of its scholarly balance this book will prove helpful to those who advocate the concept of collegiality and to those who seek to implement the principle of subsidiarity. In some places the strong stress on unity and centrality will give pause to oratory about collegiality. Hardworking administrators, likewise, will be jarred to read that their efforts may be at odds with the Gospel and crippling to the Church. For both these pages should be salutary.

Americans have a penchant for the pragmatic. Today we are challenged to discover new ways in which we may put into practice the principles of subsidiarity and collegiality. This book should prove a helpful stimulus to many in the American Church.

Paul M. Boyle, C.P.

EDITOR'S PREFACE

The sub-title of this book is descriptive of the Church. The expression, "a communion of freedom," is rooted in the ancient concept of *communio ecclesiarum,* the fraternity of the local communities of faith. It takes its inspiration from that "communion" in the body and blood of Christ which is shared at the table of the Lord. Admission to the eucharistic banquet in the early Church was the clear and distinctive sign that a person truly belonged to and held the faith of the local community. Analogously, *communio* was used to describe the relationship between the churches—commonness of faith, mutual recognition, reciprocity of membership—in short, the kinds of interchange which were the measure of unity in the Church.

The communion of the churches did not mean their uniformity. It was the expression of their mutual acceptance and fundamental unity of faith and discipline. But to say that local assemblies were "in communion" did not imply that they were identical, similarly governed, or that there was a formal structural relation among them. It was a communion in freedom. Local differences, regional practices, and community autonomy were respected, prized, and safeguarded. In other words, the concept of "communion" bridged the gap between the need for unity in the Church and the desire for self-direction and adaptation in the local churches. A "communion of freedom" can be the answer to the problem of unity and subsidiarity in today's Church.

Subsidiarity is a key issue on all levels of Church life:

a) in the tension between papal authority and the national conferences of bishops (or national pastoral councils);

b) in the delicate balance between the adoption of policies at a national conference and the independence of the diocesan bishop;

c) in the relationship between "The Chancery" and local pastors;

d) in the interplay between lay initiatives and the parish clergy;

e) in the struggle between the leadership of religious communities and the new satellite small-group-living experiments.

And the great project of reuniting the Christian Churches is placed in an entirely different focus by a true appreciation of the notion of subsidiarity.

Who will make the decision? Where is the authority? How "far up" must the matter be referred? To what extent can the local group regulate itself? These are the age-old questions of subsidiary function. They are central to the present renewal of the Church.

In order to come to grips with the problem of decentralization in the Church one must reflect on these issues:

—— the doctrine of collegiality;

—— the principle of subsidiarity;

—— the synodal tradition in the Church;

—— the historical process of centralization;

—— the failure of subsidiary function;

—— the authority of episcopal conferences;

—— the role of papal diplomats.

The studies in this book are addressed to these issues. They were written in preparation for the 1969 Synod of Bishops because the chief subject of that meeting was the relationship between Rome and the national conferences of bishops. Our authors examine diverse facets of the problem of subsidiarity from the viewpoint of their own expertise.

Richard McBrien gives the post-conciliar "state of the question" on the doctrine of collegiality. He surveys the theological literature of the past ten years and organizes his analysis around the critical issues involved in the episcopal collegiality/papal primacy tension.

William Bassett writes of the principle of subsidiarity and the need to restore it in the Church. He explores the history and rationale of the world organization of the Catholic Church and the changes in the direction of freedom indicated by the Second Vatican Council. He concludes with a telling list of practical recommendations.

In the strong historical section of the book, Francis Dvornik begins with a vivid description of the synodal structure of the early Church. He shows that the pattern of local conciliar action was firm and widespread (from Spain to Persia, from Gaul to Africa) in the fourth and fifth centuries only to decline and nearly disappear in the Middle Ages.

John E. Lynch traces the movement toward centralization of ecclesial authority from the post-apostolic period to the fifteenth century. "In the interests of unity, if not uniformity, the papacy in the course of history exerted an increasing control over the local churches by concentrating a number of administrative, legislative, and judicial functions in its own hands."

Robert McNally, employing the illustrative method rather than the survey, gives the case of Martin Luther as an example of a local problem too quickly catapulted to Rome. The issue was magnified and intensified out of all due proportion because of inept handling and inadequate procedures. A prompt assertion of regional responsibility could have produced a vastly different result.

Returning to the post - Vatican II period, Frederick McManus provides a complete and accurate analysis of the authority of national conferences of bishops. He outlines the debate and the decisions of the Ecumenical Council on this question and places the result in the context of the historical development of the episcopal conference in the United States.

James Hennesey examines one of the key elements in the centralization problem: papal diplomacy. He describes both the secular (Vatican to civil government) and ecclesiastical (pope to local church) roles of the diplomatic corps, the origins out of which those functions grew, and their questionable appropriateness today. His reminders of the historical American reactions to Vatican legates are of particular interest.

These studies were commissioned for a symposium on "Unity and Subsidiarity in the Church" which took place just before the Synod of 1969.[1] The participants in that meeting framed a statement of consensus directed to the Synod delegates.[2] That statement is included here both because of its theological content and because several of the practical recommendations it contains were enacted at the Synod of Bishops. Its final urgings regarding areas of local decision-making remain issues of the highest importance today.

William Leahy has provided a valuable appendix to this book. It is a compilation of the references to episcopal conferences in the conciliar (and certain post-conciliar) documents. These ordered citations should prove helpful to students of the Church.

Our special gratitude goes to the Canon Law Society of America, the University of Dayton, and the John XXIII

---

1. The meeting took place on September 12-14, 1969, at Bergamo, the John XXIII Center for Renewal, Dayton, Ohio. It was the fifth in a series of interdisciplinary and ecumenical symposia on questions of church order sponsored by the Canon Law Society of America. The preceding studies were published as follows: *Law for Liberty: The Role of Law in the Church Today*, ed. James Biechler, Helicon, Baltimore, 1967; *We, The People of God . . . : A Study of Constitutional Government for the Church*, ed. James Coriden, Our Sunday Visitor, Huntington, 1968; *The Bond of Marriage: An Ecumenical and Interdisciplinary Study*, ed., William Bassett, University of Notre Dame Press, 1968; *The Case for Freedom: Human Rights in the Church*, ed. James Coriden, Corpus, Washington, 1969.

2. The names of the symposium participants are appended to the consensus statement, p. 275.

Center for Renewal who co-sponsored the symposium, to Our Sunday Visitor, Inc., whose financial contribution helped make it possible, and to those many wise and kindly counsellors who provided the ideas and encouragement for the project.

May these studies assist us, under the Spirit's guidance, to rebuild the Church we love into a true communion of freedom.

James A. Coriden

COLLEGIALITY: STATE OF THE QUESTION

By Richard P. McBrien

Collegiality is not a single theological question; it is a cluster of questions. Is the Church essentially collegial in structure? Is there evidence of collegiality in the period of its biblical origins? Was there an apostolic college? Did Peter have a unique place and function within this college? Is the episcopal college the successor of the apostolic college? Has supreme power for governing the universal Church been conferred on the pope? Has supreme power for governing the universal Church been conferred on the episcopal college? What is the relationship between the papal primacy and the episcopate? Are there two subjects of power, or only one? How should this collegial relationship be realized in practice?

The first five questions do not readily provoke controversy in Catholic theology today, except insofar as they are

1

linked with the rest, and particularly the question concerning the relationship between the primacy and the episcopacy. Indeed, the heart of the discussion is there, although not its totality.

At the beginning of the decade and before the council, Karl Rahner wrote that "the theology of the relation between the papal primacy and the episcopate is undoubtedly one part of ecclesiology which has yet to find its final form."[1] Considerable progress has been achieved since that time, but in certain important respects, Rahner's judgment remains valid even today. Clearly we have not yet created a juridical or pastoral situation in the Church at large which satisfactorily and faithfully embodies the best theological findings and insights produced by the combined scholarship of this decade alone. Secondly, Rahner's own reflections on the episcopacy and the primacy, offered in a tentative and hypothetical manner (indeed, as one in a series of *questiones disputatae*), have not yet been surpassed or modified substantially. Finally, the papal-episcopal relationship itself admits of no final and absolute formulation. There is reason now to suggest that the theology of collegiality in the wider sense (i.e., embracing the canonical and pastoral implications) will always pursue a flexible and accommodating course in response to this radically insoluble, because mysterious, dialectic within the Church's structure.

Nevertheless, some lines of development do seem clear: certain opinions hesitantly or sketchily proposed earlier in the decade are now generally accepted, and other opinions

1. *The Episcopate and the Primacy* (with J. Ratzinger), New York, 1962, p. 64.

presented at the same time with considerably less reserve and restraint are now generally rejected.

This chapter offers an interpretative survey of the literature surrounding these questions, with particular emphasis on the papal-episcopal interrelationship. But the survey is not without its own conscious limitations. It proposes only a state of the question, not a history.[2] It is concerned principally with the discussion as it has taken root and developed within the past decade. This is not an arbitrary limitation, for it embraces the period of greatest literary production, including, of course, the exchanges prompted by the Second Vatican Council and the writing of its central *Dogmatic Constitution on the Church*. In the decade preceding Vatican II, much of the work touching directly on the question

---

2. A most useful collection of historically-oriented essays is provided by *La collégialité épiscopale. Histoire et théologie* (Unam Sanctam, 52; introduction by Y. Congar), Paris, 1965. An earlier volume in the same series contains additional historical materials and interpretation, *L'épiscopate et l'église universelle* (Unam Sanctam, 39; edited by Y. Congar and B. Dupuy), Paris, 1962. The historical discussion centering on the First Vatican Council is presented in four articles in this latter volume: G. Dejaifve, "Primauté et collégialité au Premier Concile du Vatican"; W. Dewan, " 'Potestas vere episcopalis' au premier Concile du Vatican"; G. Thils, " 'Potestas ordinaria' "; and O. Rousseau, "La vraie valeur de l'épiscopat dans l'Eglise d'après d'importants documents de 1875," pp. 639-736. Cf. also J.-P. Torrell, *La théologie de l'épiscopat au premier Concile du Vatican* (Unam Sanctam, 37), Paris, 1962. The period between the Council of Trent and Vatican I is covered in H. Jedin, "Zur Theologie des Episcopates vom Tridentinum bis zum Vatican I," *Trierer Theologische Zeitschrift* 74 (1965) 176-181, and in G. Alberigo, *Lo sviluppo della dottrina sui poteri nella chiesa universale. Momenti essenziali tra il XVI e il XIX secolo*, Freiburg, 1964. A portion of this study has been published in *La collégialité épiscopale*, "La collégialité épiscopale selon quelques théologiens de la papauté," pp. 183-221. The most recent addition to the conciliarist controversy, particularly as it applies to the Council of Constance and the doctrines enunciated at Vatican I, is F. Oakley's *Council over Pope?*, New York, 1969.

of collegiality was biblical, historical, and liturgical in character, and many of these studies were not brought together, in readily accessible form, until the very eve of the council.[3] The dogmatic and speculative aspects of the question emerged with fullest force only during the conciliar years. The opponents of collegiality perceived the theological and canonical implications at once, and the ensuing debate was at times severe. It seems now to have waned almost completely since the council's adjournment, at least at the academic level, but the issues are still sharply joined at the procedural and the pastoral levels.

The survey is also limited by its preoccupation with Catholic theological literature. There are several references to Orthodox, Anglican, and Protestant contributions, but these are provided for the sake of clarifying the debate as it has developed in Catholic theology.[4] Since the heart of the col-

---

3. E.g., *L'évêque dans l'église du Christ* (edited by H. Bouëssé and A. Mandouze), Bruges, 1963, and the Congar-Dupuy volume, *L'épiscopate et l'église universelle,* already cited.

4. See, for example, A. Schmemann, "La notion de primauté dans l'écclésiologie orthodoxe," in N. Afanasieff, *La primauté de Pierre dans l'église orthodox,* Neuchâtel, 1960; P. L'Huillier, "Collégialité et primauté. Réflexions d'un Orthodoxe sur les problèmes historiques," in *La collégialité épiscopale,* pp. 331-344; and J. Panagopolous, "An Orthodox Study of Ministerial Office," *Journal of Ecumenical Studies* 4 (1967) 27-46. An Anglican point of view is presented by D. W. Allen and A. M. Allchin, "Primauté et collégialité. Un point du vue anglican," *La collégialité épiscopale,* pp. 371-390; cf. also Allchin's essay, "Collégialité et papauté dans le rapport final de la Conférence de Lambeth en 1968," *Irénikon* 41 (1968) 443-7. (The first article is available in translation in *Journal of Ecumenical Studies* 2 (1965) 63-80, with the title, "Primacy and Collegiality: An Anglican View.") For a Calvinist opinion, cf. F. J. Leenhardt, "Les fonctions constitutives de l'église et l'épiscopat selon le Nouveau Testament," *Revue d'histoire et de philosophie religieuses* 47 (1967) 111-149, and A. Ganoczy's commentary, "La structure collégiale de l'Eglise chez Calvin et au IIe Concile du Vatican," in *La collégialité épiscopale,* pp. 345-369.

legiality problem has to do with the relationship between pope and bishops, the major burden of the discussion has been carried principally by Catholics.

Thirdly, the survey is directly concerned with the dogmatic and speculative aspects of the question, rather than the biblical, the historical, the liturgical, or the canonical. This limitation, however, is one of emphasis rather than of total exclusion. But there has been no attempt to amass an exhaustive bibliographical arsenal.

Finally, I do not offer any detailed and critical analyses of the conciliar teaching on collegiality. Almost all of the theological participants in the discussion have been, and still are, in conscious dialogue with *Lumen Gentium*. The conciliar point of view, therefore, is always of interest insofar as it is a reflection, positively or negatively, of the discussion in current and recent Catholic theology. But the concern of this survey is with theological rather than magisterial literature.

A word also on method. In a work which proposes to offer a survey of contemporary literature, one can organize his material around the principal participants in the discussion, or around the issues to which they have addressed themselves. I have chosen the second method. The issues are these: (1) In what sense and with what justification can it be said that the episcopal college is the successor of the apostolic college? (2) Has supreme power for governing the universal Church been conferred upon the Pope, and what is the nature of this primacy? (3) What is the theological basis for episcopal collegiality? (4) What is the relationship between the papal primacy and the episcopacy? In the manner of an ecclesiastical procession, the most important question is reserved until last.

THE EPISCOPAL COLLEGE AND THE APOSTOLIC COLLEGE

J. Ratzinger has argued that the doctrine of episcopal collegiality is based on two historical facts: the collegial character of the apostolic office and the collegial character of the ecclesiastical office in the ancient Church.[5] One can deduce the collegial character of the apostolic office from the number of disciples Jesus selected to fill it. The eschatological symbolism is clear: the *twelve* apostles are a sign of the new Israel which will be the fulfillment of the promises of God in history.[6] Indeed, when Judas's place in the group was left vacant, Matthias was promptly elected in order to maintain the symbolism of "the Twelve." With the addition of Paul, however, the apostolic office assumed a new function: testimony to the Resurrection (Acts 1:22).[7]

Ratzinger is critical of the usual syllogistic argument for episcopal collegiality: the apostolic office was collegial; bishops are the successors of the apostles; therefore, their office must be collegial, too. "By itself (the syllogism) is insufficient to support this doctrine because the decisive realities of the Church are not a matter of conclusions but of his-

5. "The Pastoral Implications of Episcopal Collegiality," *Concilium* vol. 1, no. 1 (January, 1965) 20-34.

6. Cf. G. Klein, *Die zwölf Apostel,* Göttingen, 1961; K. H. Rengstorf, "απόστολος," *Theological Dictionary of the New Testament* (G. Kittel, ed.), Grand Rapids, 1965, vol. I, pp. 424-443; K. H. Schelkle and H. Bacht, "Apostel," *Lexikon für Theologie und Kirche,* I, 734-8, and A. Vögtle, "Zwölf," *Ibid.,* X, 1443-5; and A. Javierre, "Apostle," *Sacramentum Mundi,* I, 77-79.

7. For further studies on the idea of collegiality in the New Testament, see D. M. Stanley, "The New Testament Basis for the Concept of Collegiality," *Theological Studies* 25 (1964) 197-216; J. Lécuyer, *Etudes sur la collégialité épiscopale,* Lyons, 1964; and M. J. LeGuillou, "La parallélisme entre le Collège apostolique et le Collège épiscopal," *Istina* 10 (1964) 103-110.

torical facts. This syllogism has value only insofar as it is an explanation of the historical development of the ecclesiastical office in the ancient Church."[8]

In these earliest years, the Christian community developed on a local basis. These local churches were not simply administrative units in a larger corporate apparatus, but rather living cells containing the whole mystery of the one body of the Church. Within these local churches there existed a close bond among bishops, presbyters and deacons, and the community as a whole, and this fraternal relationship was a principal basis for the apostolicity of each community. There were also important links among the various local churches: bishop with bishop, community with community. It was clear, from the earliest liturgical testimony (e.g., the consecration of a bishop by several other bishops rather than one only), that the individual bishop could have his episcopacy in no other way than in communion with the other bishops. And this is what catholicity means. The history of the Catholic Church has been, in large measure, preoccupied with the tasks of balancing one value against the other, of preserving the integrity of the local Church (apostolicity) without diminishing the reality of the Church universal (catholicity).

Before the third century, these relationships within and among the local churches were described in such evangelical terms as *fraternitas.*[9] *Ordo* and *corpus* were also used, but *collegium* as such was not. "This variety of concepts," Ratzinger notes, "is significant because it shows the insufficiency of the categories offered by Roman law and contem-

8. *Art. cit.,* p. 22.
9. Cf. Ratzinger's own essay, "Fraternité," in *Dictionnaire de spiritualité,* V, 1, 1143-49.

porary philosophy to express adequately the reality of the communal character of the episcopal office." [10] Indeed, this is a judgment which recurs throughout the decade of discussion on collegiality. In the final accounting, the papal-episcopal relationship does not admit of legal or philosophical categorization. One distorts the collegial principle and suppresses the collegial mystery when he defines them by the standards of Roman law, scholastic philosophy, or any other time-conditioned way of apprehending and circumscribing reality. It is clearly the consensus of contemporary Catholic theology that the relationship must be defined in terms of the Church's essence rather than on the basis of extraneous systems of thought.

Certain legalistic developments between the third and fifth centuries tended to alter the original balance between apostolicity and catholicity, fraternity and communion. The term "brother" is now reserved for one's fellow bishop alone, and the word *collegium* replaces *fraternitas* to express episcopal solidarity. Ratzinger places heavy emphasis on these terminological changes because, in his view, "collegiality can unfold its full pastoral fruitfulness only when it is related back to the fundamental reality of those who through 'the First-born of the Father' become brothers."[11]

THE PAPAL PRIMACY IN THE CHURCH

The tendency to exaggerate the place and function of the pope in the Church has had its source in certain canonical writings as well as in the works of theologians strongly

10. "The Pastoral Implications...," p. 23.
11. *Ibid.*, p. 24.

influenced by a canonical perspective. Thus, J. Beyer once suggested that the pope should assume to an even greater extent the responsibility which the bishops had been exercising in their dioceses,[12] and W. Bertrams has argued that the pope alone has full power over the Church, to such an extent that he is not bound, by dogmatico-juridical necessity, to share the government of the Church with the bishops.[13] The one theologian to whom Bertrams appeals is F. Gagnebet, who has explicitly rejected the classic position of J. Bolgeni (1732-1803).[14] Bolgeni's views on episcopal collegiality have proved closer to the teaching of the Second Vatican Council than Gagnebet's.[15]

Bertrams' concern for the prerogatives of the pope has been embodied in the *Nota explicativa praevia* of *Lumen Gentium,* which J. Ratzinger has analyzed at some length.[16] While the canonico-juridical orientation espoused by the minority opposition at the Second Vatican Council continues to hold the allegiance of an influential group of office-holders and others within the Catholic Church, it does not enjoy any support at all among the principal participants in the *theological* discussion. Karl Rahner states the relevant principle as succinctly as possible: ". . . the primacy of the pope is a primacy *within* and not *vis-a-vis* this college."[17]

---

12. Cited by S. Ryan, "Episcopal Consecration: Trent to Vatican II," *Irish Theological Quarterly* 33 (1966) 149, n. 63.

13. *The Papacy, the Episcopacy, and Collegiality,* Westminster, 1964, p. 139.

14. See Gagnebet's article, "L'origine de la jurisdiction collégiale du corps épiscopal au concile selon Bolgeni," *Divinitas* 5 (1961) 431-493.

15. Cf. Bolgeni's works, *Fatti dommatici* and *L'episcopato ossia della potestà di governar la Chiesa,* Rome, 1788.

16. Cf. *Commentary on the Documents of Vatican II* (H. Vorgrimler, ed.), New York, 1967, vol. I, pp. 297-305.

17. *The Episcopate and the Primacy,* p. 77.

Ontologically and juridically, the apostolic college and Peter
as its head comprise one entity. The Church, therefore, is a
community which is "ruled by *college*, without its head
thereby becoming the mere elected representative of the
college; the head truly rules the college, without the college
thereby becoming his mere executive organ." The relationship, needless to say, "cannot be reduced to legal terms."[18]
While it is true that the college of bishops always includes
the pope as its head, without whom it would not exist at all,
it is also equally true that "the pope, precisely when he acts
ex sese, acts not as a private person but as pope, that is, as
head of a college of bishops *iuris divini*."[19] Rahner fully rejects the tacit assumption made by theologians and canonists
in the past; namely, that the infallibility of the pope, when
he defines "alone," is completely distinct and independent
from the infallibility of the college of bishops.

Ratzinger's view of the papacy within the larger context
of collegiality is similar to Rahner's. "The primacy," he
argues, "cannot be patterned on the model of an absolute
monarchy as if the pope were the unrestricted monarch of a
centrally constituted supernatural State called Church; but
it means that within the network of the Churches communicating and thus forming the Church of God there is
one official point, the *Sedes Romana*, by which the unity of
faith and communion must be orientated."[20] This means that
the pope has the faculty and the right to decide authoritatively, within the network of communication, where the
Word of the Lord is witnessed correctly, and, consequently,
where there is true communion. For the pope, as successor

18. *Ibid.*, pp. 79-80.
19. *Ibid.*, p. 87.
20. "The Pastoral Implications...," p. 25.

of Peter, shares in Peter's function; to be the principal witness of the Resurrection. He has the special office of "the
Rock," which, like the expression "the Twelve," is taken from
the eschatological symbolism of Israel. Therefore, the papal
office is not simply the result of human need or purpose but
exists because the Lord himself established it. The primacy
of the Bishop of Rome, however, is not opposed—in its
original meaning—to the collegial character of the Church
but is "a primacy of communion in the midst of the Church
living as a community and understanding itself as such. . . .
It presupposes the *communio ecclesiarum* and can be understood correctly only in reference to it."[21]

Hans Küng's discussion of the Petrine office in the
Church manifests an abiding concern to redress the theological and canonical imbalances of the post-Vatican I era.[22]
Papal primacy, he insists, is by no means an arbitrary absolutism, even in the view of the First Vatican Council.[23] The
power of the pope is neither absolute, arbitrary, nor without limits. It is limited by Christ, by the apostles and their
successors, and by both natural and divine law. More con-
cretely, papal primacy is limited by the existence of the
episcopate, which the pope can neither abolish nor dissolve
as regards its position or its rights; by the ordinary exercise
of office by the bishops (since he cannot intervene in the
daily exercise of office by the bishops); by the ultimate purpose of the Petrine office, which is the edification and unity
of the whole Church; and by the manner of the papal exer-

21. *Idem.* Cf. also J. McCue, "The Roman Primacy in the Second
Council and the Problem of the Development of Dogma," *Theological
Studies* 25 (1964) 161-196.

22. *The Church*, New York, 1967, pp. 444-480.

23. Cf. note 2, above.

cise of office, i.e., it must not be arbitrary, inopportune, or exaggerated, but must be dictated by the needs and welfare of the Church. Küng adds the principle of subsidiarity, enunciated by Pope Pius XI in *Quadragesimo Anno,* which he interprets in this way: as much freedom as possible, curtailed only as much as necessary.[24] The Petrine primacy is always a pastoral primacy—a primacy of service, not domination.

THE EPISCOPAL COLLEGE WITHIN THE CHURCH

Although a unanimity of opinion exists regarding the *fact* of collegiality, there is no general agreement among theologians regarding the ultimate *basis* for the episcopal college. However, no contemporary theologian has been satisfied with the argument that the episcopal college exists simply by a free act of Christ. More specific reasons have been proposed by various theologians: collegiality is a deduction from the doctrine and practice of *communio;*[25] the

24. *Op. cit.,* p. 449.

25. Cf. the following contributions of Y. Congar: "De la communion des Eglises à une ecclésiologie de l'Eglise universelle," in *L'épiscopate et l'Eglise universelle,* pp. 227-260; his "Conclusion" to the volume *Le Concile et les conciles,* Chevetogne-Paris, 1959, pp. 301ff.; his "Introduction," to *Vraie et Fausse réforme dans l'Eglise* (Unam Sanctam, 20), Paris, 1950; the section on *Sobornost* in *Jalons pour une théologie du laïcat* (Unam Sanctam, 23), Paris, 1954 (revised edition, 1964), pp. 380-386 (this material does not appear in the English translation); "Confession, Eglise, et Communion," *Irénikon* 23 (1950) 3-36; and "Notes sur le destin de l'idée de collégialité épiscopale en Occident au Moyen Age (VIIe – XVIe siècles)," in *La collégialité épiscopale,* pp. 99-129. Congar's perspective is faithfully reflected in the work of his disciple, J. Hamer, *The Church is a Communion,* New York, 1964. Cf. also Hamer's "Note sur la collégialité épiscopale," *Revue des sciences philosophiques et théologiques* 44 (1960) 45-50. Cf. also L. Hertling, *Communio: Chiesa e Papato nell'antichità cristiana,* Rome, 1961, and "Communio und Primat: Kirche und Papsttum in der christlichen Antike," *Una Sancta* 17 (1962) 91-125.

episcopal college parallels the apostolic college;[26] collegiality developed as the bishops of the early Church began to sense the unity that existed among them;[27] the proclamation of the Word demands many witnesses working together;[28] collegiality is disclosed by the liturgical practice of the early Church,[29] or, by—what Rahner calls "the decisive consideration"—the existence of general councils.[30] No single explanation is sufficient in itself, and the adoption of one does not exclude the possibility of accepting one, or two, or several of the others. But while it is difficult to determine which explanation is decisive or most adequate, it seems that various historical and liturgical studies have already made several items clear: (1) the mission of the bishop is collegial, not individual; (2) *potestas ordinis* and *potestas iurisdictionis* are basically one; and (3) bishops have the fullness of the sacrament of Order.[31] An earlier view had so separated order

26. In addition to the works by Stanley, Lécuyer, and LeGuillou, already cited in note 7, cf. B. Botte, "La collégialité dans le NT et chez les Pères Apostoliques," in *Le Concile et les conciles*, pp. 1-18. The parallel between the apostolic and episcopal colleges has been drawn by J. Ratzinger, "The Pastoral Implications . . . ," and by several others.

27. See, for example, J. Coulson, *L'épiscopat catholique. Collégialité et primauté dans les trois premiers siècles de l'Eglise*, Paris, 1963; J. Lécuyer, "Collégialité épiscopale selon les papes du Ve siècle," *La collégialité épiscopale*, pp. 41-57; J. McCue, "Bishops, Presbyters, and Priests in Ignatius of Antioch," *Theological Studies* 28 (1967) 828-834; and S. Ryan, "Episcopal Consecration: The Fullness of the Sacrament of Order," *Irish Theological Quarterly* 32 (1965) 295-324.

28. H. Schauf, *De Corpore Christi Mystico*, Freiburg, 1959, pp. 298-310.

29. In addition to the items mentioned in notes 27 and 28 above, see J. Lécuyer, "La prière d'ordination de l'évêque. Le pontifical romain et la 'Tradition Apostolique' d'Hippolyte," *Nouvelle revue théologique* 89 (1967) 601-606.

30. *Commentary on the Documents of Vatican II*, p. 197.

31. Cf. S. Ryan, *art. cit.*, n. 28, above.

from jurisdiction, for example, that the bishop was distinguished from the priest simply by reason of his power to ordain and to confirm. The discovery of evidence that priests were able to ordain in the Middle Ages, however, did much to undercut this earlier assumption. Other narrow views on the episcopacy were set aside by the Second Vatican Council.[32]

The separation of the *potestas ordinis* from the *potestas iurisdictionis* has made collegiality, in the minds of those who adhered rigidly to this distinction, a matter of moral value alone. Collegiality, in this view, means only that the bishops should feel a common bond with other bishops in the exercise of the Church's mission, and that all the bishops in turn should share the universal concern of the pope who alone must bear the burden of total leadership. J. Ratzinger,[33] K. Mörsdorf,[34] S. Ryan,[35] and others have indicated that such a distinction, created in the twelfth century, has been at the basis of the shift from a sacramental to a juridical understanding of episcopal collegiality. Canonists and historians have tended to agree with this judgment.[36]

The sacramental, as opposed to the juridical, understanding of collegiality rests in large part on the biblical, patristic,

32. Cf., for example, J. Beyer's view that the episcopate is not a sacramental office but merely an office of jurisdiction. "Nature et position du sacerdoce," *Nouvelle revue théologique* 86 (1954) 356-73, 469-80.

33. "The Pastoral Implications . . . ," pp. 27-29.

34. "Bishop: IV. Canon Law," *Sacramentum Mundi*, vol. I, pp. 230-2; "Weihegewalt und Hirtengewalt im Abgrenzung und Bezug," in *Miscelanea Comillas* 16 (1951) 95-110; and "Die Entwicklung der Zweigliedrigheit der Hierarchie," *Münchener Theologische Zeitschrift* 3 (1952) 1-16.

35. *Art. cit.*, n. 28, above.

36. Cf. G. D'Ercole, "Research Notes on Episcopal Collegiality," *Concilium*, vol. 1, no. 4 (January, 1968) 74-79; and B. Tierney, "Collegiality in the Middle Ages," *Concilium* vol. 7 no. 1 (September, 1965) 4-8.

and theological notion of *communio*. Collegiality, according to Y. Congar and his disciple, J. Hamer, means a unity of faith and sacrament coalescing around the bishop and his priests, as well as the brotherhood of local communities among themselves.[37] G. Dejaifve similarly insists that the ministry of the Apostles, as instituted by Christ, prolongs the very mission of Christ insofar as he is the founder of a community of salvation. The principal concern is always the growth and unity of the Body of Christ. This apostolic ministry, whether we are speaking of a function or of a power, is in reality one and undivided. The function is the building up of the Church as sacrament of salvation, and therefore the power is always unified around this single purpose. Although the mission and the power are one, they are exercised by a plurality of subjects. Why the plurality? Because the Twelve are meant to be a sign of the new Israel, sent into the whole pluralistic world. The unity of this apostolic college is insured interiorly by the Holy Spirit and mutual love, and exteriorly by Peter, who receives the mission to strengthen the brethren (Lk 22:32) and therefore to insure unity in the mission of the Church as such. The relationship between pope and bishops must be one of reciprocity, reflecting the *communio* within which this episcopal college has been set.[38]

37. Congar ties the notion of collegiality very closely to the Russian idea of *Sobornost*. See n. 25, above. Cf. also R. Murray, "Collegiality, Infallibility, and Sobernost," *One in Christ* (1965) 19-42, and G. Dejaifve, "Sobornost ou papauté," *Nouvelle revue théologique* 84 (1952) 355-371, 466-484.

38. "Peut-on concilier le collège épiscopal et la primauté?" in *La collégialité épiscopale*, pp. 289-303. Cf. also his "Les douze Apôtres et leur unité dans la tradition catholique," *Ephemerides Theologicae Lovanienses* 39 (1963) 760-778; "Episcopal Collegiality According to *Lumen Gentium*," *Lumen Vitae* 20 (1966) 637ff.; "Le 'Magna Charta' de Vatican II," *Nouvelle revue théologique* 87 (1965) 3-22; and "Der Erste unter den Bischöfen," *Theologie und Glaube* 51 (1961) 1-21.

The collegial relationship does not admit of a juridically precise formulation because it is rooted in the mystery of the Church as a *communio* in the Spirit.[39]

PRIMACY AND EPISCOPACY

"Today we risk seeing Christians split into two groups," Cardinal Jean Daniélou wrote recently in the *Osservatore Romano*,[40] "those who make the authority of bishops spring from the pontiff, and those who make the authority of the pontiff spring from the bishops." Daniélou rejects this contrast as doing damage to the interests of both parties: the pope and the bishops alike. His own concern seems to be clearly on the side of preserving the traditional authority of the papacy in the Church: "But if what is meant by collegiality is a change in the structure of the Church, limiting the sovereign exercise of the authority of the sovereign pontiff and placing him under the episcopal college, then it is clear that this concept would be unacceptable. . . . The existence of a strongly organised central power is, today more than ever, a need of the Church. In effect, it is the only thing

39. For further discussion of episcopal collegiality, cf. also J. Ratzinger, *The Episcopate and the Primacy*, pp. 75-92, and "Zur Theologie des Konzils," in *Catholica* 15 (1961) 292-304; S. Ryan, "Episcopal Consecration: The Legacy of the Schoolmen," *Irish Theological Quarterly* 33 (1966) 3-38, "Episcopal Consecration: Trent to Vatican II," *Ibid.*, 133-150, and "Vatican II: The Re-Discovery of the Episcopate," *Ibid.*, 208-241; J. Lécuyer, "Orientations prèsents de la théologie de l'épiscopat," in *L'épiscopat et l'Eglise universelle*, pp. 781-811; P. Rusch, "Die kollegiale Strucktur des Bishofsamtes," *Zeitschrift für Katholische Theologie* 86 (1964) 257-285; and M. J. LeGuillou, "L'unité de l'Eglise: Eucharistie, collégialité, primauté," *Istina* 12 (1967) 361-374.

40. Cited in *The Tablet* 223 (19 July 1969) 724.

that allows legitimate differences to be expressed without a danger to unity."

If Rahner, Ratzinger, Congar, Küng, and all the other theologians who have addressed themselves over the past decade to the issue of collegiality are correct in their judgments, the imbalance has been toward an exaggeration of the papal primacy and a corresponding diminution of episcopal authority within the Church. Rahner isolates several earlier views which were the explicit or implicit basis of opposition to the doctrine of collegiality. He rejects these views and replaces them with the following theological principles: (1) The pope is not an absolute monarch in the political sense. (2) The episcopate exists always by divine right. (3) The papal primacy juridically constitutes the Church only when conjoined with this episcopate. (4) Bishops have episcopal power distinct from the pope's, and not as delegated by the pope.[41]

A proper understanding of the relationship between the papal primacy and the episcopacy is also conditioned by one's prior appreciation of the role of the local church and its relation to the universal Church. The local church is not simply an administrative unit within the whole Church. On the contrary, the Church as a whole becomes "event" only in the local celebration of the Eucharist. The local church is the "event" itself of this universal Church.[42] The unique relationship between the power of the episcopacy and the power of the pope is "grounded in the unique essence of the Church."[43] Again, there are no juridical or political analogues for this relationship. Our canonical distinctions are always

41. *The Episcopate and the Primacy*, pp. 16-18.
42. *Ibid.*, pp. 20-30.
43. *Ibid.*, p. 33.

a human attempt at realistic adjustment; only the Holy Spirit can guarantee the ultimate balance. He alone can preserve the unity of the Church despite the existence of these two powers, "one of which cannot be adequately reduced to the other in such a way that the Church could really be called a kind of absolute monarchy."[44]

The primacy of the pope is always a primacy *within* rather than *over against* that of the episcopal college. And that is why the contrast noted by Cardinal Daniélou is, in the final analysis, an improper one. Ontologically and juridically, Peter and the apostolic college are one entity. The Church is ruled by a college "without its head thereby becoming the mere elected representative of the college" (he is truly the head of the college), and "without the college thereby becoming his mere executive organ."[45] The college is nothing without the pope; and the pope is nothing without the college. And yet it seems that we have two separate sources of supreme and absolute authority in the Church: the pope's and that of an ecumenical council. Some have actually held such a position,[46] but Rahner vigorously rejects

44. *Ibid.*, p. 36. Cf. also the comment of J. Ratzinger, "The Pastoral Implications . . . ," p. 30: "The relations of sacrament and order, of the Petrine and episcopal offices, of the collegiality of the bishops and the fraternity of Christians, of the plurality of the Churches and the unity of the Churches, which we recognize as original realities, exceed all categories of political philosophy by such a degree that no model taken from them could do justice to our subject."

45. *Ibid.*, pp. 79-80.

46. Cf. W. Bertrams, "De subjecto supremae potestatis Ecclesiae," *Periodica de re morali canonica liturgica* 54 (1965) 173-232, and "De subjecto supremae potestatis Ecclesiae: respondetur objicienti," *Ibid.*, 490-499; and J. Beumer's review of P. Rusch's article (see n. 39, above) in *Scholastik* 40 (1965) 287. Bertrams' argument is that there are two subjects of supreme power in the Church, and that they are only inadequately distinct.

it. There can be only one subject of supreme and absolute authority in the Church, although with different modes and forms of activity.

Lumen Gentium does not resolve the dilemma. In fact the text leaves many questions open, in much the same way as the Dogmatic Constitution on Divine Revelation left open the question of the sources of revelation. But what was significant about *Dei Verbum's* stance was its refusal to endorse what many "orthodox" theologians had assumed to be the only official position; namely, that there are two separate and independent sources of revelation, the one written and the other unwritten. By declining to accept this post-Tridentine opinion, the council, in effect, removed it from the zone of doctrinal immunity. And the same is true with regard to this question of collegiality, and particularly with regard to the precise relationship between the papal primacy and the episcopate. Vatican II clearly did not want to endorse those exaggerated views of papal authority which have tended to dominate the ecclesiological and canonical discussions throughout much of this century. Indeed, the Theological Commission explicitly rejected the proposal of the pope to insert the words that the pope is "answerable to the Lord alone" in his action. This amendment was opposed on the grounds that it constituted an oversimplification of the truth and that it ignored the fact that "the Roman Pontiff is also bound to revelation itself, to the fundamental structure of the Church, to the sacraments, to the definitions of earlier councils and other obligations too numerous to mention."[47] Rahner argues finally that the authority of the pope is ultimately one and cannot be regarded as disparate in composi-

47. *Commentary on the Documents of Vatican II*, p. 202.

tion. Thus, "if he makes full use of his power as visible head of the Church, he acts at once as head of the college, without which the Church is unthinkable."[48] Rahner insists that his view is perfectly reconcilable with the Constitution and its *nota explicativa praevia:* "To 'act alone' does not mean to act as a 'private person' but as visible head of the Church, which the Pope is only when he is a member of the Church, living from its Spirit and from the institution as a whole. If he has to act as visible head of the Church, then he has to act as head of the college. Hence the collegiate possessor of supreme power in the Church is strictly one but has two modes of action, in keeping with its intrinsic structure: through the Pope 'alone' as its primatial head, and through the college acting strictly as such."[49]

G. Dejaifve describes the papal-episcopal relationship in a manner similar to the Orthodox approach. The Trinity is the principal analogue. The pope is like the Father; the bishops, like the Son and the Spirit. The pope enjoys a certain eminence of priority *(unigenitus)*, but without in any way diminishing the fullness of episcopal power and prerogatives. Within the college, as within the Trinity, there is

---

48. *Ibid.,* p. 204.
49. *Idem.* Cf. also Rahner's two articles in *Schriften zur Theologie,* vol. VI (1965): "Über den Episcopat," pp. 369-422, and "Über den Begriff des 'Ius divinum' im katholischen Verständnis," pp. 249-277. C. Duquoc agrees with Rahner's position in "Tête et corps dans le collège épiscopal: infallibilité fonctionelle et graduée, l'impossible dilemme," in *L'évêque dans l'Eglise du Christ* (see n. 3, above), pp. 81-93. Cf. also T. I. Jiminez-Urresti, "L'autorité du Pontife Romain sur le collège épiscopal, et, par son intermédiare, sur l'Eglise universelle: la collégialité épiscopale d'après les titres décernés au pape par les conciles oecuméniques," in *La collégialité épiscopale,* pp. 223-287; and G. Thils, "Unité et communion dans l'Eglise. A propos du synode épiscopal d'octobre 1969," *Nouvelle revue théologique* 91 (1969) 475-492.

diversity based on function and place, but in the operations of the college *ad extra,* it acts as one unit, even when it appears that the papal power alone is being engaged. The relationship of pope and bishops, therefore, must be one of reciprocity; the papal power is concerned most directly with preserving the unity of the Church, while the rights of the bishops are necessary for the integrity of their own churches, since the Body of Christ is a unity emerging from and sustained by a plurality (just as in the Trinity). All members of the Church share the same mission.[50]

CONCLUSION

1. Collegiality is not a single theological question; it is a cluster of questions, and the most important of them concerns the relationship between the papal primacy and the episcopacy. The theological discussion of this relationship has not yet reached its final form, but some opinions have already become part of a larger consensus.

2. The collegial relationship rests not on juridical or political realities but upon the suprainstitutional reality of the Holy Spirit, which is its source and its ground. Collegiality is rooted in the mystery of the Church and, as such, cannot be reduced to precise legal or canonical formulations.

3. Because this is so, the practico-pastoral working out of the collegial realities must follow a pattern of flexibility and accommodation, trying always to preserve the delicate balance among the various centers of power and authority within the universal Church, including, of course, the pre-

50. Cf. n. 38 above; cf. also n. 4 and n. 37 above.

rogatives and responsibilities even of those not in episcopal orders.[51]

4. The papal-episcopal relationship reflects the structure of the Church insofar as the Body of Christ is a unity emerging from and sustained by plurality. The universal Church is composed of many local churches. The Church is a *communion*, wherein the values of apostolicity and catholicity have equal claim. The unity of the Church is insured on the one hand by the Holy Spirit and Christian fraternity, and on the other hand by the presence of the college within the Church, and the pope within the college.

5. The canonico-dogmatic views of F. Gagnebet, J. Beyer, W. Bertrams, and others do not have support in contemporary Catholic theology, nor were they endorsed at the Second Vatican Council, their residual influence in *Lumen Gentium* notwithstanding. They continue, however, to shape the thinking of a major segment of the Church at the pastoral and political levels, and in some official documents.[52]

51. Episcopal conferences are but one way of fulfilling the collegial imperatives of the Church. Cf., for example, J. Hamer, "Les conférences épiscopales: exercice de la collégialité," *Nouvelle revue théologique* 95 (1963) 966-9, and also W. Onclin, "Collegiality and the Individual Bishop," *Concilium* vol. 8, no. 1 (October, 1965) 44-49. Herein, Onclin insists that the bishops "do not exercise their authority there (i.e., in episcopal conferences) by favor of the Holy See, which they do not represent, but by virtue of the episcopal authority which is strictly theirs" (p. 48). The subsequent acknowledgement of the decrees of such conferences by the Holy See does not constitute approval. Such acknowledgement does not, in fact, affect the juridical character of these decrees. Cf. also F. Houtart, "Les formes modernes de la collégialité," in *L'épiscopat et l'Eglise universelle,* pp. 497-535.

52. Such orientations are evident in the *Schema de quo disceptabitur in primo extraordinario coetu synodi episcoporum secundum conferentiarum episcopalium animadversiones exaratum,* Vatican City, 1969, and in the motu proprio *Sollicitudo Omnium Ecclesiarum,* 24 June 1969.

6. The pope never acts as a purely private person when he acts as head of the Church. He is always head of the college and a member thereof. Unilateralism, based on the idea of the papacy as an absolute monarchy, has no theological justification at all.

7. The papal office, nonetheless, exists not simply as a function of the college or of the Church as a whole but by the will of the Lord himself. The special mission of "the Rock" has eschatological significance just as the symbolism of "the Twelve." But the papacy and the episcopacy are always subordinate to the higher mission of the Church, which is the signification, celebration, and realization of the Kingdom of God in history, and the anticipation of its final coming at the end of history.[53]

8. The ultimate theological basis for episcopal collegiality is not generally agreed upon by contemporary theologians. Rahner argues that the existence of general councils is the decisive consideration, but the major weight of opinion seems to favor the idea and practice of *communio*, as collegiality's principal theological foundation.

9. The generally wide acceptance of the earlier distinction between *potestas ordinis* and *potestas iurisdictionis*, of twelfth century origin, is held responsible for the shift from a sacramental to a juridical understanding of the episcopacy. Theologians now insist that these powers are essentially one.

10. The primacy of the pope is a primacy within rather than over against the episcopal college. The Church is ruled

53. Collegiality cannot be fully understood except in the larger context of the mission of the Church. Such a discussion would have brought us far afield in this survey of current and recent theological literature. I have made an attempt at a critical reconstruction of this larger ecclesiological context in my own book, *Do We Need the Church?*, New York, 1969.

by a college in such wise that the pope is not the mere elected representative of the college, while the college is not merely his executive organ. There is one subject of supreme power in the Church and that is the episcopal college with the pope at its head and center. This power is exercised in different modes and forms, but it is radically one. The pope, therefore, is not an absolute monarch in the Church, and the bishops are not his delegates. Neither is the pope merely a functionary within the college or within the Church as a whole.

ORIGINS OF EPISCOPAL SYNODS

By Francis Dvornik

Some of the faithful, and even a few of the bishops, may have thought that something new was being introduced into the structure of the Church when the Second Vatican Council, in the Decree on the Pastoral Office of Bishops, spoke of "the Synod of Bishops," which "acting on behalf of the entire Catholic episcopate . . . will demonstrate that all bishops in hierarchical communion share in the responsibility for the universal Church."

This impression may have been caused by the fact that such episcopal synods have been almost non-existent in the recent history of the Church. However, when we study more closely the development of the Church throughout its early history, we find that proofs of the practice recommended by the Decree are to be found in the decisions of the first Councils of the Church.

It is now known that the synodal practice had developed in the early Church long before Constantine the Great. Practical reasons impelled the bishops to gather together whenever a problem arose requiring the consultation of several bishops to deal with it in such a way as to arrive at a solution consonant with the accepted Creed and ecclesiastical practice. It is also established that such meetings were held, also for practical reasons, in the capitals of the provinces of the Roman Empire, and that with time the bishops of such capitals acquired a certain supremacy over their confreres from the provinces. Thus originated the metropolitan organization of the primitive Church. The same political division of the Roman Empire into dioceses each containing a number of provinces motivated the development of patriarchates in the three most important political dioceses, namely, that of Italy in Rome, of Egypt in Alexandria, and of the Orient in Antioch. This development in ecclesiastical organization was clearly sanctioned by the First Ecumenical Council of Nicaea in 325.[1]

METROPOLITAN AND PROVINCIAL SYNODS

So far, Church historians have concentrated primarily on the study of the origins of the metropolitan and patriarchal organization of the primitive Church. Among the canons of the First Ecumenical Council, Canon Six,[2] which establishes the jurisdiction of the three Patriarchs, has attracted the gen-

1. For details see F. Dvornik, *The Idea of Apostolicity in Byzantium and the Legend of the Apostle Andrew* (Cambridge, Mass., 1958), pp. 3 sq.

2. Mansi, *Sacrorum conciliorum collectio* (Florence, Venice, 1759-1798), vol. II, col. 669 sq.

eral attention of Church historians and of canonists. Canon Five,[3] however, has escaped the scrutiny of most specialists, although it contains the first official regulation regarding the convocation of episcopal synods. It is addressed to the bishops of provinces, and asks them to hold two reunions each year, one on the fourteenth day of the Paschal period, and the second in the autumn. The main object of these synods would be to examine the excommunications pronounced by the bishops of the provinces, and to ascertain that this ecclesiastical censure was not launched "by narrowness of mind, by pertinacity, or any other vice of a bishop." The assembly of provincial bishops, after examination, was to make the sentence of excommunication definitive, provided the assembly, or the bishop who had originally pronounced the sentence, had not decided to impose a milder sentence. It should be stressed that Canon Five does not mention that any confirmation of the decision of the synod was necessary, either by the metropolitan of the province, or by any other authority. The decision made by the synod was forceful and final.

This Canon was confirmed and further expanded by the Council of Antioch, one of the most esteemed first synods of the early Church. Twenty-five canonical decisions are attributed to this synod. Canonists have long debated the date of its convocation, and many have proposed the year 341, a date when Constantius called a synod in Antioch on the occasion of the consecration of the great, new church of that city. The contents of the canons, however, indicate that the synod must have been assembled soon after that Council of

3. *Ibid.*, col. 687.

Nicaea, perhaps in 332, for the purpose of electing a successor to Bishop Paulinus.[4]

Most of the canons purpose to regularize the relations of priests with their bishops, and those of bishops with their metropolitans. Canon Nine confirms Canon Four of Nicaea which declares that the bishop of the capital of a province must have similar rights to those of a metropolitan, over all the bishops of his province. Without his permission, a bishop is unable to act outside the limits of the district, but, on the other hand, a metropolitan may make no decision without consulting his bishops. Canon Fifteen is more precise as to the authority of episcopal synods. Should a bishop be accused of trespassing and be found guilty by his confreres assembled in the provincial synod, the decision of that synod is definitive, and no appeal is admitted.

If, however, the bishops of the province are not unanimous in pronouncing their sentence, the metropolitan of that province must invite to the synod the bishops from the neighboring provinces, who must deliberate with the others. Thus we see that for the first time, the principle of collegial jurisdiction, wider than that of a provincial synod, was introduced into Church practice. This canon completed a disciplinary procedure already indicated in the Council of Nicaea.

Canon Twelve goes even further, and introduces another type of synodal assembly, the character of which is not clearly defined. It states, "If a priest or deacon has been deposed by his bishop, or a bishop deposed by a synod, and they wish to solicit the Emperor, they must present their

4. See G. Bardy, "Antioche (Concile et canons d')", *Dictionnaire de droit canonique* (Paris, 1935), vol. I, cols. 589-598. The canons in Mansi, II, col. 1308-1320.

cause at a more general council; they must state their reasons before a larger assembly of bishops, and they must submit to the inquest and the decision. But, if they neglect these legitimate provisions, and if they insist on going before the Emperor, they are not worthy of any pardon, for they will have no means of presenting their defense and must lose all hope of reintegration."

The Fathers of the synods had in mind another type of synod more competent than the provincial ones, and even more important and higher than those synods reinforced by the assistance of bishops from other provinces. Most probably they were thinking of the synods so often assembled by the Emperors during the Arianist crisis and which, although not ecumenical, consisted of bishops from many provinces. It would seem reasonable to expect that a further important synodical meeting would be convened in order to specify clearly the character of this higher synod.

It seems that the logical institution would have been the creation of diocesan synods which would serve as an instance of appeal from the decisions of the provincial synods. Surprisingly, the Second Ecumenical Council of 381 in Constantinople, which was a council in the oriental part of the Empire, did not take this step. Canon Two of the Council says simply:[5] "According to the canons, the bishop of Alexandria should limit himself to the administration of Egypt, the bishops of the Orient should administer only the Orient, provided that the rights of the church of Antioch described in the Canons of Nicaea be respected, the bishops of the dioceses of Asia, Pontus and Thrace, respectively, should ad-

5. Mansi, III, cols. 572, 573.

minister the affairs of only those dioceses." This canon shows only that the Fathers were anxious to keep the organization of the Church in strict conformity with the framework of the political division of the Empire. The sixth canon confirms the impression that Church organization was progressing along the lines of the political division of the Empire towards the formation of supra-metropolitan units corresponding to imperial dioceses. This same canon establishes that complaints against a bishop must first be examined by the provincial synod. The plaintiff could appeal the judgment of the provincial synod to a larger synod composed of bishops from the civil diocese.

Canon Six is couched in rather general terms and does not state by whom this larger synod is to be convoked. But, even if we admit that the larger synod is to be convoked by the same metropolitan who had presided over the first provincial synod, it must be admitted that the tendency to create a supra-metropolitan organism as a second instance of appeal is clear. It was to be applied to all civil dioceses of the eastern part of the Empire, not only to Egypt and the Orient, but also to the minor dioceses of Asia, Pontus and Thrace. That such was the tendency is also indicated in the ordinance issued by Theodosius I in July, 381.[6] The principle of adaptation to the administrative organization of the Empire is fully applied in the ordinance, and it can be rightly assumed that the bishops of the diocesan capitals soon became the most prominent leaders. There is no doubt about Alexandria and Antioch, but, in point of fact, the bishops

6. *Codex Theodisianus*, 16, 1, 3; ed. P. Krueger, Th. E. Mommsen (Berlin, 1905), p. 834.

of Caesarea, Ephesus and Heracleia, the capitals of the
three minor dioceses, are listed at the head of the Klesis of
218 as metropolitans.[7] Their prominence is indicated, too,
by the circumstance that each of them bore the title of
exarch, a title found also in the signatures of the Council
of 680.[8]

CONSTANTINOPLE AND THE PERMANENT SYNOD

Although the above-mentioned tendency of the Fathers
is quite clear, they did not extend the privileges of the three
major dioceses of Italy, Egypt and the Orient to the three
minor dioceses. We cannot even deduce from the canons
voted on by the first Councils that diocesan synods had ever
been introduced as a last instance of appeal.

The main reason which explains this fact seems to be
Canon Three which attributes to the See of Constantinople
an honorary primacy as the second see after Rome because,
as residence of the Emperors, Constantinople had become a
second Rome. This promotion was accepted in the East without protest as it was a logical consequence of the adopted
principle of adapting Church organization to that of the
Empire. As I have shown, not even Pope Damasus rejected
this canon,[9] which is also found in the first Latin collections
of Canon Law.[10]

7. E. Gerland, *Die Genesis der Notitiae episcopatuum* (Kadiköy,
1931), p. 8.

8. Mansi, XI, cols. 688, 689.

9. F. Dvornik, *The Idea of Apostolicity*, pp. 1-38.

10. *Idem*, "The See of Constantinople in the First Latin Collections
of Canon Law," *Recueil des travaux de l'Institut d'Etudes byzantines*,
no. VIII (Beograd, 1963), pp. 97-101.

There is a question which cannot be answered easily. Did the Fathers of the Council of 381 decline to extend the patriarchal privileges to the three exarchs because, in 381, Constantinople was already thought of as the supra-metropolitan instance of appeal for Thrace and all of Asia Minor? There is no doubt that once Constantinople became the residence of the Emperors, the prestige of her bishops had risen. It was certainly felt in the diocese of Thrace.

It should be noted that in the ordinance of July 30, 381, Theodosius I omitted to mention the diocese of Thrace, and it is justifiable to suppose that already in 381, the Bishop of Constantinople was regarded as the most competent authority in that diocese. The bishop of Heracleia, Sisinnius, is referred to in the *Acts* of the Council of 680 as only "bishop of the metropolis of Heracleia of the European eparchy," although the bishops of Caesarea and Ephesus still held the title of eparch. In spite of this, Constantinople does not appear to have played any marked role in the Church before the year 380. The prestige granted to Constantinople by the honorary primacy only began to grow after the Council. The fact that the introduction of a diocesan synod was never completed helped, of course, to increase the prestige of Constantinople and of her bishop, and he was regarded as a natural intermediary in conflicts among the bishops of minor dioceses. On the other hand, the Easterners recognized the need for a synod of bishops possessing greater authority than that of the provincial synods. This is clearly indicated in Canon Six of the same Council. We have also seen in Canon Twelve of the Synod of Antioch that a bishop wishing to appeal to the Emperor must first present his case before a larger assembly of bishops. The Fathers of Antioch and of

Constantinople were most anxious to protect their rights of jurisdiction, and to prevent appeals to the Imperial Court. Since the Emperor resided in Constantinople, it would seem logical to suppose that the larger synod, whose function was to hear appeals intended for presentation to the Emperor, should be convened in that city. Such was the custom during the Arianist struggles, for the Emperors summoned the bishops to the cities in which they resided. So it came about that the "permanent" synod, *synodos endemousa,* in Constantinople was born. Synods were not assembled with any regularity, unlike the provincial synods, but only when a matter of general interest had to be decided upon. Any bishop, present in Constantinople, had the right to assist and to decide on the case with the Patriarch.

This was sanctioned by the Council of Chalcedon in 451: "If a cleric is in conflict with his own bishop or another bishop, he must present his affair to the provincial synod. But, if a bishop or a cleric is in conflict with the metropolitan of the province, he must present his affair either to the exarch of the diocese, or to the See of Constantinople."[11] It has sometimes been thought that according to this canon, appeals from all the Eastern patriarchates were to be sent to the Patriarch of Constantinople. In reality, the Fathers had in mind only those dioceses without exarchs, which means patriarchs. This was the case of the three minor dioceses. The bishops of Egypt or the Orient had their own exarchs-patriarchs and presented their appeals only to them. Canon Seventeen contains a similar instruction. This tribunal of Constantinople became thus the last instance in the chain of ecclesiastical tribunals of appeal in the Orient.

11. Mansi, VII, col. 361; cf., canon 17, col. 365.

It should be stressed that the delegates of Rome who protested vehemently against Canon Twenty-eight which had placed the three minor dioceses under the direct jurisdiction of Constantinople, accepted without protest Canons Nine and Seventeen although both canons increased the prestige of the bishop of Constantinople.[12]

Although these two canons make no reference to the "permanent synod," this institution was mentioned, and sanctioned, during the fourth session[13] of the Council which was set apart to deal with the jurisdictional conflict between Photius, metropolitan of Tyre, and Eustathius of Beyrouth, who had obtained the elevation of his See from both the Emperor and from the "permanent synod" to the detriment of the titulary of Tyre. When the Imperial judges asked the Fathers if Anatole of Constantinople was entitled to excommunicate Photius, and if the synod which he had assembled for this occasion could be regarded as a veritable synod, the Fathers declared this procedure legitimate, with the consent of the pontifical legates. From that time on the "permanent synod" became a canonical and permanent institution in the Eastern Church.

The "permanent synod" should not be regarded as an instrument of supreme appeal. It was convoked and presided over by the Patriarch of Constantinople. It was a straightforward synod which exercised legislative, judiciary, and also administrative authority. It was exclusively a tribunal of superior instance. It had to respect all ordinary instances of ecclesiastical judiciary power, and judged only major causes of general interest to the Church. It had also to de-

12. Cf., F. Dvornik, *The Idea of Apostolicity*, pp. 88 sq.
13. Mansi, VII, cols. 85-96.

fend the purity and integrity of the traditional faith. In disciplinary matters, the synod together with the Patriarch, usually followed the Byzantine principle of "economy"— which meant avoiding a sentence which might provoke bitterness, or re-open old wounds. It was inclined to compromise as far as ecclesiastical law and dignity allowed. Administrative functions were exercised only in a later period.[14]

The synod was unthinkable without a patriarch, as the patriarch also was unthinkable without his synod. He convoked it, he presided over it, but the decisions were made by him only in collegiality with the bishops. The relationship between the Patriarch and his permanent synod is very well characterized by the declaration of Patriarch Pyrrhus, as preserved in the *Acts* of the Roman synod of 840, which assembled in the Lateran.[15] He says, "We have decided in accord with our most holy bishops assembled by us. . . ." Even more telling is the declaration of Patriarch Paul II in his letter to Pope Theodore in 646. This is how he begins his profession of faith:[16] "Because that we, that is the jurisdiction of our church and the synod are confessing. . . ."

Photius on several occasions described in his *Responsa Canonica*,[17] the functioning of the episcopal perpetual synod and its relations with the Patriarch. Let us quote only his letter to the archbishop of Calabria: "The questions which your Piety have sent us have been made known to our most

14. On the functioning of the synod see J. Hajjar, "Patriarche et Synod dans l'Eglise byzantine," *Proche-Orient Chretien*, 4 (1954), pp. 118-140, and especially the work of the same author *Le Synode permanent*, Orientalia Christiana Analecta, vol. 164 (1962), especially pp. 52 sq.

15. Mansi, X, cols. 1001-1004.

16. *Ibid.*, col. 1024.

17. P. G. 120, cols. 773-781. Cf. also *ibid.*, col. 891.

pious metropolitans and they have been asked to examine them. . . ." After replying to the questions, Photius ends his letter thus, "This is the decision given by our most pious metropolitans in unanimous approval, which our Mediocrity has found just, and confirming it, is sending it to your Holiness."

From similar expressions made by other patriarchs we see that the permanent synod was a deliberative assembly which pondered in collegiality important ecclesiastical problems, making decisions which the presiding patriarch pronounced.

The question arises whether or not there was any appeal possible against the decision of this synod. We have seen that the Fathers of the first synods mentioned the possibility of appeal to the Emperor. Although he was regarded as the highest authority in many ecclesiastical matters, we cannot find an example of any Emperor changing a disciplinary judgment of the synod. In this respect the Fathers of the Eastern Church succeeded in safeguarding their rights concerning ecclesiastical discipline and other matters.

However, there was yet another possibility of appeal, namely, to the See of Rome. The Synod of Sardica (modern Sofia) in 343, which was rather a synod of the Western part of the Empire and thus of the Western Church, decided in Canon Three:[18] "If any among the bishops has been accused, but thinks his cause is just and that a new synod should be called, let us, if you consent, honor the memory of the Apostle St. Peter, and let them who examined the case write to Bishop Julius of Rome." The Pope's decision should be ac-

18. Mansi, III, col. 40. Cf. also canon three, *ibid.*, col. 8.

cepted. It must not be forgotten that some of the canons of Sardica, and Canon Three among them, were included in the Greek canonical collection of John Scholasticus in the sixth century.[19]

In spite of this, appeals from Byzantium to Rome concerning disciplinary matters were rare. Appeals which involved doctrinal questions had, of course, been quite numerous, as is understandable. Most interesting is the case of the priest, John of Chalcedon, and of the monk, Athanasius, who appealed to Pope Gregory the Great with the authorization of their superior, Patriarch John IV of Constantinople who had sent to the Pope the documents which contained without doubt the decision of the perpetual synod in this matter. Gregory actually gave a definite decision on the case, confirming the innocence of John and recommending mercy for the monk Athanasius.[20]

In has been said that in the ninth century, the Patriarch Ignatius appealed to Pope Nicholas I against the "usurpation" of Photius, but recent discoveries have shown that Ignatius did not make any appeal, and this is proved by his own categorical declaration at the Synod of Constantinople in 861: "*Ego non appelavi Romam, nec appello.*" The appeal made to Rome by the monk Theognostus in 863, allegedly in the name of Ignatius, was therefore false. But some of the bishops in the group supporting Photius, such as Gregory Asbeatas of Syracuse, Zacharias, later Metropolitan of Chalcedon, Peter of Sardis, Eulampius of Apama, and Theo-

---

19. *Syntagma L Titulorum,* ed. V. Beneševic, Abhandlungen der bayerischen Akademie, Phil. hist. Kl. (1937), Heft 14.
20. *Gregorii papae Epistolae,* VI, pp. 15-17, P. L. 77, cols. 807 sq.

philus, Bishop of Amorium whom Ignatius judged for canonical reasons, had appealed to Rome on the basis of the
Canons of Sardica.[21]

The Synod of 861, convened to judge Ignatius in the
presence of the pontifical legates, appears to have finally
accepted the Canons of Sardica. Following the declaration
of the legates that they came to reexamine Ignatius' case
because the Fathers of Sardica had decided that the Bishop
of Rome was possessed of the power to reopen the case of
any Bishop, Bishop Theodore replied in the name of the
church of Constantinople, "This is a source of pleasure to
our church; we have no objection to it and we find it in no
way offensive." Unfortunately the Synod was rejected in 863
by Nicholas I, and its *Acts* destroyed. Only a Latin extract
containing these important declarations has been preserved.[22] It is on this basis that the Roman church should
commence her promised dialogue with the Eastern Church,
but, so far, no action of this kind has been taken.

From all this we must conclude that the organization of
the primitive Church was built on a synodal basis of bishops
who, in collegiality, were bound to deliberate with their
metropolitans and patriarchs on important questions concerning the faith and its disciplinary measures. The Byzantine church continued this practice in the East by means of
its permanent synod of bishops united with the Patriarch.

21. For details see F. Dvornik, *The Photian Schism* (Cambridge, 1948), pp. 16-19, 21-36, 48-52, 70-90.

22. Deusdedit, Cardinal, *Canonical Collection*, ed. V. Wolf von Glan-vell (Paderborn, 1905), pp. 603-616.

SYNODS IN THE PERSIAN CHURCH

There were, however, other Christian churches outside the Roman Empire, and it is valuable to know how they organized their religious life. The most important of these was the Persian church. What were its main features? Because of the hostility which for centuries had divided the Roman and Persian Empires, it had become a necessity for the Persian Christians to build their own independent ecclesiastical organization, and to maintain the least possible contact with the Christian churches of the Roman Empire. Thus the Persian church had become a kind of national church over which the Bishop of Seleucia-Ctesiphon wielded well-nigh unlimited authority.[23] It adopted, none the less, the organization it had grown up with, that of Roman Christianity complete with patriarch, metropolitans, synods and bishops, ruling from definite sees over carefully delineated dioceses as the necessary framework to carry on its Christian mission to the East. This organization the Persian church owed to the assistance of Marutha, Bishop of Maniferkat, between the Tigris and Lake Van, who went to Persia as the ambassador of Theodosius II, and represented the "Western Fathers" at the Persian synod of 410. Seleucia-Ctesiphon had all the makings of a patriarchate for Persia and for the communities that were to spring from the Persian missions.

And yet the sense of unity with the Western Christians was very much alive, and more than once in the first period of Persian church history found adequate expression. The

23. On the Persian Church see F. Dvornik, *National Churches and the Church Universal* (London, 1944), pp. 6-13. For more details see K. Lübeck, *Die altpersische Missionskirche* (Aachen, 1919).

Persian church was certainly conscious of its old connexion with Edessa and Antioch, so much so that Papa Bar Aghai (Jahbalaha) (415-420) considered it necessary to reduce opposition to his authority by appealing to the "Western Fathers," the Patriarch of Antioch and the Metropolitan of Edessa. It is questionable whether or not the Persian church was represented at the Council of Nicaea, but at its general synod of 410 the decisions of Nicaea were accepted by the church of Persia. The Western Fathers sent Bishop Akakios to Persia to settle the difficulties, and to their decisions the Persian church submitted at a synod held in 420. At that synod the Persian church also accepted the canons of some other Western synods, even admitting into her legislation other decrees on religious matters issued by the Roman Emperors.

But in all other things, the Persian church followed the direction of her own growth. The works of her greatest priest, Father Afrahat, written in the first half of the fourth century, reveal a mentality all its own. Christian, no doubt, yet Syriac and Persian for all that, and unaffected by the course of Greek Christianity. The head of the church was the bishop of the capital city who did not take the title of Patriarch, but of Katholikos. He reigned over the church in collegial union with his bishops assembled at numerous synods, to discuss with him major matters. In 424, the Persian synod decreed that thereafter there would be no appeal from the judgment of the Katholikos to the Western Fathers: "Easterners shall not complain of their own Patriarch to the Western Patriarch. Any case that cannot be settled by him shall await the tribunal of Christ."

This decision of the Persian synod which proclaimed a kind of autocephaly was made after a persecution of the

Christians by the Persian King of Kings. It did not mean a separation of Persian Christianity from the Church Universal, but was dictated by the desire to show that the Persian church should not be suspected of a relationship with the Roman Emperors, who were thought of as enemies of the King of Kings. It should be stressed that these synods were assembled when the Persian church still professed the Orthodox faith, which reveals to us that the basis of its organization was that of collegial union with the bishops at their synods, presided over by their Katholikos or Patriarch. Nestorianism was introduced only in 486 in Persia. But even the Nestorian church considered the assemblies of bishops in union with the Katholikos[24] to be the basis of its organization.

ARMENIAN SYNODAL STRUCTURE

The Armenian church[25] was founded by the missionary efforts of Gregory the Illuminator, who was consecrated bishop in Cappadocia. He converted King Tiridates III at the end of the third century. The bishopric was at Valarshapat, and was considered a suffragan of Cappadocia, but remained hereditary in Gregory's family. The church at Valarshapat also accepted the synodal practice as it had developed in the Byzantine Empire. Gregory's son assisted

24. "The Acts of the Persian Synods" were published by J. B. Chabot, *Synodicon Orientale,* Notices et Extraits de Mss. de la Bibliothèque Nationale et autres Bibliothèques (Paris, 1902), vol. 37.

25. Cf., F. Dvornik, *The National Churches,* pp. 13 sq.; H. Gelzer, "Die Anfange der Armenischen Kirche," *Berichte* of the Sächs. R. Academy. Cl. Phil. Hist., vol. 47 (1895), pp. 109-174. T. Markwart, *Die Entstehung der armenischen Bistümer,* Orientalia Christiana, no. 80 (Rome, 1930).

at the Council of Nicaea, and Bishop Isaak was present at a synod of Antioch and signed a letter addressed to the Emperor Jovian (363-364). Nerses the Great, who became bishop in 353, held an important synod in Ashtishat, which voted on canons concerning certain Armenian customs. Another national episcopal synod held in Ashtishat (435) accepted the decrees of the Ecumenical Council of Ephesus. The synodal practice continued during the time when Armenia was Orthodox, and during the struggle surrounding the acceptance or rejection of the Council of Chalcedon. The church became more and more national, possessing its own alphabet, and its own translation of Greek religious literature. In the fifth century, the Metropolitan of Armenia took the title of Katholikos, and his relationship with his bishops was characterized by collegiality in the synods. And so it went on, also after the rejection of Chalcedon by the Armenian synod of Ctesiphon in 614.

SYNODS IN AFRICA

We have less information concerning the synodal practice in the church of Ethiopia, which depended hierarchically on the Patriarchate of Alexandria. In the Western world of Christianity the synodal practice first developed in North Africa.[26] Christianity penetrated into the African provinces mainly through Carthage, the chief commercial and administrative center most frequently in touch with Rome and Italy in general. The episcopal sees were numerous. In 225,

26. Cf. H. Leclercq, *L'Afrique chretienne* (Paris, 1904); F. Heiler, *Altkirchliche Autonomie und papstlicher zentralismus* (Munich, 1941), pp. 3-50.

there were seventy bishops in Africa Proconsularis and Numidia. By the year 411, there were two hundred and seventeen bishoprics and their number increased to nearly six hundred by 430. St. Cyprian of Carthage with his genius for organization, firmly established the supremacy of the see over the whole of third-century Africa. This predominant position of Carthage remained untouched even after the administrative division of Africa into nine provinces by Diocletian.

In one respect, however, the church organization of Africa differed from that of other churches. The bishops of the provinces together formed a synodal unity, but when they convened in synods the chairmanship was reserved, not to the bishops of the provincial capitals, but to the oldest bishops. The provincial assemblies were, however, very much overshadowed by the universal synods of the whole African church, which were convoked and directed by the bishop of Carthage. Although his jurisdiction over the entire African church was absolute, extending over all bishoprics, he had to content himself with the modest title of *primae sedis episcopus*, as was decreed in Canon Twenty-six of the third Carthaginian synod.[27]

The African synods introduced the old Roman senatorial system into the internal structure of its assemblies.[28] This can be traced in Cyprian's letters and in the Acts of the first African synods that have come down to us. The same forms of convocation and procedure were used for the synods as for the Senate: *convocare, concilium, vocare, convocare*

---

27. H. T. Bruns, *Canones apostolorum et conciliorum* (Berlin, 1839), I, p. 127.

28. F. Dvornik, "Emperors, Popes and General Councils," *Dumbarton Oaks Papers,* 6 (1951), pp. 4-23.

senatum; habere concilium, habere senatum. Like the Senate under the Emperors, the council was a deliberative assembly, and the bishops had equal rights as did the senators. When Cyprian, as a bishop of the capital city, summoned a synod, he followed the procedure once used in the Senate. He read his *relatio*, or outline in the discussion, as the magistrate who represented the Emperor did in the Senate, then added a few words of explanation. Then followed the discussion and the *interrogatio* of all the bishops present, each of whom gave his *sententia*, using the senatorial formula: *censeo, decerno, mea sententia est, existimo.* The *sententia* was subsequently announced in a synodal letter addressed to the parties concerned. It was thus with this senatorial procedure, that the ecclesiastical gatherings built up their system. It was further developed at the first four General Councils.

Although in constant contact with Rome, the church of Africa spiritedly defended its autonomous status, as shown by Cyprian's attitude regarding the question of the Christians during Decius' persecution who had denied their faith, and particularly by the decision of the African Synod of 418 forbidding any appeal to Rome from the judgment of African bishops,[29] a canon which was strongly reaffirmed in a synodal letter of 426, in which the synod of Carthage forbade any further Roman intervention in African ecclesiastical matters.[30] The Africans protested, in the same document, even against the sending of legates from Rome to Africa, "We found no synodal decree which would authorize such a practice." From that time on Rome no longer inter-

---

29. Canon 17, Mansi, III, col. 822.
30. H. T. Bruns, *Canones,* I, p. 202.

vened in the interior affairs of the African church. Unfortunately, any further development of this African synodal practice was stopped by the invasion of Africa by the Vandals. The African synodal practice elaborated by Cyprian, by Aurelius, Allippius, and Augustine rendered great service to the Church in the struggle with Donatism, Manicheism, and Pelagianism.

COUNCILS IN SPAIN

The early Spanish church also accepted the synodal practice as is illustrated by the Acts of the Synod of Elvira, about 305.[31] The synod represented all five provinces of Spain, and its numerous canons are important for the study of early Spanish Christianity. With the nineteen bishops, twenty-four priests attended and were seated with the bishops. Other clerics attended, but they stood. The canons, however, are announced only in the names of the bishops. Sulpicius Severus speaks in the second book of his *Chronica*[32] of the synod of bishops from Spain and Aquitania who assembled in Saragossa in 380. The bishops condemned those of their number who adhered to the doctrine of Priscillianism. The synod voted on eight canons. The first synod of Toledo[33] convoked in 400 by the bishop of that city together with eighteen other bishops, voted on twenty canons but had still to deal with the Priscillianists. This was also the main

31. Mansi, II, col. 1 sq.
32. Ed. C. Halm in *Corpus scriptorum ecclesiast. latin . . .*, vol. 1 (Vienna, 1866), II, cap. 47, p. 100. On Spanish Church, see H. Leclercq, *L'Espagne chretienne* (Paris, 1906).
33. For decrees of all Councils of Toledo see H. T. Bruns, *Canones*, I, pp. 203 sq.

subject of the provincial synods of 563 and 572.

The synodal system of the Spanish church was thus well developed in the early period of its expansion. It suffered a setback during the invasion and occupation by the Visigoths (507). However, the invaders were a small minority, and were quickly romanized. When in 587 the Visigothic King Reccared had become a Catholic, abandoning the Arianist creed, the synodal system of the Spanish church flourished again displaying very interesting and particular features.[34] The bishops of the provinces formed a provincial council presided over by the Metropolitan. His see was the first tribunal of appeal for the whole province. Besides the provincial councils there existed a national council, as in the African church, called *concilium universale* or *generale*, presided over by the Archbishop of Toledo, capital of the Visigothic Kingdom. It was assembled by the King who also proposed the agenda. He often interfered in the debates, and would sign the decrees before the bishops, publishing them as state laws. The council often concerned itself with state affairs, but the King claimed juridical power over the bishops, especially the Metropolitans of Toledo. The general council was the most important institution of the Visigothic state, exercising an authoritative influence not only in the church, but in matters of State as well. The most important of the national councils is that of 589 which hastened the process of unification between the two nations.

At this council the Visigothic nation embraced the Catholic faith, even including some of the Arianist bishops. It was at this council that the *Filioque* was added to the Creed.

34. Cf., K. Ziegler, *Church and State in Visigothic Spain* (Washington, 1930).

In spite of a nationalistic particularism which this synodal system presented, the Visigothic church respected the primatial position of Rome, and the decisions made by other councils, general or particular. The bishops were well aware of their high position in the church and any intervention in their internal affairs by Rome or anyone else was repugnant to them. When in 638 Pope Honorius reproached the Spanish bishops for their laziness in suppressing heresy, the Sixth Council of Toledo (638) delegated Bishop Braulio to reply to the Pope's charge. Braulio accused His Holiness of slandering the Spanish church, as long ago the Spanish King had ordered the persecution of heretics, and thus Rome had nothing to fear.[35] On another occasion, Pope Benedict II reproached Bishop Julian of Toledo for certain inaccuracies in one of his theological commentaries. Bishop Julian made a self-confident defense of his declarations at the Fourteenth Council of Toledo (684), asserting at the finish that "to all lovers of truth, his answer, by divine judgment, will appear sublime, even if considered by ignorant, covetous men as unteachable."[36] The bishops present agreed with the speaker. We can see that the Spanish bishops at their synodal meetings evinced a similar, energetic reaction against the intervention of Rome as did the Bishops of Africa at their synods.

The Visigothic Spanish church produced several prominent ecclesiastical figures, such as Leander of Seville, Isidore of Seville, the encyclopaedist, theologian and canonist, Braulio of Saragossa, and especially Ildefonsus of Toledo, a great churchman and theologian. But intimate relations with the State sapped its energy and secularized its life. With the

35. Braulionis *Epistulae*, P. L. 80, letter 21, cols. 667-669.
36. Mansi, XII (XV. Conc. Toled.), cols. 10-18, especially col. 17.

destruction of the Visigothic Kingdom by the Arabs in 711, the national, synodal system of the Spanish church broke down.

In Gaul, ancient Gallia, Christianity had from its beginning a character not Roman, but rather oriental and Greek in character. The first bishop of Lyons, about the year 130 A.D., was Photinus, from Asia Minor, and he was succeeded by his compatriot, St. Irenaeus, rightly called the father of Catholic dogmatics. His theological thinking was Eastern in character, and continued contact with the East gave the early Gallic church rather an eastern and Greek stamp. This oriental influence is seen particularly in the tendency to independence in theological thinking, ecclesiastic administration and discipline in the church of Gaul. It was more attracted to the church of Milan than to that of Rome.[37] Many of her bishops took part in synods organized by the Metropolitans of Milan, and this contact with Milan was of assistance to the church of Gaul in developing its metropolitan organization during the fourth century. But it was never so well organized as in Africa or Spain, chiefly because of the continuous rivalry between the sees of Vienne and Arles for primacy in Gaul.[38] However, the system of episcopal synods progressed well in Gaul. The first synod was held in Arles

37. Cf., T. Scott Holmes, *The Origin and Development of the Christian Church in Gaul during the First Centuries* (Cambridge, 1911). H. Leclercq, 'Gallicane (Eglise) *Dictionnaire d'archéologie chrétienne et de liturgie*, vol. 6 (Paris, 1924), cols. 310-473.

38. Cf., on this rivalry F. Dvornik, *The Idea of Apostolicity*, pp. 36-39, 46.

in 314 A.D. The synods held in Paris in 335 and in 360 voted for strong measures against Arianism. The synod of Agde (506) stressed the obligation of celibacy of priests, and the obligation of the faithful to assist at Mass on Sundays. It was presided over by Caesarius of Arles, who also directed the Second Synod of Orange (529) known for its rejection of Semi-Pelagianism and for the definition of the doctrine on grace according to St. Augustine. During the second and third centuries, Roman authority, although respected, was hardly felt in Gaul. But by the fourth century, Rome had succeeded in eliminating the influence from Milan and thus restored her lost authority. The elevation by the popes of the bishop of Arles to a kind of apostolic vicar of Gaul provoked strong protest from the bishops of Vienne and Marseilles. The Synod of Turin (417) convoked on their initiative, rejected the pope's decision, but a compromise was reached and a break with Rome was avoided. The bishop of Marseilles, Proculus, persisted in his opposition in spite of his excommunication, which illustrates the independent spirit of the bishops of Gaul.[39]

The furtherance of more intimate relations between the church of Gaul and Rome were interrupted by the occupation of Gaul by the Franks. The independent position of the Frankish national church is illustrated by the fact that the Frankish Kings approved, or appointed, the bishops, and placed the synodal system under their sovereignty. They convoked the national councils, prepared the agenda and confirmed the canons and conclusions. Provincial episcopal synods also came under their authority and were convened

39. On the Councils of Gaul and of the Franks see H. Leclercq, *op. cit.*, col. 457-467 with all documentation.

by them. The vicariate of Arles lost all importance for Rome and the primatial rights were transferred to the See of Lyons, where the bishops presided over the national episcopal synods and even pretended to the title of Patriarch. This spirit of independence in the Frankish church, shown so often in its episcopal synods, was completely broken during the Carolingian period. The political alliance of the papacy with Pepin and Charles the Great naturally had its consequences in the ecclesiastical organization of the Frankish church. Charlemagne, anxious to unify the different customs and particularities in the life of the Frankish church, introduced Roman canon law and customs, including the Roman liturgy, and he strengthened Roman jurisdiction in the church. The decadence of the Frankish church which had commenced in the seventh century helped him to bring the church completely under his control. The synods became provincial and national assemblies in which, beside the bishops and the abbots, counts and barons discussed ecclesiastic and state affairs. The decisions were promulgated by the Emperor and called *Capitularia*.

There was a certain amount of resistance to this wholesale romanization and secularization of the Frankish church. An heroic, solitary figure was that of Hincmar, Archbishop of Rheims, who defended the rights of the metropolitans to convoke provincial synods, the rightful tribunal of appeal, and he protested against appeals directed by bishops and priests to the papal Curia, without reference to their Metropolitans. His work *De jure metropolitarum* was his swansong on the decline of the episcopal synods, once a respected organ in the administration of the early Church.

SYNODS IN THE ROMAN CHURCH

We must stress the fact that even the Bishops of Rome followed the synodical practice, at least during the early period. As a matter of fact, Pope Miltiades (311-314) had explained to Constantine the Great that the episcopal synods were the customary procedure by which the Church solved her problems. When the heretical Donatists, and the schismatics of northern Africa, dissatisfied with their condemnation by the African bishops, petitioned Constantine the Great to appoint independent judges from Gaul to examine their case, the Emperor agreed and appointed five bishops, including the Bishop of Rome. This was the first ecclesiastical case submitted to him, and he applied to its solution Roman juridical procedure by setting up a court of investigation empowered to give judgment. Pope Miltiades transformed the court into a council to which he invited fourteen Italian bishops (313). Once Constantine had learnt of the church's method, he adopted it, and when the Donatists repudiated the decision of the Roman synod, he decided to summon another council at Arles (314).[40] This was presided over by one of the judges, Marinus, Bishop of Arles; Pope Sylvester (314-335) sent only two priests and two deacons, as his representatives. At the conclusion, Constantine confirmed the decision of the Synod of Arles, and after that the Emperors used the synodical procedure in all doctrinal disputes.

Pope St. Damasus (366-384) is known to have convoked four synods for the purpose of confirming his election and for the condemnation of heretics. A fifth synod was assem-

40. For details see F. Dvornik, "Emperors, Popes, . . ." pp. 4 sq.

bled by Damasus in 385.[41] Innocent I held another in 402
which voted on sixteen canons in reply to questions sent to
Rome by the bishops of Gaul. It is known that Pope Celestine[42] condemned Nestorius in 430 at a Roman synod and
inaugurated the same decision made by the Ecumenical
Council of Ephesus in 431.

With the growth of papal authority based on the petrine
tradition, which Damasus had already begun to stress, the
popes inaugurated a new custom, that of making decisions
alone as the holders of the *Cathedra Petri,* and by promulgating their *Decretalia* and *statuta sedis apostolicae.* Siricius
(384-398) is the first known author of such a *Decretale,*
which was addressed to Bishop Himerius of Tarragona.[43] Innocent I (402-417) in one of his *Decretale* claimed that all
important decisions of episcopal synods should be sent to
the Roman See for approval.[44] The pattern of the *Decretalia*
changed gradually, and often emulated the style and form of
imperial constitutions. Gelasius went even further than Innocent I when he claimed full papal sovereignty over all
episcopal synods.[45]

In spite of this new development the old synodal practice
was not forgotten in Rome. For example, Leo the Great
(400-461) is said to have held a synod in Rome in 444, to
discuss the case against a Manichaean sect discovered in the
city. The *Acts* are not preserved. He also condemned the
Latrocinium of Ephesus at a Roman synod. Pope Hilarius
(461-468) convoked a synod in 465 together with forty-eight

41. Mansi, 111, cols. 459-462, 485, 624.
42. *Ibid.,* col. 1019.
43. P. L. XIII, col. 1146.
44. *Epistolae,* P. L. 20, col. 473.
45. P. L. 59, col. 66.

bishops, which dealt with questions presented to the Pope by the Spanish synod of Tarragona. Pope Felix II (III), when dealing with the Patriarch Acacius who had accepted the Henoticon which favored Monophysitic ideas, did not content himself with letters or decretals. Instead he convoked a synod of seventy-seven bishops in 484, excommunicated not only Patriarch Acacius himself but also the papal legates suspected of intercourse with partisans of the Patriarch. Another synod of forty-three bishops sent its synodical decree to the oriental monks. Another Roman synod of 487 protested against the persecution of Catholics in Africa.[46] Even Gelasius (492-496) held a Roman synod in 494 to deal with Italian ecclesiastical matters. A further synod assembled by Gelasius in 495 rehabilitated the legate excommunicated by Felix II. *Acta* are preserved.[47] However, the famous *Decretum* on the Holy Books is not a decree of the Gelasian synod as is still believed by many, as it was composed in the sixth century by an anonymous author.

The synods during the reign of Symmachus (498-514) of 499, 501, and 502 dealt with the election of popes and of accusations against Symmachus. They contributed to the declaration that the first See cannot be judged by anyone.[48] Hormisdas (514-523) who ended the Acacian schism, followed the new method, fighting and defending his rights by letters and *Decretalia* sent to the Church in the East. There is no evidence that Roman synods were held on the Acacian affair. It appears, however, that the reconciliation may have been confirmed in 517 by a Roman synod. From the seventh century on let us mention especially the Roman synod under

46. Mansi, VII, cols. 1106, 1137, 1166, 1171.
47. Mansi, VIII, cols. 145-151, 178-184.
48. *Ibid.*, 230, 246, 247, 262, 295.

Severinus in 640, which condemned the imperial decree, the Ecthesis, and the first great Lateran synod convoked by Martin I in 649 to condemn Monotheletism.

The synodal practice was again revived in the ninth century by Pope Nicholas I during the Photian affair. His example was also followed by Hadrian II, who condemned Photius and reinstated Ignatius at a Roman synod in 868. The *Acta* of this synod were brought by the legates to the Ecumenical Council (869-70) and were read during the seventh session. The legates simply asked that all the bishops should accept the decision of the Roman synod without further inquiry. This simple request caused great astonishment because, according to the easterners, only an ecumenical synod could deal with a case of this kind. This embarrassed Ignatius who was reinstalled as Patriarch, and angered the Emperor Basil who intended to convoke a council in Constantinople to discuss and reach a decision on this question. This explains why only about one hundred and ten bishops assisted at that Council, and why the great majority of the bishops ignored the decision of the Council and remained faithful to Photius even though he had been condemned by both synods.[49]

PAPAL AUTHORITY AND THE DECLINE OF SYNODS

As regards the provincial episcopal synods, their importance declined in the same measure as the prestige of the Roman Curia increased in the eighth and ninth centuries. The centralization of Church administration in the Roman

49. See for details and documentation, F. Dvornik, *Photian Schism*, pp. 132, sq.

Curia was accelerated by the appearance of one of the biggest falsifications of the Middle Ages, namely, the *Pseudo-Isidorian Decretals.*[50] The falsification originated somewhere between 847 and 852 in the Frankish Empire, probably in the diocese of Rheims, and was directed against Hincmar's defense of the rights of the Metropolitans. Pope Nicholas I accepted them as genuine documents. Among the false papers was a decree that any major synod could be assembled only with permission from the Holy See. The falsity spread rapidly in Gaul and in Germany during the tenth century, and was rediscovered in Rome by the reformists under Pope Leo IX and Gregory VII. The sixteenth principle of Gregory's *Dictatus Papae*[51] declares that no synod can be called "general" without permission from the pope. Applied to the provincial synods this dictum meant the disappearance of this old institution, and ended the last remnants of the old Christian autonomous direction of ecclesiastical affairs by the episcopal synods.

The many synods held by the reformist popes, from Leo IX to Paschalis II, had quite a different aspect. The struggle against Investiture forced the popes to hold their synods outside Rome, and to invite to the gatherings those counts and barons whose help in the struggle with the Emperor was most welcome. The papacy won its struggle for the reform of the Church, and this was publicly proclaimed in the First Council of the Lateran in 1123. It was also the first Ecumenical Council of the Western Church.

This short study shows how the administration of the early Church was based on the synodical system. The

---

50. Ed. Paul Hinschius (Leipzig, 1863).

51. Ed. E. Caspar, *Das Register Gregors VII,* vol. 1, (Berlin, 1920), pp. 201, sq.

bishops assembled in collegiality in either provincial or national synods, together with their Metropolitans, possessed equal rights in the discussions and decisions on problems that had arisen in their churches. Their common faith united them with the bishops of Rome whose primacy in the Church was reverently respected by them. In matters of faith, the bishops looked to Rome for guidance, regarding her as the highest tribunal of appeal.

This system, which also made the bishops responsible for the development of religious life in their dioceses, ecclesiastical provinces, and in their nations, slowly disappeared in the Middle Ages in proportion to the growth of Roman centralization of administration. The almost complete disappearance of the primitive system of episcopal synodical rule in ecclesiastical affairs has not been of advantage to the Church as the present crisis in the Roman Catholic Church manifests.

THE HISTORY OF CENTRALIZATION:
PAPAL RESERVATIONS

By John E. Lynch, C.S.P.

For the first 250 years of its history the Christian Church was far from being a highly centralized institution.[1] The numerous local churches, each eventually headed by a single bishop, were held together in a loose confederation. What ties existed were largely due to geographical divisions of the Roman Empire. Quite understandably, the churches of a certain area soon experienced the realities of political community exerting a noticeable influence on religious life.[2]

1. For a recent bibliography see E. Corecco, "The Bishop as Head of the Local Church and Its Discipline," *The Sacraments in Theology and Canon Law, Concilium*, Vol. 38, New York, 1968, 88-104; H. Marot, "The Primacy and the Decentralization of the Early Church," *Historical Problems of Church Renewal, Concilium*, Vol. 7, New York, 1965, 15-28; R. Markus and E. John, *Papacy and Hierarchy*, London, 1969.

2. A. H. M. Jones, *The Later Roman Empire 284-602: A Social and Administrative Survey*, University of Oklahoma, 1964.

Proximity led to a sharing, in addition to the Gospel faith, of customs and usages—liturgical, disciplinary, and organizational.

Since the New Testament, in contrast with the Old, deals only in general principles with extraordinarily little in the way of concrete and specific detail, customary usages were justified on the basis of apostolic tradition. At first it was commonly assumed that the apostles were unanimous in programing the Christian life. Thus, early Church orders were entitled *The Teaching of the Twelve Apostles* (the *Didache*), *The Apostolic Tradition* (Hippolytus), *The Catholic Teaching of the Twelve Apostles (Didascalia Apostolorum)*, and *The Apostolic Constitutions.* In the second century controversy over the celebration of Easter, churches passionately defended their practice as apostolic.[3] In time, when it was accepted that churches could differ in custom, the Church Orders, obviously not an apostolic consensus, lost their popularity.

What institutional unity existed during this period was to a large extent regional. Provincial capitals, especially the great cities, such as Rome, Alexandria, and Antioch, set the tone or acted as models throughout zones of influence,[4] as regional cooperation developed. Since Christianity spread so rapidly in the Eastern part of the Empire, organizational ties were stronger there and found expression in synods which sought to formulate a common policy.

On the level of the Church universal, when the Gospel itself and not mere custom was at stake, it was assumed that

3. B. Altaner, *Patrology*, trans. H. Graef (based on 5th German ed. of *Patrologie*, 1958), New York, 1960, 50-61.

4. P. Batiffol, *Cathedra Petri, Études d'Histoire ancienne de l'Église*, Paris, 1938, 41-59.

apostolic succession would guarantee unity. Irenaeus and Tertullian[5] argued vigorously for this standard. In view of the strong conviction of the early Church, it is ironical to note the subtitle of a recent *Concilium* volume on Apostolic Succession: "Rethinking a Barrier to Unity."[6] St. Cyprian was one of the first to run into this barrier. His ecclesiology, based on the unity of the bishops,[7] could not surmount the impasse between himself and Stephen of Rome over the validity of heretical baptism.[8] Apostolic succession and the consultation of bishops did not automatically work for the maintenance of unity. The course of events, prescinding from theology, demanded a certain center of unity to hold the Universal Church together. This leadership the papacy supplied.

In the interests of unity, if not uniformity, the papacy in the course of history exerted an increasing control over the local churches by concentrating a number of administrative, legislative, and judicial functions in its own hands. The present study will trace a movement towards centralization that has its spurts and checks, but almost no reverses. In the first two centuries the Christian Church, necessarily preoccupied with survival, made only a few faltering steps in the direction of overall coordination. The subsequent emergence of the Christian Emperor (c. 325 A.D.) found the bishops of

---

5. *Adv. Haer.* 3, 2-5 (SCh. 34:98-126); *De Praescrip.* 28 (CSEL 70: 34). See J. N. D. Kelly, *Early Christian Doctrines,* London, 1958, Chap. II "Tradition and Scripture."

6. Ed. H. Küng, New York, 1968.

7. Ep. 66, 8 (CSEL 3.2:732-733); Ep. 48, 2 (CSEL 3.2:611).

8. *Sententiae Episcoporum* (CSEL 3.1:436). See G. S. M. Walker, *The Churchmanship of St. Cyprian,* Richmond, 1969; J. Colson, *L'Episcopat Catholique: Collegialité et Primaute dans les Trois Premièrs Siècles de L'Église,* Paris, 1963, 79-121.

Rome unprepared to assert a significant role. With Pope Leo the Great (c. 440) and Pope Gregory the Great (c. 590), however, the papacy inaugurated a policy of forceful leadership which, despite the promise of Nicholas I (c. 860), did not really get underway until the Gregorian reform (c. 1050). At once the movement gathered momentum until it was almost complete in the age of Pope John XXII (1316-1334). At this point the papacy controlled appointments to almost every significant post in the Western Church along with the supervision of the most minute aspects of ecclesiastical discipline. The rise of nationalism, Conciliarism, and the Reformation severely challenged the highly centralized Church.

THE FIRST TWO CENTURIES

The origin, theory, and development of papal reservations is inextricably bound up with the exercise of primacy on the part of the bishop of Rome.[9] The earliest historical evidence usually appealed to in support of the primacy is not without a certain ambiguity. Some Catholic historians have questioned whether the *First Epistle of Clement,* the letters of St. Ignatius of Antioch, and certain texts in Irenaeus constitute a recognition of Rome's unique authority.[10] Perhaps the first act of papal primacy occurred during the Easter controversy (c. 190 A.D.) which involved the Holy See and re-

9. For the relevant texts see E. Giles, *Documents Illustrating Papal Authority A.D. 96-454,* London, 1952.

10. J. F. McCue, "The Roman Primacy in the Second Century and the Problem of the Development of Dogma," *Theological Studies,* 25 (1964), 161-196.

gional conferences of bishops.[11] Meetings were held throughout the Empire to consider the divergent traditions regarding the celebration of Easter. Except for Asia Minor all the conferences favored a Sunday observance. Polycrates, however, in the name of the Asiatic bishops wrote to the Church of Rome that Asia intended to follow its ancient custom of keeping the feast on the 14th day of the Passover. In the letter Polycrates states that the Asiatic bishops met in council at the request or demand of the Roman Church. The request seems to have involved some intimidation, for Polycrates adds that he is "not afraid of threats."[12] Upon the refusal of the Asiatics to adopt the practice of the other churches, Victor, bishop of Rome, "tried to cut off from the common unity the dioceses of all Asia." Irenaeus among others sharply rebuked Victor for this harsh action.

Other instances of papal intervention in the next century are rare. Callistus (217-222) sought to impose his doctrine of penance "over the whole world."[13] Stephen (254-257), though he refused to accept Cyprian's position on baptism, did adopt the latter's phrase *cathedra Petri* and made a specific claim to the primacy.[14] Soon came the persecutions

11. Eusebius, *The History of the Church*, V, 23-24 (SCh 41:66-71). Colson, *op. cit.* "Cette attitude des évêques vis-à-vis de la sentence du pape Victor est une des plus belles affirmations de la primauté de l'évêque de Rome, à l'occasion de l'une de ses toutes premières manifestations..." (p. 51).

12. Polycrates in his argument lays great stress on the fact that "great luminaries sleep in Asia." From this approach one may surmise that Victor based his claim to authority on Rome's possession of the apostolic tombs, rather than on Mt. 16:18.

13. GCS *Hippolytus Werke*, III:251 (*Philosophumena* IX, 13).

14. Firmilian's letter to Cyprian 256 A.D., in Cyprian's Ep. 75 (CSEL 3.2:821 #17): "qui sic de episcopatus sui loco gloriatur et se suc-

of Decius, Aurelian, and Diocletian. Questions of unity among the local churches yielded to the more urgent concern of survival.

THE CHRISTIAN EMPEROR

Once the Constantinian turning-point was reached, it was the Emperor who pressed for unity in the Church in order to bolster a sagging state. The Council of Arles in 314 and the Council of Nicaea eleven years later were imperial attempts to deal with the divisive Donatists and Arians.[15] The sudden *volteface* of the Empire from bitter persecution to favor caught the Church largely unprepared. The popes between Stephen (d. 257) and Damasus (366-384) with the exception of Julius (337-352) were undistinguished, "if not entirely shadowy figures, who simply reacted to events without showing any real capacity to shape the new relationship."[16] Ambrose, the first ecclesiastic to attempt a clarification of the relationship between Church and state, was not a pope, but bishop of Milan (c. 374-397).

One important development, to be sure, did take place in this period of papal passivity. During the chaotic years after Nicaea when councils and creeds succeeded one another with kaleidoscopic speed, Constantine's sons, emperors of East and West, agreed to a council at Sardica or Sophia

cessionem Petri tenere contendit . . . Stephanus qui per successionem cathedram Petri habere se praedicat nullo adversus haereticos zelo excitatur . . . ."

15. V. C. de Clercq, *Ossius of Cordova: A Contribution to the History of the Constantinian Period* (The Catholic University of America Studies in Christian Antiquity, 19), Washington, D.C. 1954, *passim.*

16. G. Barraclough, *The Medieval Papacy*, New York, 1968, p. 21.

in 343. Though the Eusebian or semi-Arian representatives soon withdrew, the remaining bishops, 38 Greek-speaking and 33 Latin, enacted a number of canons.[17] The historical importance of this council derives from three of those enactments, the so-called appeal canons, which were to affect profoundly the jurisdictional position of the papacy. It was provided that a bishop could appeal to Rome for redress against the judgment of a provincial synod. Rome would then appoint judges from the neighboring provinces to reconcile the case. Representatives from Rome could also participate in the re-trial. While the appeal was being heard, the sentence of deposition was to be suspended. Note that complete jurisdiction over all cases of deposition is not here conceded, nor is the pope to be the sole judge, despite later papal claims. These canons, frequently appended to those of Nicaea, were transmitted in all the Greek collections and immeasurably enhanced the judicial role of the papacy.

Throughout the doctrinal controversies of the fourth and fifth centuries the Emperors continued to press for a unified Church as a base of political support and recognized the value of Rome as a standard of discipline. Gratian in 378 sustained Pope Damasus' claim to authority over the Western bishops.[18] Theodosius I in 380 made Christianity the state religion and defined it as "the religion which it is clear that the Pontiff Damasus and Peter, Bishop of Alexandria, a man of apostolic holiness, follow."[19] Valentinian III in 445 lent the full weight of the state to enforce papal authority.[20]

17. H. Hess, *The Canons of the Council of Sardica A.D. 343*, Oxford, 1958, p. 46.

18. *Ad Aquilinum Vicarium Urbis* (PL 13:586 B; CSEL 35.1:54).

19. *Theodosian Code*, XVI, 1, 2 (trans. Pharr p. 442).

20. N. Val. 17, 1 (trans. Pharr, p. 530-1; PL 54:637).

It will not be lawful for the bishops of Gaul or of other
provinces to attempt anything contrary to the ancient
custom without the authority of that venerable man the
Pope of the Eternal City; but let whatever the authority
of the Apostolic See decrees or shall decree, be accepted
as law by all, so that if any bishop summoned to trial
before the Roman Bishop shall fail to attend, he shall be
compelled to be present by the Governor of the province
in question, due regard being paid at every stage of the
proceedings to the rights which our divine parents bestowed on the Roman Church.

The pressure of political events which left Rome no
longer the seat of imperial government roused the popes
from Damasus (366-384) to Gregory the Great (590-604)
to extraordinary activity in order to maintain the Roman
primacy. In the West the imperial court moved first to Milan
(286 A.D.) and then to Ravenna (402 A.D.). Constantinople
was the "New Rome" in the East and despite the lack of
Roman representation a council there in 381 was recognized
as ecumenical. A Roman synod the next year rebuked the
pretensions of Constantinople with the declaration that papal
primacy derived not from synodal decree but from the right
conferred upon Peter by Christ.[21] To emphasize his unique
position, Damasus then began to speak of Rome as "The
Apostolic See" and to address the bishops as "sons" instead
of the customary "brothers."[22]

21. "Sancta tamen Romana Ecclesia nonnullis synodicis constitutis
caeteris Ecclesiis praelata est: sed et evangelica voce Domini Salvatoris
nostri primatum obtinuit . . ." (PL 13:374).
22. Battifol, *Cathedra Petri*, pp. 151-168. Also see P. Battifol, *Le
Siège apostolique* 359-451), Paris, 1924 (PL 13:370; Jaffé 234).

THE DECRETAL

Undoubtedly the most significant development in this period of papal assertiveness was the emergence of the decretal. The origin and juridic basis for papal legislative activity have not been settled to the historian's satisfaction. Although it is debated whether Damasus issued the first known decretal, his successor Siricius (384-399) undoubtedly intervened in several affairs.[23] He transmitted to the African bishops the decisions of a Roman council held in 386.[24] He responded authoritatively to an inquiry from Bishop Himerius of Tarragonna in Spain forbidding the rebaptism of Arian converts.[25] On his own initiative he communicated certain disciplinary regulations to the bishops of Italy.[26] His directives, he claimed, had the same binding force as the decrees of synods. Siricius maintained that the very nature of his office obligated him to act in this way.

> . . . zeal for the Christian faith surpassing that of all others is incumbent upon us; . . . we bear the burdens of all who are troubled; rather the blessed Apostle Peter bears them in us; he protects and guards us, we trust, in all things as his heirs in government.[27]

23. J. Gaudemet, *L'Église dans L'Empire roman* (*IVe-Ve siècles*) (*Histoire du Droit et des Institutions de l'Église en Occident* Tome III), Paris, 1958, p. 220.

24. Mansi 3:669-671 PL 13:1155; Hefle-Leclercq II. 1:68-75.

25. Ep. 1 (PL 13:1131-1147); Jaffé 255.

26. PL 13:1162. E. Caspar, *Geschichte des Papsttums,* Tubingen, 1930, I, 262-264.

27. "Et quamquam statuta sedis apostolicae vel canonum venerabilia definita, nulli sacerdotum Domini ignorari sit liberum . . ." PL 13:1146; Jaffé 255. Caspar calls attention to the fact that Siricius in laying down the law speaks of his connection with Peter in the legal terminology of a juristic succession, *haeredes.*

From the pontificate of Innocent I (401-417), 29 decretal letters to such sees as Rouen, Toulouse, and Gubbio have survived.[28] They treat matters as diverse as clerical continence, the sacraments, conjugal fidelity, penal justice, and the canon of Scripture. The letter to Victricius of Rouen lists fourteen rules to be observed.[29] The tempo of legislative activity quickened during the rest of the century. From all over the West requests poured into Rome seeking solutions for present problems and norms for future guidance. Since officials in the Roman Empire were accustomed to seek rescripts from the Emperor to deal with unusual cases,[30] it is not surprising that bishops would turn to the bishop of Rome, the successor of Peter, for similar help. The pontifical *responsa,* originally addressed to a local situation, quickly assumed the character of a general law on a par with synodal enactments.[31] Soon the papacy did not wait to be consulted but adopted a legislative stance on any issue it considered important. It claimed to be speaking with the voice of God; those who violated the decrees of the Apostolic See could

28. Ep. 2 to Rouen (PL 20:469); Ep 6 to Toulouse (PL 20:495); Ep. 25 to Gubbio (PL 20:551).

29. PL 20:470; Jaffé 286.

30. The most famous in Church History is a rescript of Trajan (98-117) to Pliny the Younger concerning the legal status of Christians, Ep. X, 96, 97 "Conquirendi non sunt." See A. N. Sherwin-White, "Trajan's Replies to Pliny: Authorship and Necessity," *Journal of Roman Studies,* 52 (1962), 114f.

31. Pope Leo the Great Ep. 1, 1 "per auctoritatem canonum decretorum-que nostrorum." (PL 54:593). "... omnia decretalia constituta, tam beatae recordationis Innocentii, quam omnium decessorum nostrorum, quae de ecclesiasticis ordinibus et canonum promulgata sunt disciplinus, ita a vestris dilectione custodiri debere mandamuus." Ep. IV, 5 (PL 54:614); Jaffé 403. The decretal thus becomes part of canon law in the Western Church.

expect the same fate as those who transgressed the divine ordinances.[32]

Quite early these papal decretals were brought together in collections. One of the most popular was that made by Dionysius Exiguus at the beginning of the sixth century.[33] He compiled a chronological series of 38 papal decretals from Pope Siricius (384) to Pope Anastasius II (d. 498) inclusive; 21 decretals came from Pope Innocent I. The various collections circulated widely in the West, thus promoting the legislative authority of the papacy.

In addition to his decretal activity Pope Innocent I made an important contribution to papal reservations. Writing to Victricius of Rouen in 404, he states that if a "major cause" arises at a local synod, the decision is to be referred to the Roman See for confirmation or revision.[34] The formulation suggests Ex. 18:22 where Jethro says to Moses: "let them act as judges for the people on all ordinary occasions; all important cases they shall bring to you." Quite likely Rome's claim to review all major cases is an outgrowth of the appellate jurisdiction recognized at the Council of Sardica. The imperial rescript *Ordinariorum sententias* of Gratian (already referred to), assigning the trial and appeal of bishops to the Roman pontiff, marks a further step in this direction.

32. Pope Hilary at the Roman Council of 465, the first to preserve exact minutes and the pope's allocution. "... nulli fas sit sine status sui periculo vel divinas constitutiones vel apostolicae sedis decreta temerare." *Canones Apostolorum et Conciliorum saec. VI-VII*, ed. Bruns, Berlin, 1839, II, 282.

33. PL 67:230-316.

34. "Si majores causae in medium fuerint devolutae, ad sedem apostolicam, sicut synodus statuit, et beata consuetudo exigit, post judicium episcopalae referantur." Ep. 2, 6 (PL 20:473); Jaffé 288.

Innocent makes no attempt to spell out what these *causae majores* include. This jurisdictional development need not be attributed to papal aggrandizement. Nicaea had been forced to set up appellate procedures on the provincial level. Later, as Church affairs grew more complex, a more universal forum was needed.

PAPAL LEADERSHIP: LEO I AND GREGORY I

With the pontificate of Leo the Great (440-461) the papacy began to exert an influence on the universal Church such as to suggest monarchical control.[35] To Leo belongs the distinction of having constructed on a juridical basis a full-blown doctrine of the prolongation of Petrine power in the pope. The papacy is identified with Peter to whom was given the power of the keys, the power to bind. Leo buttresses the main argument which bases pontifical jurisdiction on divine law with the appellate recognition accorded Rome by Nicaea (with which Sardica was confused).[36]

What distinguishes Peter's authority from that of all the other Apostles is its universality. It is this universal authority which the pope has inherited, "care of all the churches."[37]

---

35. T. J. Jalland, *The Life and Times of St. Leo the Great,* London, 1941.

36. W. Ullmann, "Leo I and the Theme of Papal Primacy," *Journal of Theological Studies* 11 (1960), 25-51. W. W. Buckland, *A Textbook of Roman Law,* Cambridge, 1932, p. 317. Ep. 43 (PL 54:821; Jaffé 437).

37. Serm. 4, 4 (PL 54:152); Ep. 5, 2 (PL 54:615 B). The formula derives from II Cor. 11:28. "Et quia per omnes Ecclesias cura nostra distenditur, exigente hoc a nobis Domino, qui apostolicae dignitatis beatissimo apostolo Petro primatum fidei suae remuneratione commisit, universalem Ecclesiam in fundamenti ipsius soliditate constituens, necessitem sollicitudinis quam habemus." J. Rivière, " 'In partem sollicitudinis'. . . evolution d'une formule pontificale," *Revue des sciences religieuses* 5 (1925), 210-231.

Though the authority of the bishops is not thereby diminished, Leo reminds them that their power is derived through
him: the Lord's gifts were bestowed primarily on Peter and
through him on the whole body so that "whoever dares to
withdraw from the stability of Peter may know that he is
torn away from the divine mystery."[38]

> Although every pastor looks after his own flock with spe-
> cial care . . . we share that care with all; each one's ad-
> ministration is part of our own work; so that when men
> resort to the see of Peter from all over the world . . . , the
> greater our duty to all, the heavier we feel the burden
> resting on our shoulders.[39]

Pope Leo the Great sought juridical control over the various churches. He sent Bishop Potentius to Africa to ascertain the facts about ecclesiastical abuses in the wake of the
Vandal invasions.[40] Leo then wrote the African bishops in
446 requiring a full report so that he could review the decisions taken. He granted a sanation to laymen who had been
directly promoted to the episcopate, thus allowing them to
retain their offices. He emphasized that, in the event of an
appeal to Rome, the sentence of a local synod is thereby
suspended. In a letter to the bishops of Gaul, Leo deprived
Hilary of Arles of metropolitan status for "claiming the
rights of consecration in a province to which he had no
right" and reduced his position to that of a simple bishop

---

38. "Qui ausus fuisset a Petri soliditate recedere" Ep. 10, 1 (PL
54:629; Jaffé 407).
39. Serm. 5, 2 (PL 54:153 C).
40. Ep. 12 (PL 54:646, 656; Jaffé 410).

(suae tantum civitatis illi sacerdotium).[41] Later a petition came from Arles that Leo restore what that church "had either received from of old or subsequently possessed by authority of the Apostolic See."[42] Leo was particularly anxious to assert jurisdiction in the Prefecture of Eastern Illyricum, midway between the two rival spheres of influence, Rome and Constantinople. He wrote to the bishop of Thessalonica granting him many powers but requiring that a report be made to Rome in a *major causa* so that in accord with ancient tradition and due respect for the Apostolic See a decision may be given. Leo adds that he also reserves to himself any appeal that may be made.[43]

The many wise and clear decisions that Leo made in response to inquiries submitted, particularly with regard to the practical administration of penance, profoundly influenced subsequent canon law. Certainly in his firmness and willingness to assert authority Leo stands out among the early popes.

He orders, decides, reprehends, deposes, corrects, threatens, defines, sentences, suspends, prescribes—in short, Leo's language is the language of him who possesses the *gubernacula ecclesiae universalis:* his tone is the tone of him who governs.[44]

41. Ep. 10, 7 (PL 54:634-635; Jaffé 437).
42. Ep. 65, 4 (PL 54:883).
43. Ep. 6, 5 (PL 54:619 B): "Si qua vero causa major evenerit, quae a tua fraternitate illic praesidente non potuerit definiri, relatio tua missa nos consultat . . . qui vocem appellationis emiserit, reservamus." Jaffé 404.
44. W. Ullmann, *art. cit., JTS* 11 (1960), 25. *Gubernaculum* in fifth-century language, however, is not "government" but the rudder of the [ship of] the Church — quite a different emphasis.

Succeeding popes continued to deal with the problems of church organization in the West, particularly in Gaul and Spain, warning that the decrees of the Apostolic See should be observed just like the precepts of the divine law and the Nicene canons. Pope Gelasius (492-498) gave classical expression to the supreme jurisdiction exercised by the Roman pontiff, superior even to that of a synod. By ancient custom the papacy has frequently "absolved those who had been unfairly condemned by a council and condemned without a council those who deserved condemnation."[45] The Apostolic See has the "right to loose what has been bound by the sentence of any bishop because it has the authority to judge all churches but can be judged by none."[46] Bishops are not to dispense from the canons without the consent of the Apostolic See.[47]

During the period of temporizing with the Monophysites in the reign of Justinian, however, the Roman pontiffs were indeed judged by other churches. Milan, Ravenna, and Aquileia refused to follow Vigilius, and papal influence declined. The second pontiff to be accorded the title "Great" rescued the Roman See from this eclipse. The vast correspondence of Gregory I (590-604) bears convincing witness

45. "Apostolica sedes frequenter, ut dictum est, more majorum etiam sine ulla synodo praecedente et absolvendi, quos synodus inique damnaverat, et damnandi nulla existente synodo, quos oportuit, habuerit facultatem." Ep. 26 (*Epistolae Romanorum Pontificum Genuinae et Quae ad Eos Scriptae Sunt a S. Hilaro usque ad Pelagium II,* ed. A. Thiel, Brunsbergae, 1868, p. 400; Jaffé 664).

46. "Ac per hoc illam de tota Ecclesia judicare, ipsam ad nullius commeare judicium ..." Ep. 10, 5, ed. Thiel, p. 344; Jaffé 622.

47. Ep. 14, 9, ed. Thiel, p. 367. See J. L. Nelson, "Gelasius I's Doctrine of Responsibility: A Note," *Journal of Theological Studies,* 18 (1967), 154-162.

to his supervision of the universal Church.[48] He does not seem to have made innovations in the process of concentrating power in the hands of the papacy, but was content to consolidate the policies of his predecessors.

Far from seeking to diminish the jurisdiction of bishops, Gregory sought to maintain ancient practices: "we defend our own rights and also respect the rights of each church . . . I desire to honor my fellow bishops in everything and strive to uphold the honor of each, provided there is no conflict of rights between them."[49] When on one occasion the African bishops asked him to confirm their customs, he did so with one reservation: no bishop converted from Donatism was to be made a primate.[50] This limitation imposed by Gregory indicated that he had the authority to overrule or modify local practices if he deemed fit.

Gregory was particularly concerned to enhance the judicial function of the papacy. In the face of some African opposition, he insisted that appellants to the Apostolic See were not to be impeded in any way.[51] He reserved to the papacy those cases that were especially grave: "If any question of faith or of some other matter should arise among the bishops which is difficult to settle, it should be explored and settled before twelve bishops; if it still cannot be solved, let it be referred to our judgment."[52] Gregory insisted that he had the right to "reverse the sentence of others."[53] He actu-

48. F. H. Dudden, *Gregory the Great: His Place in History and Thought*, New York, 1905 (reissued 1967), Vol. I, Bk. II, "Gregory's Pontificate."
49. Ep. II, 52 (MGH Ep. I, 156; Jaffé 1199).
50. EP. I, 75 (MGH Ep. I, 95; Jaffé 1144).
51. EP. I, 72 (MGH Ep. I, 95; Jaffé 1141).
52. Ep. V, 58 (MGH Ep. I, 2, 370; Jaffé 1374).
53. Ep. X, II (MGH II, 2, 246; Jaffé 1779).

ally did so in a case arising in the patriarchate of Constantinople. Later on, defending papal competence against those at Ravenna who claimed he was violating the canons, Gregory wrote:

> Do you not know that the case of the priest John against John of Constantinople, our brother and fellow bishop, was referred to the Apostolic See according to the canons and was decided by our judgment? If, therefore, a case was brought to our attention from the Imperial City, how much more should a dispute against you be terminated here after the truth has been determined.[54]

As a result of the Lombard invasions, the political dependence of the papacy on Byzantium gradually slackened. The practice of seeking imperial confirmation of a papal election which began with Justinian ended in 741. At the same time the Islamic conquests eliminated three of the five patriarchates: Alexandria, Antioch, and Jerusalem. Carthage, the only serious rival of the papacy in the West, was also to exalt Rome upon the ruins of the great towns of the East which was the cradle of Christianity."[55] The papacy turned westward and in 754 Pope Stephen II concluded an alliance with the Frankish king, Pippin.

At this critical period St. Boniface, the Apostle of Germany, sought to ensure papal control over the ecclesiastical affairs of western Europe. In a reorganization of the Frankish

54. Ep. VI, 24 (MGH Ep. I, 2, 401-402; Jaffé 1404).

55. F. Lot, *The End of the Ancient World and the Beginning of the Middle Ages,* Eng. trans. M. and P. Leon 1931, Harper Torchbook 1961, p. 303.

church Boniface recognized that the metropolitan system then almost moribund had definite advantages as a unifying factor. True unity, however, demanded that the metropolitans be closely tied to Rome. To this end a Frankish synod over which he presided in 747 decreed that metropolitans must apply to Rome for the pallium.[56] The pallium eventually became the distinctive sign of almost all the metropolitans in the West. Pope Nicholas insisted that metropolitans not exercise their power until they received the pallium and it would not be given until they made an oath of allegiance to the papacy.[57] At the Council of Ravenna in 877 under Pope John VIII it was ordered that all metropolitans within three months of their consecration send to the Apostolic See a profession of faith and a petition for the pallium; otherwise they would lose the right of consecrating bishops.[58] In time the bestowal of the pallium came to have great juridical significance; the metropolitan could not exercise jurisdiction before obtaining it. As a symbol of unity and submission the pallium seemed to confer upon the archbishop a share in the universal primacy and to identify him as the pope's vicar. A forged papal privilege, fabricated under Archbishop Frederick of Salzburg (c. 975) speaks of

56. Hefele-Leclercq III, 2, No. 554 "Metropolitanos pallia ab illa sede quaerere et per omnia praecepta sancti Petri cononice sequi desiderare."

57. Ad Bulgar. c. 73 (PL 119:1007; MGH Ep. XI, 593). See A. S. Popek, *The Rights and Obligations of Metropolitans*, Catholic University of America Canon Law Studies [CUA Canon Law], no. 260), Washington, D.C. 1947.

58. Hefele-Leclercq, IV. 2, #523 (p. 661); Mansi 17:337. For a discussion of the pallium see J. P. Whitney, *Hildebrandine Essays*, Cambridge, 1932, 46-53.

the Apostle Peter's successors appointing *archiepiscopos qui eorum vices tenerent in ecclesiis.*[59]

The identification here realized of archbishop and apostolic vicar must have shown that a characteristic feature of the ancient Christian metropolitan constitution, that is, its autogenous origin, based on the collegiality of the episcopate, had disappeared from the living consciousness of Western Christendom. The victory of the Roman idea was only a matter of time.[60]

Through the efforts of Boniface and Gregory before him the newly converted peoples were imbued with a profound sense of devotion to St. Peter which was reflected in their docile attitude toward his successor in Rome.

NICHOLAS I

Nicholas I (859-867), deservedly called 'the Great,' moved quickly and firmly to establish papal control over the churches of the West, both old and new. He reserved to the Apostolic See the right to convoke, direct and confirm general councils, or what today would be called national councils: *facto concilio generali, quod sine apostolicae sedis*

---

59. PL 135:1081; Mansi 19:58; Brackmann, *Reg. Rom. Pont., Ger. Pont.* I, no. 35.

60. F. Kempf, Chap. 35 "Metropolitans, Primate, and Papacy," *The Church in the Age of Feudalism. Handbook of Church History,* III, New York, 1969, 290.

Praecepto nulli fas est vocandi.[61] The Roman Church by its authority "confirms councils, by her directions gives them the value they possess."[62] He appealed to history to make the point that "no council has ever been received without its consent,"[63] indeed, such a council loses its force. Nicholas' objective was to lessen the hold of the Carolingian rulers upon the Church; they had not even bothered to refer conciliar decisions to Rome for approval. Nicholas gained a measure of success. Whereas the Council of Frankfort in 794 spoke of itself as convoked: *apostolica auctoritate atque jussione Caroli regis,*[64] now the Synod of Soissons wrote to Nicholas: *Synodo Suessionis habita jussu et auctoritate sanctissimi apostolatus vestri.*[65] Nicholas did not, however, claim the same supervisory rights over provincial councils. It remained for the pseudo-Isidorian Decretals to assert that every council needed papal approbation.

Nicholas sought to clarify what were the *causae majores* reserved to the papacy. He wrote that a metropolitan, primate, or patriarch could be judged only by the pope.[66] In fact, since any case involving a bishop is a matter of grave importance, it could be judged in the first instance at Rome.[67] Here is possible evidence of the pseudo-Isidorian influence.

---

61. Ep. 71 (PL 119:891). See Y. Congar, "S. Nicolas Ier (d. 867): Ses Positions Ecclesiologiques," *Rivista di Storia della Chiesa in Italia*, 21 (1967), 393-410. J. Roy, *Saint Nicholas I*, trans. M. Maitland, London, 1901.

62. Ep. 86 (PL 119:947).

63. Ep. 65 (PL 119:822 C).

64. C. 1 (Mansi 13:909).

65. III Council of Soissons 866 A.D. (Mansi 15:728).

66. Ep. 65 (PL 119:882 D).

67. Ep. 71 (PL 119:892) "quia sacra statuta et veneranda decreta episcoporum causas, ut pote majora negotia, nostrae diffiniendas censurae mandarunt."

He ordered Hincmar of Rheims to affirm at the Council of Troyes that archbishops and bishops can only be deposed with the consent of the Apostolic See.[68] The appellate jurisdiction of the papacy was in his view mainly protective, a refuge for the oppressed: "we must support those of our brethren who have suffered any injury."[69]

When Nicholas claims any right, he is careful to set forth Gospel texts and deduce arguments from them. To Photius in 862 he wrote that Peter received the primacy over the churches from Christ; through Peter the Roman Church is the head of all the churches.[70] These churches find in the Roman Church the perfect rule regarding ecclesiastical institutions; no decision of the Apostolic See may be departed from under any pretext. He tells the archbishop of Bourges to "read the holy canons, examine the acts of councils and see that the Apostolic See by a special prerogative . . . has the right to make laws, establish decrees and promulgate sentences in the universal Christian Church."[71] From the head of the churches came regulations about monastic vows, divine worship, the functions of the chorepiscopi, certain marriage cases, and a host of other practical concerns. Truly he was convinced that he held the place of Jesus Christ in the universal Church that divine providence had put him at the head of the universal Church and had made his apostolate, as it were, the cornerstone of the Church.

Just before the reign of Pope Nicholas there appeared a group of canonical collections of the same general prov-

68. Hefele-Leclercq IV, 1: no. 327 (PL 126:76).
69. Ep. 104 (PL 119:1084).
70. Ep. 12 (PL 119:786).
71. Ep. 65 (PL 119:882) "cui facultas est in tota Christi Ecclesia leges speciali praerogative ponere, ac decreta statuere, ac sententias promulgare."

enance and tendency which are now known as the pseudo-Isidorian forgeries.[72] These works were probably produced at Le Mans or Rheims during the mid-ninth century.[73] The author sought to protect the Church from unprincipled political interference, to limit the power of metropolitans over their suffragans, and to extol papal primacy. The overall objective was to strengthen the position of the local bishops vis-a-vis the lay lord and immediate ecclesiastical superior, the archbishop. Provincial synods were restricted in their competence and cases against bishops were reserved to Rome. The forgeries, especially the *False Decretals,* proved to be especially useful to the reform popes of the Gregorian era. It was through the various canonical collections of the tenth and eleventh centuries that the forgeries made their impact; but, paradoxically, they then served to tighten the control of the papacy, rather than to advance the cause of episcopal independence.

Shortly after Nicholas I, the papacy entered upon a century and a half of almost continual degradation. The collapse of the Carolingian empire, the last wave of invasions by the Danes, Magyars, and Saracens, and the rapacity of the Italian aristocracy combined to render papal leadership all but impotent. What rescued the papacy was a reform movement originating at the monastery of Cluny in Burgundy as well as in monasteries of Lorraine. Fostered by the monarchy, the movement gathered momentum until, through the Emperor Henry III, the papacy itself was liberated from

72. See W. Ullmann, Chap. VI "The Age of Pseudo-Isidore," *The Growth of Papal Government in the Middle Ages,* London, 2nd ed. 1962, pp. 167-189.
73. W. Goffart, *The Le Mans Forgeries: A Chapter from the History of Church Property in the Ninth Century,* Cambridge, Mass., 1966, p. 66.

Italian factionalism. Pope Leo IX (1049-1054), an Alsatian and a relative of the Emperor, inaugurated the Gregorian Reform and set the papacy firmly upon its course of monarchical centralization.

GREGORY VII

Renewed activity on the part of the papacy coincided with that of the canonists, and the interaction worked to advance the Roman primacy. The most important of the early collections, *The 74 Titles* or the *Diversorum patrum sententiae,* attributed by many scholars to Cardinal Humbert, appeared between 1051 and 1073.[74] Quickly becoming a handbook for the reformers, it was incorporated in succeeding collections down to Gratian. Most of the themes stressed in the Sentences have close parallels in the *Dictatus Papae,* which appeared early in the reign of Gregory VII (1073-1085) after whom the whole reform period takes its name. The *Dictatus Papae* consists of 27 rubrics dealing with papal prerogatives which probably served as chapter headings for a canon law collection drawn up by Gregory. The material can be traced back largely to the ninth century *False Decretals.*[75] What was new in the reform came mainly from interpretation and application of old law.

74. J. T. Gilchrist, "Canon Law Aspects of the Eleventh Century Gregorian Reform Programme," *Journal of Ecclesiastical History,* 13 (1962), 21-38.

75. MGH, Ep. Sel. (Caspar ed.), 201-8; Reg. II, 55a. K. Hofmann, "Der 'Dictatus Papae' Gregors VII als Index einer Kanonessammlung?," *Studi Gregorianni,* ed. G. Borino, Rome, 1947, pp. 531-537. R. Morshen, "Richerche sulla formazione del Registro di Gregorio VII," *Annali di Storia del Diritto,* 3-4 (1959-60), 35-63.

Gregory adopted the following rubrics in the *Dictatus Papae* which are particularly relevant to a discussion of reservations.[76] (1) The Roman Church was founded by God alone. Upon this contention, the medieval papacy based its claim to special jurisdiction over and above the other apostolic churches. (2) Only the Roman pontiff can rightly be called universal. (3) He alone can depose bishops and reinstate them. (4) His legate, even if of inferior rank, takes precedence over bishops in council, and he can pass sentence of deposition against them. (7) He alone, if necessity demands, can make new laws, establish new congregations, raise a collegiate church to abbatial status and, on the other hand, divide a rich bishopric and combine poor ones. (13) If necessary, he can transfer bishops from one see to another. (16) No general synod may be called without his consent. (17) No chapter and no book shall be considered canonical without his authority. (18) His verdict should not be altered by anyone; he alone can review the decisions of all. (19) No one should venture to condemn a person appealing to the Apostolic See. (21) The major suits of every church must be referred to Rome. (25) Without the meeting of a synod he can depose and reconcile bishops.

The explicit statement that a pope could depose an emperor (12) seems to be the most significant innovation on the part of Gregory. For the rest one could find some historical precedent. In the long struggle over lay investiture, procedures that previously had been applied to bishops and clerics began to be used against seculars. The excommunica-

76. S. Ehler and J. Morrall, *Church and State Through the Centuries: A Collection of Historic Documents with Commentaries*, Westminster, Md., 1954, pp. 43-44.

tion and deposition of Emperor Henry IV is the most famous instance.

The claims of the *Dictatus Papae* were formulated by the Gregorian reformers as weapons to eliminate abuses from the Church. Because of vested local interests, it was recognized that only a vigilant and vigorous central authority could deal with unworthy ecclesiastics, who were the source of all the evils. Only the papacy with its Petrine heritage had the supra-national standing to cope with the problems, and to this end its authority had to be strengthened.

If the reform program were not to remain a merely pious hope, some means of execution and enforcement had to be found. Pope Leo IX adopted a strategy of synods and papal legates, which was also followed by his successors. He held a synod in Rome almost every year of his pontificate.[77] Since the prestige of the papacy at that time was not sufficiently high to guarantee that the decrees of a Roman synod would be accepted everywhere, he himself, after the pattern of the secular rulers, journeyed from region to region summoning the bishops: Pavia, Rheims, and Mainz in 1049; Siponto, Salerno, Vercelli in 1050; Mantua and perhaps Bari in 1053. The presence of Peter's successor in the flesh, bearing the keys of salvation, binding and loosening, gave powerful impetus to the reform spirit.

The papal claim of sole competence over all general synods was not accepted without a struggle. The German national synods were too fresh and too valuable for the king to let them slip from his control without protest. Peter Damian wrote the *Synodical Debate Between the Emperor's*

---

77. Hefele-Leclercq, IV. 2: pp. 99f.

Advocate and the Defender of the Roman Church in response to a German synod's refusal to accept the new papal election provision of 1059.[78] Since the canonical foundation for exclusive papal rights over councils was slight, Damian had to argue that the pope acts in the place of Christ, the *institutor sanctarum legum.*

Gregory VII sought to make the Lenten synods which met in the Lateran an annual institution.[79] Participation was enlarged to include France and England, as well as northern Italy. This device was intended to offset the "general assembly of all the princes of the kingdom" which Henry IV had arrayed against him. Gregory's efforts to secure recognition of the synods from the whole Church anticipated the future significance of these councils. Urban II (1088-1099) convoked eleven councils in all; only the ones at Melfi, Benevento, Troia, Piacenza, Clermont, and Rome found a place in the canonical collections.[80] He strove to make regional and diocesan synods subject to papal confirmation. When the investiture issue flared up again, Paschal II (1099-1118) held councils in Spain, France, and Italy, as well as at the Lateran in 1112. The next synod to be held at the Lateran in 1123 to ratify the Concordat of Worms has been accorded recognition as the ninth Ecumenical Council, the first such council to be held in the West. The Gregorian reform synods thus shaded off into the great medieval councils of the next four centuries, posing many problems for scholars concerned with the theology of ecumenical councils.

78. PL 145:67-90.

79. *Concilia Romana* (PL 148:750-823).

80. F. Gossman, *Pope Urban II and Canon Law* (CUA Canon Law, no. 403), Washington, D.C., 1960, p. 146.

A second agency used to implement the Gregorian reform was the papal legation.[81] Though the employment of legates was not new, Leo IX began to make unaccustomed use of them. He assembled an especially capable entourage which he dispatched all over Christendom on important errands of reform. Cardinal Humbert, who went to Constantinople on momentous business in 1054,[82] and Cardinal Peter Damian were the most famous of these emissaries. Alexander II (1063) sent Peter Damian to Gaul with full authority to act for the pope.[83] Gregory VII used legates with great effectiveness, sending them to Denmark, Norway, Sweden, Poland, Hungary, and Spain.[84] He was convinced that business could be carried out most expeditiously on the spot.[85] He assigned his legates a wide assortment of charges: to resolve monastic disputes, to discipline those receiving lay investiture, to absolve and reconcile penitents, to regularize marriages, and to confirm those elected to the episcopacy.[86] Above all, the legates were to work through councils in establishing the reform. The pope continued to reserve *causae majores* to himself, though he did permit the legates to initiate the process. Henceforth the legates became an indispensable organ of papal government and centralization. They were present everywhere, extending the jurisdiction of the papacy and resisting independent claims of the bishops.

81. G. Paro, *The Right of Papal Legation* (CUA Canon Law, no. 221), Washington, D.C., 1947. F. J. McDonough, *Apostolic Administrators* (CUA Canon Law, no. 139), Washington, D.C., 1941.
82. PL 143:1001 A-1002C.
83. Mansi 19:958, "Pleno iure commissimus."
84. Reg. Greg. II, 51; VI, 13; VIII, 11; II, 73; II, 13; IV, 28.
85. IV, 17.
86. IV, 16; VIII, 421; VII, 16; VI, 20, 21.

Not all bishops submitted meekly to close papal control. The bishops of Germany—undoubtedly under imperial pressure—complained to Gregory VII in 1076 that he was trying his best to deprive them of the power that had been bestowed by the Holy Spirit.[87] A little later St. Bernard of Clairvaux articulated "the groaning and complaints of the churches" to Pope Innocent II: "They cry out that they are being amputated and dismembered . . . because abbots are taken out from under their bishops, bishops from their archbishops . . . you have been appointed to preserve for each the rank and order of his honor and dignity, not to prejudice them."[88]

Other significant developments during the reform shifted more powers from the bishops to the papacy. Though it is difficult to pinpoint the origin of monastic exemptions, it became more and more common at this time for monasteries to be withdrawn from the jurisdiction of the local ordinary and made subject directly to Rome.[89] What had begun as mere papal protection was transformed by the concession of various immunities into a status of immediate subjection to the Holy See. Gregory V granted (c. 990) privileges to

87. MGH, Const. I, 107, "Sublata enim, quantum in te fuit, omni potestate ab episcopis quae eis divinitus per gratiam S. Spiritus, qui maxime in ordinationibus operatur, collata esse dinoscitur, omnîque rerum ecclesiasticarum administratione."

88. *De consideratione,* III, 4 (Leclercq, III, 442). See E. Kennan, "The 'De Consideratione' of St. Bernard of Clairvaux and the Papacy in the Mid-twelfth Century: A Review of Scholarship," *Traditio* 23 (1967), 73-115.

89. It is often stated that Honorius I in 628 gave the monastery of Bobbio a complete exemption (Jaffé 2017). But Schwarz maintains there is no instance before c. 1000 A.D. (*Zeitschrift der Savigny-Stifing für Rechtsgeschichte* 79 [1959], 34-98; Bobbio p. 57).

the monastery of Cluny which were to become typical.[90] The abbot was to control ordinations within the monastery, inviting whatever bishop he wished and at a time that was convenient for the monastery. John XIX in 1025, after the bishop of Mâcon fought with Cluny, granted an exemption from episcopal excommunication and interdict.[91] Thus the monastic movement, freed from secular and local encroachments, could work with the papacy to lift the spiritual tone of the Church. In fact, the reform movement succeeded only when an alliance was forged between Rome and the monasteries. Gregory VII and his successors withdrew not only individual foundations, but also affiliated abbeys and priories from the juridical control of bishops. By the time of Urban II (1088-1099) monastic exemption was more common than not.[92] He frequently moved to place monasteries directly under the Apostolic See. The exemptions applied to internal affairs; in matters pertaining to the *cura animarum* the authority of the bishops prevailed.

Gregory VII also sought to impose the Roman liturgy on certain churches of the West. In 1074 he wrote to the kings and bishops of Spain reminding them that the first missionaries had brought the Roman rite to that land. He ordered them to abandon the Toledo rite and return to the ancient practice.[93] The Council of Burgos in 1085 capitulated to Roman demands and gave up the Mozarabic rite, though

90. PL 137:932. See N. Hunt, *Cluny under Saint Hugh* 1049-1109, Notre Dame, 1967.

91. PL 141:1136.

92. E. Fogliasso, "Exemption," *Dictionnaire de Droit Canonique* (1953), V, 646-665.

93. MGH, Ep. Sel. Reg. 1, 63; 1, 64; F. Cabrol, DACL 12. 1, 390-491.

as a compromise six parishes in Toledo were permitted to observe the old rite. The Council of Léon, forbidding the use of Gothic letters, prescribed new service books in Latin characters.[94] Attempts to achieve uniformity at Milan proved largely unsuccessful; a non-Roman ritual has persisted there to the present day. For the most part the Roman authority did prevail. Bernold of Constance (d. 1100) in his liturgical treatise, the *Micrologus,* argued for reform on the basis of the Roman usage. Phrases such as these dot almost every page: *secundum consuetudinem Romanam, juxta ordinem Romanum, more Romano, Romana auctoritas.*[95] For Bernold any precept of the Apostolic See must be accorded religious obedience:

> Hanc puram obedientiam cum omnibus spiritualibus nostris praeceptoribus certissime debeamus maxime tamen apostolicae sedi ex intimo corde debemus quae totius Christianae religionis caput est et origo.[96]

The Concordat of Worms in 1122 signaled the victory of the Gregorian reform over lay investiture, at least in principle. The First Lateran Council the next year ratified the agreement and opened a new chapter in which legal activity was to play a dominant role. The canonical collections of the reform, stressing papal authority and reflecting

94. H. F. Williams, "The Diocesan Rite of the Archdiocese of Braga," *Journal of Ecclesiastical History,* 4 (1953), 123-138, at p. 125.

95. PL 151:974-1022. See V. L. Kennedy, "For a new edition of the Micrologus of Bernard of Constance," *Mélanges en L'Honneur de Monseigneur Michel Andrieu,* Strasbourg, 1956, 229-241.

96. PL 151:998B.

papal policy, charted the course for the next two centuries. When Gratian published his *Concordia discordantium canonum* (c. 1140), the need to distinguish between *auctoritates* became urgent.[97] The very structure of the *Decretum* provoked discussion and uncovered difficulties. Efforts toward a more efficient administration of the Church and new developments in theology posed further legal problems. Glosses and *Summae* multiplied as the lawyers came to grips with new questions.

As administrative centralization tightened, legal business preoccupied the popes.[98] Instructions or decisions concerning particular lawsuits flowed from Rome. Papal responses to specific questions on points of law were recorded. The four Lateran councils, later recognized as ecumenical, were held within a century. For 42 years the Church was ruled by Alexander III (1159-1181) and Innocent III (1198-1216), popes with extensive legal training. Their pronouncements were collected, analyzed, and studied in the law schools of Western Europe. The new papal legislation was officially promulgated by Pope Gregory IX in 1234. His book of 2,139 decretals arranged the material in five books: *judex, judicium, clerus, connubia, crimen.* By this time the papacy was looked upon as the real legislative authority in the Church. Lateran Council III employed a symbolic formula: the conciliar decisions are proclaimed by the pope "with the approbation of the holy council."[99]

---

97. See S. G. Kuttner, *Harmony from Dissonance,* Latrobe, Pa., 1960.
98. G. Le Bras, *Histoire du Droit et des Institutions de L'église en Occident,* T. VII *L'age Classique,* 1140-1378, Paris, 1965, 133-166.
99. *Conciliorum Oecumenicorum Decreta,* p. 187, no. 1. See C. Andreson, "History of the Medieval Councils in the West," *The Councils of the Church: History & Analysis,* ed. H. J. Argull, (trans. from Ger. ed. 1961), Philadelphia, 1966, at 132-133.

Pope Innocent III affirmed that insofar as he had received plenitude of power from God, he is fully responsible for the flock committed to his care. Since there is no judge superior to the pope, he is competent to settle all affairs brought to his cognizance. Appeals have been instituted, not to enhance papal power, but "for the protection of the oppressed, so that one may always have recourse to the Roman Church as the mother of all the churches, the unique refuge of all the faithful of Christ."[100]

Pope Innocent vigorously maintained the right to modify diocesan boundaries, to suppress and establish bishoprics as circumstances warranted. In the Iberian peninsula he personally settled the differences between the archbishops of Compostella and Braga over their suffragan sees.[101] In Portugal he defined diocesan limits and forced the Knights Templar to restore usurped territory to the bishop of Coimbra.[102] Similar settlements were made in France, Germany, and Hungary. He also provided for the organization of the Church in Bulgaria.[103]

Litigants in the highly centralized church of Innocent III recurred more and more to Rome for rulings on administrative and disciplinary matters. A casual inspection of the papal registers reveals the trivial cases handled. Innocent intervened at Poitiers, for instance, to effect the transfer of a canon, at Léon to force the cathedral chapter to accept a certain member; he ruled on problems of burial in a Cis-

---

100. 1, 490 (PL 214:456); 1, 109 (PL 214:96); 1, 240, (PL 214: 206B). See A. Fliche, "Innocent II et la Réforme de l'Église," *Revue d'Histoire Ecclesiastique*, 44 (1949), 87-152.

101. 11, 103 (PL 214:653).

102. 1, 221 (PL 214:191).

103. 11, 82 (PL 214:625); XIV, 84 (216:447) etc.

tercian monastery. It is estimated that there are 250,000 letters in the Registers preserved in the Vatican archives from 1198 to 1417.[104] Perhaps no more than a tenth of those dispatched was recorded. Only a fraction of the letters, however, are rulings; most are grants. Pope John XXII used 71,566 pounds of lead during his 18-year pontificate to seal letters, another indication of the vast correspondence flowing through the *Cancelleria Apostolica*.[105]

Though the prestige of the papacy declined after the heady days of Innocent III, the Avignon popes managed to extend the jurisdiction of the Apostolic See. The peak of centralization in administrative and financial affairs was reached in the reign of John XXII. He laid down the first definite regulations for the Rota, the tribunal which tries the cases brought to the Apostolic Palace.[106] These cases dealt mainly with benefices. The Apostolic Penitentiary, empowered to lift censures and grant marriage dispensations in certain cases, employed about 30 persons. The Apostolic Camera was charged with collecting and administering the papal revenue. The net effect of these developments was to create a huge bureaucracy concerned mainly with financial and legal matters, to the detriment of the Church's spiritual mission.[107]

104. G. Battelli, "Le ricerche storiche nell'Archivo Vaticano," *Relazioni of the Tenth International Congress of Historical Sciences*, Rome, 1955, 1, 451-477, 457.

105. J. E. Weakland, "Administrative and Fiscal Centralization under Pope John XXII 1316-1334," *The Catholic Historical Review*, 54, (1968), 39-54, 285-310, esp. p. 51.

106. *Ratio iuris* 1331, *Dict. de Droit Canonique*, VII, 745.

107. Weakland *op. cit.*, p. 52 Raymond of Pennafort was one of the first penitentiaries. Gregory IX in promulgating the Decretals spoke of him as *capellanum et peonitentiarum nostrum* (*Rex pacificus*, Potthast 9694).

Pope John XXII sought to prevent the Curia from building an independent power base. The various officials were bound by an oath of loyalty and honesty to the pope himself. The formulas used in letters of supplication emphasized that it was the pope who was the source of the favor: *quod —gratiam non expediat sine expressa conscientia domini nostri.*[108]

During the period from Gratian's *Decretum* (c. 1140) to the end of the Avignon residency of the popes (1378), *"l'Age Classique"* of canon law, rapid developments occurred in several areas of papal reservations: appointment to bishoprics and other benefices, the grant of dispensations, the absolution of censures. The remainder of this paper will trace the growth of papal control over these functions.

APPOINTMENT OF BISHOPS

In the election of bishops the practice in the West differed from that in the East.[109] The laity were excluded from participation in the selection of bishops in the East at a much earlier date. Canon 3 of Nicaea II in 787 finally declared that every election by princes is invalid: the right belongs exclusively to the bishops of the province.[110] It

108. Weakland, *op. cit.*, p. 50.
109. A convenient entry to the vast bibliography on episcopal elections may be found in R. L. Benson, *The Bishop-Elect, A study in Medieval Ecclesiastical Office*, Princeton, 1968, esp. chap. 11 "Constitutional Background; Gratian's Decretum," 23-55. For an older but still useful summary see A. Parsons, *Canonical Elections*, (CUA Canon Law, no. 118), Washington D.C. 1939.
110. COD, 116.

must be noted, however, that this legislation did not inhibit imperial interference. In the West both the clergy and the people continued to have an important voice in elections for some time. Pope Celestine in 428 wrote to the bishops of Gaul and formulated the principle that no bishop was to be foisted on people who did not want him.[111] Pope Leo the Great in a letter to the bishops of the province of Vienne in 445 declared that one who is to rule over all should be elected by all.[112] In time, particularly in the Carolingian and feudal periods, the secular ruler usurped the right of appointment to the episcopal offices. The bishop as a result tended to become a royal functionary. Canonical elections either disappeared or were reduced to a mere formality, an approval of the prince's choice.

The heart of the Gregorian reform program was to free the Church, especially the episcopate, from secular domination. Toward the middle of the twelfth century the tendency was to place the election of the bishop in the hands of the cathedral chapter, thus eliminating lay interference and limiting the role of the lesser clergy and monks.[113] In Dist. 63, Gratian lined up eight texts prohibiting lay interference and seventeen texts, on the other hand, which recognized such influence, particularly on the part of the king. He harmonized the apparent contradiction by restricting lay

111. Ep. 10, 5 (PL 50:434) "Nullus invitus detur episcopus. Cleri, plebis et ordinis consensus ac disiderium requiratur." D. 61, c. 13.

112. Ep. 4, 5 (PL 54:634A) "Qui praefuturus est omnibus, ab omnibus eligatur." (D. 63, c. 27: I: 243).

113. II Lateran Council, c. 28 (COD, 179) forbade the canons to exclude religious men from the election. Gratian's rubric to this enactment (D. 63, c. 35) states that the major clergy should not *elect* without the *counsel* of religious men.

participation to acclamation and consent. As for the privileges of rulers, these resulted from emergency situations which, remarked Gratian, no longer existed. The authority which the *Decretum* received ensured that election by cathedral chapters would dominate canonical thinking by the end of the century.

Election alone did not suffice; a candidate had to be confirmed. The Council of Nicaea had stipulated that the confirmation of the metropolitan was necessary.[114] In the case of a disputed election, according to Leo the Great, it was up to the metropolitan to decide which candidate was "aided by greater zeal and merit."[115] Church councils from the fifth through the seventh centuries continued to insist upon the metropolitan's consent before the one elected to a bishopric could enter upon his duties. Gratian incorporated in the *Decretum* the texts requiring the metropolitan's confirmation.[116] Rufinus in his *Summa* (1157-1159) and Stephen of Tournai a few years later distinguished between the bishop's sacramental power of orders and his jurisdiction. Jurisdiction came only from confirmation: bishops "from their election are approved; from the confirmation of their election, they obtain power."[117] Almost immediately the decretists agreed that one could not exercise jurisdictional powers until he was confirmed. It was up to the superior

114. Canon 4 (COD, 6).

115. Ep. 14, 5 (PL 54:673), "qui majoribus et studiis juvatur et meritis."

116. D. 64, c. 1 (I: 247-248): D. 63, c. 36 (I:247).

117. Rufinus, *Die Summa decretorum des Magister Rufinus*, ed. H. Singer, Paderborn, 1902. D. 21, cap. 2 (p. 45). Stephen of Tournai, *Die Summa des Stephanus Tornacensis Über das Decretum Gratiani*, ed. J. F. von Schulte, Giessen, 1891. D. 23 (p. 35) Text is from Stephen. Benson, *op. cit.*, 90-108.

to confirm the inferior: the archbishop would confirm the bishop; the pope would confirm the metropolitan.[118]

The emphasis on confirmation as the key factor bestowing rights and jurisdiction strengthened the position of the superior at the expense of the electors. The English canonist Alanus realized the logical conclusion of this development when he wrote: "every bishop has his bishopric from the pope," but then immediately added, "It is not he, however, who bestows it, but the canonical election of the clerics."[119] By the end of Innocent III's reign papal confirmation of metropolitans was the regular practice.[120]

Gradually the papacy took over from the metropolitan the right of confirming the suffragan bishops. For a long time the pope had been empowered to transfer a prelate from one See to another. Similarly, when a candidate lacked some legal qualification for office, the electors had been accustomed to postulate the Holy See rather than the metropolitan.[121] The most important advance in papal control was jurisdiction over disputed elections. The direction of appeals to Rome originated with the aggrieved parties not with an aggressive papacy. Appeals were taken to the Curia because justice could more likely be found there. A declaration of Alexander IV, reaffirmed by Gregory X at Lyons

118. See, for example, Bernard of Pavia, *Summa decretalium*, ed. E. Laspeyres, Regensburg, 1860, p. 320.

119. A. M. Stickler, "Alanus Anglicus als Verteidiger des Monarchischen Papsttums," *Salesianum* 21 (1959), 362: "Set quilibet episcopus habet episcopatum a papa, set tamen papa non tribuit set canonica clericorum electio." See Benson, *op. cit.*, p. 131 who has called attention to these references.

120. IV Lateran Council c. 26 (COD, 223).

121. C. 7, X, 1, 6 (II: 51-52) III Lateran Council, c. 3 (COD, 188-189).

II (1274), reserved such cases to the Holy See alone.[122] Since it was possible for one elector to challenge an election, that council tried (c. 9) to limit frivolous appeals. From the settlement of disputed elections to the simple confirmation of bishoprics was an almost unnoticed step. Gregory IX, for example, in 1236 confirmed the election of Walter de Cantelupe after his election to the see of Worcester.[123]

As the thirteenth century progressed, the confirmation of bishops was transformed on an increasing scale into direct appointment. It was a period marked by clerical worldliness: the vigor of the reform had spent itself; selfish and material considerations hampered the work of the Church. Oftentimes cathedral chapters for unworthy motives neglected to fill an episcopal vacancy. Lateran Council IV in 1215 decreed (c. 23) that if an election were not held within three months of a vacancy, the right to appoint devolves upon the next immediate superior.[124] Boniface VIII in 1298 asserted the right of the papacy to intervene if the electors had chosen an unqualified person or proceeded irregularly.[125] Local authorities could not be trusted to function unsupervised. The papacy in the interests of order and efficiency shifted from a predominantly judicial control over the selection of bishops to a more administrative role.[126]

122. C. 9 (COD, 296).
123. Matthew of Paris, *Abbreviatio Chr. Ang.* (ed. Madden, Rolls Series II: 393).
124. COD, 222.
125. C. 18, in VI°, 1, 6 (II: 959).
126. G. Barraclough, "The Making of a Bishop in the Middle Ages; the part of the Pope in Law and Fact," *The Catholic Historical Review,* 19 (1934), 275-319. "The earlier situation under which the control

PROVISIONS

Papal appointment of bishops was directly connected with the system of provisions whereby Rome nominated individuals to certain ecclesiastical benefices.[127] A letter of Innocent II to the archbishop of Compostella in 1137 asking that a benefice be conferred on a certain cleric is the first recorded instance of a papal provision.[128] By the time of Hadrian IV (1154-1159) a papal mandate requiring an appointment to a certain office was common; as yet no right was bestowed by the fact of the papal nomination.[129] Soon the popes moved to confer a vacant benefice before the bishop acted, the *jus concursus*. Pope Celestine III (1191-1198) seems to have been the first to take such action.[130] Since the pope was unlikely to be aware of an opening before the local bishop, the exercise of the *jus concursus* was limited. An important advantage to the pope would accrue when the holder of a benefice died at Rome.

In 1199 the climax of papal provision was reached with the reservation: the pope so appropriates a benefice that

of elections lay practically exclusively with the local ecclesiastical authorities, had passed; but the system of Reservations, which gave the Pope very nearly a free hand, had not yet arrived ... The Papacy (rightly it seems to me) did not trust the local hierarchy to function alone. During the period of transition, a number of temporary expedients for coalescing the new central and the old local powers were used," p. 309.

---

127. See G. Barraclough, *Papal Provisions*, Oxford, 1935. J. Haydt, *Reserved Benefices* (CUA Canon Law, no. 161), Washington D.C. 1942.

128. PL 179:323 (Jaffé 7831).

129. Ep. 230 (PL 188:1603): Ep. 235 (PL 188:1606). Haydt, *op. cit.*, p. 15.

130. Referred to by Innocent III in Potthast 117.

its conferral by another authority is invalid. The practice of reservation began with Pope Innocent III who instructed the bishop of Orleans that the first vacancy in his diocese should be reserved for the papal nominee.[131] The pope declared that he was acting in virtue of the *plenitudo potestatis nobis concessa*.[132] At the start of the practice reservation was particular, that is, it affected a certain benefice or the benefices belonging to a certain individual. Although in 1249 during the struggle with the Hohenstaufens Innocent IV inhibited all elections in Germany *absque nostra licentia speciali*, general reservations are usually said to date from the *Licet ecclesiarum* of Clement IV.[133]

This document, issued in 1265, made three claims: the disposition of all ecclesiastical benefices belonged to the Roman pontiff; by ancient custom any benefice that became vacant at the Apostolic See was reserved to the pope; lastly, papal policy would henceforth demand the strict observance of the custom so that any conferral in contravention would be invalid.[134] The ancient custom referred to does not seem to be a true reservation but rather the exercise of the *jus concursus:* the papacy had *de facto* conferred such benefices, but some collators had tried to forestall the appointment. Canonists agreed that the decretal *Licet ecclesiarum* did not affect major benefices such as bishoprics and metropolitan sees, but disputed whether abbacies were included. The phrase *vacans apud Sedem Apostolicam* was not quite clear.

131. Potthast 677 (PL 214:586) I, 589.

132. 1, 89 (PL 214:77).

133. P. Hinschius, *Das Kirchenrecht der Katholiken und Protestanten in Deutschland,* Berlin, 1869-1897, 111, 127.

134. 2, in VIº, 3, 4, (11: 1021). Haydt, *op. cit.,* pp. 23-29.

It certainly reserved all minor benefices whose holders *died* at Rome. Between 1265 and 1298 the interpretation varied; sometimes a benefice was considered vacant when the pope accepted a resignation or removed a beneficiary. Though this decretal did not in fact reserve many benefices, it set the precedent for later popes to revolutionize the medieval Church. The practice of reservations, as much as any single factor, stimulated the hostility to the papacy that would culminate in the Protestant Reformation.

Boniface VIII declared subject to reservation benefices rendered vacant by deaths taking place within a two-day's journey of Rome.[135] Clement V in 1305 brought major benefices within the ambit of the decretal: henceforth, patriarchal, archiepiscopal, and episcopal sees which became vacant by a death at Rome were reserved.[136] The next step was to extend the reservations to vacancies arising from other causes. John XXII in 1316 explicitly included transfers and depositions which took place while the incumbent was at the Holy See; soon the actual presence of the beneficiary at the papal court was not a condition. Pope John XXII also reserved benefices involved in an election or a postulation which was later declared null or benefices which were renounced and accepted by the Holy See.[137]

Various other categories were gradually brought within the scope of reservations, but the most important covered all patriarchal, primatial, archiepiscopal, and episcopal sees. Here was the outcome of an ever increasing use of particular reservations. Pope John XXII, for example, reserved a large

135. C. 34, in VIº, 3, 4, (11:1031).
136. C. 3, in Extrav. Com., 3, 2 (11:1258).
137. C. 4, in Extrav. Com., 1, 3 (11:1240-1241).

number of episcopal sees.[138] Urban V in 1363 climaxed this movement with a general reservation applicable to all sees. When he included this legislation in his *Regulae Cancellariae*,[139] it became part of the Church's universal law. During the early years of the Great Western Schism his successor, Gregory XI, asserted "the right to appoint to all patriarchal, archiepiscopal, and episcopal churches, as well as to all houses of monks and friars, regardless of their revenue, wherever and however they fell vacant."[140]

Not only was the episcopal appointment itself reserved, but also that dignity next in importance, such as provost or dean. The principal dignity in a collegiate church with an annual income of over 10 gold florins was later included.[141] Eventually the *regula mensium* reserved all ecclesiastical benefices which became vacant in the months of January, February, April, May, July, August, October, and November.[142] This most extensive of all reservations was gradually modified by the privilege of alternate months. Residential bishops were allowed to confer benefices which became available every other month. The effect was to reduce the papal reservation from eight to six months of the year.

The papacy acted in virtue of its plenitude of power in

138. See *Lettres Communes des Papes d'Avignon Jean XXII 1316-1334*, ed. G. Mollat, Paris, 1933, XIV (Index) "Reservationes ecclesiarum cathedralium," p. 202.

139. E. Ottenthal, *Regulae cancellariae apostolicae, die Päpstlichen Kanzleireglen von Johannes XXII bis Nicholaus V*, Innsbruck, 1888.

140. G. Mollat, *The Popes at Avignon* (Eng. trans. by J. Love, 1963), Harper, 1965, p. 386.

141. Ottenthal, *op. cit.*, p. 124, n. 2.

142. Hinschius, *Kirchenrecht*, 111, 153; issued by Nicholas V in 1447 but not incorporated into the *Regulae cancellariae* for some time.

enforcing reservations, but the system of the reservations did not develop primarily as a means to enhance that power. The practice was instituted to protect Church offices and property. Oftentimes the ordinary collators, in order to keep revenues for themselves, did not hurry to fill benefices. Again for selfish reasons canon law would be violated to intrude the obviously unfit. It was not unusual for the election of a bishop or abbot to precipitate intrigue, rivalry, even violence. The prolonged vacancy of a position entailing the care of souls would work grave spiritual harm to the Church. There can be no doubt that abuses did exist and that in numerous instances papal reservations sought to alleviate the evil. At first the clergy welcomed this intervention to the extent that it freed them from royal domination; they rejoiced especially at John XXII's *Execrabilis* of 1317 which forbade pluralities.[143] The point was reached, however, when the secondary effects became more intolerable than the original disease. The conferral of benefices came to be especially lucrative to the Holy See. Bishops and others were expected to pay a service charge, *servitia communia*, on the occasion of their appointment or confirmation. These payments, begun as gifts, gradually, like tips today, became obligatory. These taxes had to be paid under pain of excommunication.[144] Numerous complaints testify to the burdens thus imposed. Some historians have calculated that the monies received from the common services constituted the chief source of revenue for the papacy during the Avignon

143. C. un, Extrav. Joann. XXII, 3 (11:1207-1209). W. A. Pantin, "The Fourteenth Century," the *English Church and the Papacy in the Middle Ages*, ed. C. H. Lawrence, Fordham, 1965, pp. 184-185.

144. G. Mollat, *The Popes at Avignon*, p. 319.

period.[145] The bestowal of benefices also enabled the pope to provide for his staff without paying in cash.

One may wonder whether the prelates provided by the papacy were on the whole remarkably better than those who had been elected in the past. Pope John XXII, despite his policy of reservations, had misgivings about the wisdom of such a practice.[146] He was aware that the suppression of elections did not enhance the popularity of the papacy. He was even forced to confess that experience had convinced him that those prelates who had been promoted, far from manifesting gratitude and devotion, were more likely to be a source of trouble for the Church.

DISPENSATIONS

There are a few isolated instances in the early centuries which show that recourse to the Apostolic See was considered necessary for the relaxation of certain canons.[147] In 465 the Council of Tarracona petitioned Pope Hilary to transfer Irenaeus to the see of Barcelona. Though the request was denied, the fact that it was made shows that the

145. W. E. Lunt, *Papal Revenue in the Middle Ages*, New York, 1934, 1, 82; 1, no. 179: II, no. 382.

146. *Lettres secretes du Pape Jean XXII relatives à la France*, ed. Coulon, no. 667 (to King Philip, no. 667, p. 342.).

147. M. A. Stiegler, *Dispensation: Dispensationswesen und Dispensationsrecht im Kirchenrecht Geschichtlich dargestellt*, Mainz, 1901. J. Brys, *De Dispensatione in Iure Canonico, praesertim apud Decretistas et Decretalistas*, Brugis, 1925. E. Reilly, *The General Norms of Dispensation* (CUA Canon Law no. 119), Washington, D.C., 1939. S. Kubik, *Invalidity of Dispensations according to Canon 84, §2*, CUA Canon Law, no. 340), Washington, D.C., 1953.

bishops believed that the pope had a right of dispensation, superior even to that of a council.[148] Pope Gelasius insisted that no bishop should disregard certain laws without permission of the Apostolic See.[149] It is not beyond doubt that dispensation was meant.

From the ninth century the popes began to use their dispensing power more extensively and to specify the conditions under which it would be used. Pope Nicholas I (857-867) affirmed that traditions emanate from the Roman Church; no bishop had a right to modify them.[150] During the Gregorian Reform the popes made liberal use of dispensations to straighten out irregular situations. Urban II (c. 1088) granted general sanation to the clergy of Milan who had been ordained by schismatic bishops.[151] Bernold of Constance about the same time vindicated the pope's right to grant dispensations based on his legislative power.[152] As for the bishop's power to dispense, some confusion was felt. Bernold allowed them to dispense, especially from penitential law, provided the canons conceded them this power. Anselm of Lucca (c. 1083), on the other hand, denied that bishops could dispense from any but their own laws; he based his position on ancient sources.[153] Ivo of Chartres (c. 1095) in the episcopal tradition seems to have acknowledged the right of bishops to dispense from the general law.[154]

148. Mansi VII 926-928.

149. Ep. 14, 9 (ed. Thiel 1:367); Mansi VIII, 38; Jaffé 636.

150. Ep. 98 (PL 119; 1019).

151. Jaffé 5359, 5386.

152. *De Statutis ecclesiasticis sobrie legendis*, MGH, *Libelli de Lite*, 11, 142.

153. MGH, *Libelli de Lite*, 11, 310. *Collectio Can.* 11, 32 (PL 149: 111).

154. PL 161:51. See Brys, *op. cit.*, pp. 58-59.

Meanwhile through vigorous activity the papacy was setting numerous precedents for its exclusive dispensatory rights. Pope Urban II (1088-1099) dispensed from illegitimacy, commuted vows, and voided unjust decisions of metropolitans and suffragans.[155] Pope Paschal II (1099-1118) in response to a petition granted Anselm of Canterbury power to dispense in almost every contingency.[156] Undoubtedly the disposition of bishops to seek the opinion of Rome or to refer certain decisions to the Apostolic See increased the scope of areas reserved to the pope. The Council of London in 1138, for example, reserved to the Roman Pontiff the cause of clerics ordained without letters from their proper bishops.[157] Not all bishops or canonists, of course, approved the drift towards papal monopoly of power. An author's position on dispensatory rights of bishops would largely be determined by his attitude toward papal authority.

Gratian argued that since the pope was the source of law, he could, by special privilege and favor, grant that which was forbidden by general decree.[158] Gratian noted that the *capitula* of certain councils had explicitly provided for such a contingency by adding: "unless the authority of the Roman Church rules otherwise"; or "saving the right of the apostolic authority in all things." Without treating in detail the dispensing power of bishops, Gratian did reserve certain matters to the Holy See: permission, to cite

155. F. Gossman, *Pope Urban II and Canon Law* (CUA Canon Law, no. 403), 1960, p. 145.

156. Ep. 221 (PL 163:219).

157. C. 7 (Mansi XXI:512).

158. Dictum Gratiani p. c. 16, C. 25, q, 1, (1:1010-1012).

one example, for a twice-married man to receive the diaconate.[159]

The decretists tended to make dispensation from the
common law an exclusive papal prerogative. Rufinus (c.
1165) insisted that bishops can dispense only insofar as the
law allows them.[160] Statements of the decretists that do allow
for certain episcopal powers probably refer to dispensations
in the broad sense which include remission of canonical
penalties. In early canonical literature the term "dispensation" covered exemptions, as well as abrogations of the law.
Rufinus restricted the usage: *est itaque dispensatio justa
causa faciente ab eo cuius interest, canonici rigoris causalis
facta derogatio.*[161] As incorporated in the *glossa ordinaria*
of the *Decretum,* it was accepted by most commentators.

The first decretalists, such as Bernard of Pavia, firmly
maintained that the power to dispense belonged to the pope
by right and that bishops could dispense only when the
canons allowed them to do so.[162] Innocent III, however, by
an ambiguous decree in 1199 provoked discussion on the
power of bishops. Referring to the remission of a penalty,
the pope stated: "From the fact that the founder of the
canon did not reserve the absolution of it to himself, it seems
that he has granted to others the faculty to relax it."[163] Some
canonists then argued that bishops could dispense unless
they were explicitly forbidden to do so. Others maintained

159. Dictum Gratiani ante c. 7, D. 34 (1:127).
160. *Summa* (ed. Singer), p. 423.
161. Rufinus, c. 6, C. 1, q, 7, p. 234, Gloss "plerisque," c. 5, C.
1, q, 7 (Rome 1582, p. 793).
162. *Summa Decretalium* V, 28 (ed. Laspeyres), p. 254.
163. C. 29, X, 5, 39 (11:900-901).

that in addition there would have to be a precedent for such action whereby a bishop had acted with proper authorization.[164]

From the time of the Decretals of Gregory IX (1234) the earlier and stricter position prevailed. The difference between dispensation proper and absolution was recognized. Absolution was regarded as favorable and not injurious to the common law.[165] As for dispensation in the sense of relaxing the law, bishops, according to Innocent IV, could not do so except when empowered by law. With regard to absolving from penalties, bishops were presumed to have the power unless specifically forbidden by law. Alexander III had in fact forbidden bishops to absolve from the penalties incurred by major crimes. A more probable opinion demanded that there be at least a tacit grant of power in the law before the bishop could dispense from penalties. Even if an implicit concession sufficed, the principle was eventually established that "bishops cannot dispense unless the power has been granted to them in the law."[166]

CENSURES

The practice of sending penitents to Rome for absolution can be traced back at least to the ninth century. On one occasion Nicholas I in 865 reproached the Frankish

164. Reilly, *op. cit.*, p. 31; Brys, *op. cit.*, p. 245.

165. J. Christ, *Dispensation from Vindictive Penalties*, (CUA, Canon Law), p. 39, cites *Archdiaconus*, glossa ad c. 14, de electione, 1, 6, in VI°, Guido de Baysio, *Rosarium domini Guidonis archidiaconi Bononiensis super Decreto*.

166. Van Hove, *Commentarium Louvaniense* in C.I.C. Vol. 1, tom. V, p. 326-327 cites Innocent IV *Apparatus*, ad. c. 15, Dilectus, X, de temporibus ordinationum et qualitate ordinandorum, 1, 11.

bishops for sending lay people to Rome for all sorts of problems while neglecting to consult the pope on important matters of ecclesiastical discipline.[167] The papacy repeatedly sought to maintain freedom of access to the Holy See. When the synod of Seligenstadt in 1023 ordered that the penance be performed and the documents obtained from the local bishop before one could go to Rome, Pope Benedict VIII objected strongly.[168] He even forbade the archbishop the use of the pallium. The Council of Limogues in 1031 also sought to have penitents go through the local bishop in obtaining absolution.[169] These attempts to regulate the procedure indicate the practice of sending penitents guilty of serious crimes to Rome for absolution was quite common. It was this practice that led to papal reservation of censures.

Pope Innocent II in canon 13 of the synod of Rheims (1131) decreed that anyone maliciously laying hands on a cleric or monk incurred an anathema which could only be removed, except in danger of death, by a personal petition to the Holy See.[170] The fifteenth canon of Lateran II in 1139 incorporated the Rheims statute into the general law of the Church, the famous *Si quis suadente diabolo,* the first instance of papal reservation of censures.[171] In the anarchical, anti-clerical times of Arnold of Brescia, unarmed clerics were in great danger from violent mobs and had to be given special protection. Soon other censures were accorded the reserved status of the *privilegium canonis.* Alexander III (1159-1181) reserved to himself the case of a priest sus-

167. MGH, Ep. VI, Ep. 71, p. 393.
168. MGH Const. 1, 638, c. 18.
169. Hefele-Leclercq IV: 2, 959. Mansi XIX: 546.
170. Mansi, XXI: 461.
171. COD, p. 176.

pended for daring to bless those entering a second marriage.[172] Clement III (1187-1191) declared that arsonists after the publication of ecclesiastical sentence could be absolved only by the Apostolic See.[173] The gloss on the Decretals of Gregory IX specified that the crime referred to the burning of churches and that reservations were imposed to deter others from such crimes. Pope Celestine III reserved the absolution of clerics who participated in the divine offices with those under papal excommunication.[174] He likewise withheld absolution from those who were denounced after despoiling churches.[175] Innocent III in 1198 reserved absolution of those who would not destroy counterfeit papal bulls.[176]

Canonists pointed out that, for a censure to be reserved to the pope, that fact had to be explicitly stated in the law. Hostiensis noted that of 33 censures incurred *ipso iure* only seven were reserved to the pope. The bishop had jurisdiction over the other censures and, indeed, even over reserved ones in danger of death and for other weighty reasons. Incidentally, Hostiensis lists at least 17 reasons which cause the papal reservation for striking a cleric to cease.[177]

CONCLUSION

With the development of direct papal appointment and reservation, one may wonder whether centralization instead

172. C. 1, X, 4, 21 (11:730).
173. C. 19, X, 5, 39, (11:896).
174. C. 18, X, 5, 39, (11:895).
175. C. 22, X, 5, 39, (11:896).
176. C. 4, X, 5, 20 (11:817).
177. Hostiensis, *Summa Aurea,* tit. de sent. excom. "Quis possit excommunicare," fol. 492 n. 3, fol. 499r n. 12.

of promoting efficiency and spiritual good, has reached the point where it now becomes a burden, stifling and retarding grass-roots Christianity. Here our historical account must end. We have traced the gradual concentration of power in the hands of the papacy from the almost autocephalous days of the primitive communities to the hydra-like bureaucracy of Avignon. The "solicitude for all the churches" nourished with the "plenitude of power" served, under Divine Providence, to guide the Church through the tempestuous years of Europe's adolescence.

St. Paul (Gal. 3:24) speaks of law as a "pedagogue in Christ." Strict supervision and control are necessary in an age of immaturity to train the child to do spontaneously those things which the law intends.[178] During the feudal period, at a time of near anarchy, as Western Europe reeled from one invasion to another, only strong central direction preserved the Church from subversion by local interests. To charge, as one author recently did, that "a violent, intolerant dominativeness has been a characteristic mode of papal utterance and behavior" and that "great, even saintly men have been the victims of a cruel, un-Christian system" betrays an amazing insensitiveness to the realities of history.[179] Papal leadership was eagerly welcomed by the most renewal-minded spirits of the middle ages, Peter Damian, Bernard, and Francis of Assisi. So dependent on secular authority had the bishops become that they could not raise a Christian protest. Instinctively, therefore, religious men turned to the Apostolic See for authentic guidance and impartial judgment.

178. St. Thomas Aquinas, *Summa Theologiae,* 1-11, 92, 1.
179. C. Ernst, O.P., "The Primacy of St. Peter; Theology and Ideology," *New Blackfriars,* 50 (1969), 347-355, 399-404.

No one would want to maintain that Rome's response or Rome's initiative never deviated from a course of perfect altruism. Alexander III, the first great lawyer-pope, openly admitted as much: "The Church is in constant need of being corrected and reformed."[180] Every one of the papal councils of the Middle Ages had reform high on its agenda. When the cry for reform was drowned out by the excitement of the Renaissance, then Divine Judgment had to intervene.

The medieval arrangement for unity need not be the ideal one, but rather a temporary expedient until the churches came of age. "Come of age"—that is the perennial challenge to the Church, to preach the Gospel to all nations in such a way that their highest aspirations may be fulfilled.

Pius XII speaking to the tenth International Congress of Historical Sciences in 1955 stressed that the Church is an historical fact, "with a sure instinct for what is appropriate for the different peoples and for the whole of humanity." The Church is "much more than a simple ideological system; she is a reality—just as visible nature, a people or a state are realities. She is an organism, very much alive, with her own objectives, her own principle of life.[181]

Always and everywhere adapting herself unceasingly to the circumstances of time and place, she seeks to fashion the individual and, so far as possible, all individuals, according to the law of Christ, reaching also in this manner to the moral foundations of life in society. The aim of the Church is man, naturally good, penetrated, ennobled and strengthened by the truth and grace of Christ. The

180. Mansi, XXII: 212.
181. "The Catholic Church and History," *The Tablet*, 206 (Sept. 24, 1955), reprinted in *The Pope Speaks.*

Church wishes to make men established in their inviolable integrity as images of God; men proud of their personal dignity and their salutary freedom; men rightly jealous of equality with their fellows in all that touches the most intimate roots of human dignity; men solidly attached to their lands and their tradition.

Could any of us wish more for the Church?

THE ROMAN PROCESS OF MARTIN LUTHER:
A FAILURE IN SUBSIDIARITY

By Robert E. McNally, S.J.

The theme which I propose to handle in this chapter deals with the legal process that led directly to Martin Luther's definitive excommunication (*Decet Romanum Pontificem*, 3 January 1521) and ultimately to the Protestant reform as a separatist movement. I have selected this theme not because it represents a classical example of papal reservation in the sixteenth century but because it illustrates in a striking way certain aspects of the juridical system of the Holy See that still merit serious attention. Here the accused is judged in the court of his accusers; the plaintiff, who draws the indictment, acts as judge and jury in deciding its merits. The case under consideration here arose from the initiative of a bishop who was too anxious to shift his responsibility to Rome and from the zeal of the Curia which was too willing to assume this burden. As the legal process moved forward, the theological issues which had at first called it into being were forgotten. New horizons and new perspectives opened as the dialectic developed. What had commenced as a protest against abuse in a local church terminated in protest against the authority of the whole Church. It is significant that in the last weeks before his excommunication Martin Luther publicly burnt the papal bull *(Exsurge Domine)* and the canon law.

A simple friar opposed a mighty archbishop over the formulation, the meaning and the practice of Christian piety. In itself the issue was not profound; it was more in the practical than the theoretical order. By the time that the controversy had run its natural course religious pluralism had divided Christendom. All this happened in the obscure city of Wittenberg in Ernestine Saxony in the first quarter of the sixteenth century. Albrecht of Hohenzollern (1490-1545) was the mighty archbishop; Martin Luther (1483-1546), the simple friar; indulgences, the religious issue. Fundamentally the problematic posed by the controversy was theological and logical; it should have been resolved in that context. Actually it was handled by the Roman Curia on another level. A juridical process was instigated that soon became a celebrated case.[1]

This case illustrates strikingly the character of the difficulties in which the legal system of the late Middle Ages involved the Church. What commenced on a diocesan level terminated in the Roman Court; what could have been re-

---

1. Cf. R. E. McNally, S.J., "The Ninety-Five Theses of Martin Luther: 1517-1967," *Theological Studies* 28 (1967) 439-80, for the historico-theological background of the indulgence controversy.

solved in Germany spread throughout the empire. Without denying to the Holy See its right to intervene in canonical litigation and to reserve decisions to itself as the court of last appeals, the question of expediency, of method and of prudence can be raised. The involvement of the Curia in the case of Martin Luther greatly polarized the anti-Roman sentiment of Germany into the Protestant Reformation; it contributed more than any other factor to the circumstances in which he emerged as an historically great person.

THE INDULGENCE QUESTION

In 1515 Pope Leo X (1513-1521) promulgated the concession of a plenary indulgence to those who would contribute to the building of the new basilica of St. Peter on Vatican Hill.[2] To facilitate the liquidation of certain financial obligations Albrecht of Hohenzollern allowed the indulgence to be preached in the dioceses (Mainz, Halberstadt and Magdeburg) under his direct episcopal authority. In Brandenburg and Magedeburg this preaching was entrusted to Johann Tetzel (ca. 1465-1519), a Dominican friar and competent public speaker. In his official capacity as subcommissary of the indulgence preaching he enjoyed great success. People flocked to hear his stirring sermons; and under his powerful influence they were persuaded to gain the precious indulgence by making the appropriate offering (the requisite good work) specified in Leo's bull (*Sacrosancti salvatoris et redemptoris nostri*, 31 March 1515) of

2. Cf. R. Fife, *The Revolt of Martin Luther* (New York 1957), pp. 247-52.

concession.[3] In the early autumn of 1517 Tetzel was preaching in Jüterbog and Zerbst, not very far from Wittenberg, which on order of Elector Frederick had been closed to the indulgence preachers.

What opinions did Luther form about this preaching? First, that the indulgence theology which was being propagated by Tetzel and supported by the archbishop Albrecht's *Instructio summaria*[4] was seriously defective, especially in what concerned the theology of indulgences gained by the living for the dead; second, that in consequence of this bad theology the indulgence preaching was having harmful effects on the spiritual life of the faithful; and, third, that the cause of the Christian religion was being hurt by this spectacle in which money was exchanged in the context of eternal salvation. These three opinions formed a matter of conscience, even deep concern, for a man who was at once university professor and popular confessor.

THE NINETY-FIVE THESES

Luther's opinions in this matter did not remain on a purely speculative level. In view of the religious scandal that was being created in Jüterbog and Zerbst and in other parts of Germany and in view of his own vocation and commitment to the Christian religion, this simple friar decided to act. He wrote to the archbishop; he pointed out the pub-

3. Cf. W. Köhler, *Dokumente zum Ablassstreit* (Halle 1902), pp. 83ff. for the text of the bull of March 1515.

4. Cf. *ibid.*, pp. 104ff. for the text of the *Summaria*. A translation is to be found in H. J. Hillerbrand, *The Reformation* (New York 1964), pp. 37-41.

lic scandal that the indulgence preaching was creating among the people and underlined the defective theology of both Tetzel's sermons and the archbishop's own *Summaria*. To clarify the theological issues he included in his letter a short treatise of his own on indulgences and a list of ninety-five theses.[5] There is no convincing evidence to show that these theses were publicly nailed to the door of the castle church of Wittenberg on October 31, 1517, at a date before their reception by the archbishop.[6] The style and manner in which Luther expressed his appeal, suggest respect and confidence in Albrecht's judgment and argue against a public challenge even before his letter had left Wittenberg. "I pray," he wrote, "that you may accept this humble but faithful admonition graciously as ruler and bishop, even as I submit it with a faithful and devoted heart. For I, too, am one of your sheep. The Lord Jesus guard and guide you forever. Amen."[7] At the same time Luther brought the matter of the abuse of indulgences to the attention of other churchmen, to Hieronymus Scultetus of Brandenburg whose jurisdiction made him a concerned party in this appeal. Luther's letter to Albrecht was left unanswered; the reply of Scultetus was unsatisfactory; the appeal, therefore, to episcopal authority failed.

5. Cf. J. Wicks, S.J., "Martin Luther's Treatise on Indulgences," *Theological Studies* 28 (1967) 481-518. The text of the ninety-five theses (*WA* I, 233-38), translated by C. M. Jacobs, is revised by H. H. Grimm in *Luther's Works* 31: *Career of the Reformer* 1 (Philadelphia 1957) 25-33.

6. On the solution of this problem depends the interpretation of Luther's protest. Did he at first act privately and through official channels, or did he at once make his protest public even before his letter had reached the archbishop? Cf. E. Iserloh, *The Theses Were Not Posted* (Boston 1966).

7. Cf. H. Hillerbrand, *op. cit.*, p. 51.

A careful examination of the ninety-five theses shows various levels of theological thought. Here *nova et vetera* are found side by side. The old Catholic tradition is stated, affirmed, distinguished and interpreted; but latent is a concept of the Church (elucidated later in 1520 in *The Babylonian Captivity of the Church*) that was scarcely compatible with the ecclesiological thinking of the curialists of the early sixteenth century. Luther's opponents (Johann Tetzel and Sylvester Prierias) were quick to point out the radical character of his negation of the teaching authority of the ecclesiastical magisterium.[8] But at the time (31 October 1517) that Luther formulated his theses his position was still in the hypothetical order. "If you, Reverend Father," he wrote, "so desire, you might look at the enclosed set of propositions to recognize how indefinite the concept of indulgence is, even though the indulgence preachers consider it altogether certain."[9] And in the introduction to the "Resolutions," published early in 1518 he stressed the problematical character of his theses which he described as "propositions for debate, not dogmatic definitions."[10]

It is known that Luther's letter with the theses reached the archbishop's consultors on 17 November in Calbe-Saale. A triple course of action was prescribed: first, consultation with the university doctors on the theological and canonical issues involved in the theses; second, communication of the whole matter to the North German bishops who were meeting at Halle. Both measures—the request for professional advice and collegial support—were reasonable and practical

8. Cf. R. E. McNally, S.J., *op. cit.*, pp. 461; 465-7.
9. Cf. H. Hillerbrand, *op. cit.*, p. 51
10. Cf. *ibid.*, p. 54.

from the point of prudent episcopal government.[11] Third, about the middle of December, a complete dossier of the case was transported to Pope Leo in the hope that a *processus inhibitorius* might be launched against "the rash monk of Wittenberg." By transferring the case to the papal court Albrecht abnegated his episcopal responsibility. His motivation, possibly an unwillingness to offend Elector Frederick by proceeding against one of his subjects, or possibly the consideration that the indulgence preaching was essentially the pope's concern, is not clear.[12] What is clear is that Albrecht denounced Luther to Rome without having extended him the courtesy of a reply to his letter of 31 October or the personal opportunity to discuss and defend his position. Absent is the *admonitio caritativa.*

The exact nature of the earliest charge made to Rome against Luther must remain obscure in view of the fact that the pertinent documents are no longer extant. It can, however, be reconstructed from references which have the character of citations. For example, in appealing against Cajetan in October 1518 he described the Roman Court as proceeding against him *"tamquam de haeresi suspectum et in ecclesiasticae potestatis iniuriam vilipensionem, dimin-*

11. The response of the universities was far from decisive. A proposal coming from the circle of Duke George of Saxony and the Leipzig university that a provincial (even a national) synod be summoned by Albrecht as primate of Germany to decide the issues met with little success. Cf. P. Kalkoff, "Zu Luthers römischen Prozess," *Zeitschrift für Kirchengeschichte* 31 (1910) 53-4.

12. Albrecht certainly had at his disposal in his archdiocese the canonical means of handling the case of Luther, at least in its early stages. After transferring it to Rome he seems to have lost interest in it. Cf. *ibid.,* pp. 56-65.

utionem claviumque irreverentiam machinatum."[13] Thus there was question of heresy and subversion—charges basic to the Roman case against Luther up to and including his solemn excommunication by the bull *Decet Romanum Pontificem* of 3 January 1521.

THE CASE IN ROME

By early January 1518 the case of Martin Luther was in the hands of Pope Leo X. Its general direction was assigned to Mario de Perusco, the *procurator fisci,* who collaborated with Sylvester Mazzolini (Prierias), the Dominican *magister sacri palatii,* and Girolamo de Ghinucci, *auditor camerae.* These three curial officials were formed as a special commission, not of *iudices* but *auditores* (in the technical sense), set up by the pope himself to study, investigate and report. Both Sylvester and Girolamo had the same general portfolio with regard to Luther but with different functions. The former was to examine his writings; the latter was to handle the summons and to conduct the hearing, which would be of the nature of a personal examination. The definitive sentence, when and if it were given, belonged to the pope as the supreme judge *ex officio.* In modern parlance this triad—de Perusco, Mazzolini and de Ghinucci—formed a fact-finding commission on whose report and advice the pope could rest his decision on the case.

As the case progressed (31 October 1517–3 January 1521) all three virtually disappeared from the scene; Leo

13. Cf. K. Müller, "Luthers römischer Prozess," *Zeitschrift für Kirchengeschichte* 24 (1903) 47.

remained the sole judge, and in formulating his final decision he was advised by a new commission.[14] None of the three was distinguished for either theological or canonical learning. None qualified as an expert on the highly sensitive question of the German church and its relation to Rome. They were simply officials, administrators, curialists. In February their position was further encouraged and strengthened by the failure of the general of the Augustinians, Gabriel Venetus, to silence Luther, and through the denunciation to the Curia which the Saxon Dominicans made in early March on the advice of Johann Tetzel.[15] The important influence of the Dominicans in Rome sustained the impetus of the curial process against Luther.[16]

While his case pended before the Roman Court, Luther continued his academic and pastoral activities in Wittenberg. He found that he had suddenly become celebrated, almost a national hero. His theses were now common knowledge, and so was his denunciation to the Curia by archbishop Albrecht. He enjoyed the nearly unanimous support of the university community at Wittenberg, the assurance of many friends and especially the backing of Elector Frederick who promised to prevent his transportation to Rome.[17] After the Heidelberg Disputation (April 1518) before the General Chapter of his order, it was clear that no effective measures against him could be hoped for from the higher superiors (Gabriel Venetus and Johann von Staupitz) of the Augustinians. Once again responsibility was negated until it was too late to be effective.

14. Cf. *ibid.*, pp. 49-50.
15. Cf. P. Kalkoff, *op. cit.*, pp. 368-404.
16. Cf. *ibid.*, p. 65.
17. Cf. R. Fife, *op. cit.*, p. 264.

By mid-summer 1518 the papal commission was prepared to act. On the basis of his writings and preaching
(*"fama publica et ipsa rei evidentia"*) Luther was considered
notorious with a notoriety *"facti permanentis"* well known
to the officials and others. He was charged with heresy and
subversion, accusations now no longer needing proof, since
these crimes were obviously and publicly verified in his
published works. Correct canonical procedure now required
presence, that is the physical appearance of the accused
party before the papal commission. Luther was to be heard,
not tried, but sentenced. As always the definitive sentence
remained with the pope himself who was the court of last
instance in appeals. On 7 August 1518 on the advice of
Girolamo and Prieras Luther received through the office of
Mario de Perusco his first official summons to appear in
Rome within sixty days (on or before 6 October) to answer
charges of heresy and subversion that had been made against
him. In view of this eventuality he wrote Frederick a letter,
which is no longer extant, to use his influence to have the
case heard in Germany. At almost the same time emperor
Maximilian promised the pope imperial support in executing
the papal judgment against Luther.

THE SUMMONS

The original summons has been lost and no direct copy
is on hand; but the general format of the document can be
reconstructed on the basis of the *Acta Augustana*, Luther's
appellationes and what is known of the canonical procedure
of this time. It would have contained the following particu-

larities: (1) names of those issuing the summons: Girolamo and Prierias; (2) name of the summoned: Martin Luther; (3) reason for the summons: denunciation for heresy and subversion; (4) place and date of the hearing: in Rome, before Girolamo and Prierias, within sixty days of the receipt of the summons; (5) summons issued through the office of Mario de Perusco; (6) personal appearance of Luther required; (7) summons peremptory in character; (8) inclusion of the papal *litterae commissionis;* and (9) appearance of the summoned required under threat of excommunication and other penalties.[18]

In the course of the late spring and early summer the basic pattern of Luther's position *vis-a-vis* the papal court emerged: (1) refusal to go to Rome and to entrust himself to the curial authorities there; (2) a demand that his case be heard on German soil; and (3) that German judges be appointed to preside at his trial. The strength of his position derived from the intense loyalty of his friend, the firm backing of Elector Frederick, the support of the Wittenberg university and general popular sympathy. Mindful of the miserable fate of the Bohemian heretic, John Hus (d. 1415), he asked that his case be returned from Rome to Germany, to the place of its origin, and that it be heard there in a court by German judges in whose integrity he could have confidence. The personal invective which Sylvester Prierias had heaped upon Luther in his *Dialogus* (mid-June 1518) only convinced him that the Roman tribunal before which he was asked to appear could not be impartial. Thus he wrote to the court chaplain Georg Spalatin on 8 August:

18. Cf. K. Müller, *op. cit.,* pp. 59-61.

"That 'sweetest' man Prierias is simultaneously my accuser and my judge."[19] It would not be wrong to say that at this time Luther's resentment was more with the canonical procedure than with the magisterial competence of the Church.

On 23 August Cardinal Cajetan (Thomas de Vio, O.P.), papal legate to the Diet of Augsburg, received a brief instructing and empowering him to act in the Lutheran matter. A new moment—a compromise—had been reached in the legal process. Luther's case would be heard in Germany, not by German judges, but by the papal legate himself. The brief outlined the general method the Curia wanted followed. Three courses of action were specified: (1) to pardon Luther, if he should freely appear at Augsburg and recant his errors; (2) to arrest him and send him to Rome, if force should be required to make him appear at Augsburg, or if he should not recant; and (3) to declare him a heretic, if he should refuse to appear before the papal legate and cannot be brought there by force. On 11 September the pope allowed Cajetan to hear and terminate the case at Augsburg.[20]

At the same time (23 August) the pope sent a brief to Elector Frederick requesting his cooperation in the arrest and surrender of Luther to papal authority. On the urging of the Curia, Gabriel Venetus, the General of the Augustinians, wrote to the Saxon provincial, Gerhard Hecker, on 25 August ordering him to seize Luther and transport him

19. Cf. G. Krodel, ed. and tr., *Luther's Works* 48: *Luther's Letters* 1 (Philadelphia 1963) 72.

20. Cf. R. E. McNally, S.J., *op. cit.*, p. 471, n. 80, on Luther's reaction to the brief of 23 August. He felt that by this instrument he was condemned during the sixty days period of respite granted in the citation of 7 August.

to Rome "in chains."[21] He had already appealed without success to Luther's immediate superior, Johann von Staupitz, advising him strongly to reconcile the dissident friar and bring him to his senses at once. Thus within eight months (December 1517—August 1518) the Curia had employed a strategy which essentially rested on canonical procedure. But over and above that, it brought the pressure of its prestige to bear on him through his religious superiors (General, Provincial and Prior) and tried to influence his temporal lord, the Elector of Ernestine Saxony, to cooperate with the Roman authorities. The sympathy of the aging emperor Maximilian had already been assured, and the influence of the Dominican order stood behind the process.

THE PAPAL BRIEF

Three points are to be observed about the papal brief addressed to Cajetan; they are pertinent to the understanding of the character of the legal process instituted against Luther: (1) The brief to Cajetan envisions rapid and summary proceedings—not a trial. The principal function of this confrontation is to establish *contumacia*, which will appear in his refusal either to appear before the papal tribunal or to recant his heretical teaching. In no sense is there provision made for the possibility that Luther, without recanting his position, might establish his innocence. As far as Cajetan's mission is concerned, Luther must either withdraw from his position or be arrested and transported to Rome.

21. Cf. T. Kolde, "Luther und sein Ordensgeneral in Rom in den Jahre 1518 und 1520," *Zeitschrift für Kirchengeschichte* 2 (1878) 476-78.

(2) Luther is presumed notorious on the basis of Girolamo's *inquisitio famae* which had concluded with the declaration that *diffamatio* was well-established. (3) As cited before Cajetan, Luther is regarded as *haereticus declaratus,* not *haereticus condemnatus.* The ultimate judgment, whether given by Cajetan in Augsburg or by Leo in Rome, will define and specify the condemnation. The arrest of Luther, which the brief orders, is a consequence of his citation *(citatio rei* or *realis citatio)* to Rome.

Luther recognized the competence of Cajetan to examine him. His hearing was conducted in Augsburg before the papal legate in the role of examiner and father rather than judge and prosecutor. According to the pope's instructions there was to be no disputation between the two.[22] The proceedings from 12 to 14 October terminated in Luther's refusal to forsake his position. Standing on Scripture, history and the Fathers, he argued his case against Cajetan and held firmly to his theological convictions. In a sense the hearing at Augsburg was a failure. Luther did not recant nor was he excommunicated according to the provisions of the brief. But on another level the proceedings were filled with meaning for both parties. They showed the shape of things to come.

The spirited colloquies at Augsburg revealed to Luther the essential dissonance between his theological method and that represented by Cajetan. His position polarized sharply. In matters of faith he would not accept authority as decisive and convincing against his comprehension

---

22. This part of the pope's instruction Cajetan did not obey. Under the impulse of the tense atmosphere he yielded to feeling. Cf. R. E. McNally, S.J., *op. cit.,* pp. 473-7.

of Scripture and tradition. His reaction expressed itself in three moments: (1) a request on 15 October to be released from his vow of obedience as an Augustinian; (2) an appeal on 16 October to the pope over the jurisdiction of his legate Cajetan; and (3) on 28 November an appeal to a general council over the head of the pope. Cajetan had discovered in his discussion with Luther a marked deficiency in documents on which to rest his argument from authority. Clearly the bull *Unigenitus Dei Filius* of Clement VI—the *locus classicus* from which he had argued against Luther —had proved insufficient. There was question of method here. To proceed more securely there was need of further papal amplification of the Catholic doctrine of indulgences which would provide a solid theological basis for the legal process. Pope Leo obliged with the bull *Cum Postquam* of 9 November 1518 which clarified the principal issues at stake. This, however, had no effect on Luther and his doctrine.

By the beginning of the year 1520 the Curia had reached a point of exhaustion and frustration with the progress of the case against Luther.[23] All attempts—legal, theological diplomatic—had failed to terminate it successfully. He was notorious, and he was contumacious, and that in the grave matter of faith and obedience; and he gave no evidence

23. With the approaching death of emperor Maximilian, the process of Luther was halted while the Curia sought to provide a successor. Anyone save the Spanish Hapsburg Charles would have been acceptable; even Luther's protector, Elector Frederick of Saxony, was considered. Apropos of this interlude the observation has been made: "... die landesherrliche Verantwortung war in Rom in 1519 stärker ausgeprägt als die theologische." Cf. G. Müller, "Die römische Kurie und die Anfänge der Reformation," *Zeitschrift für Religions und Geistesgeschichte* 19 (1967) 6.

of retreating from the theological and legal positions which he had taken. Protected by Elector Frederick the Wise, he was secure in distant Ernestine Saxony; and in his preaching and writing he continued to develop the very ideas and attitudes which had moved the Curia "to bring him to book." Accordingly in the late winter a special commission was appointed in Rome to draw up a bull preparatory to the condemnation of the person and the doctrine of Luther. This would serve as the Curia's definitive solution of the case which had called forth the process.

EXSURGE DOMINE AND DECET ROMANUM PONTIFICEM

On 16 June 1520 *Exsurge Domine* was published not as a bull of excommunication but as the ultimate warning that a definitive sentence would be pronounced against Luther, if he did not submit within a period of sixty days. The theologians on the commission, certain of the errors in the teaching of Luther, wanted the bull so drawn that it would simply condemn Luther as a notorious heretic. The canonists, however, on the basis of a legal technicality opposed this course of action. While agreeing with the theologians that the doctrine and the writings of Luther should be condemned, they thought that his person should be exempted, at least for the moment. Granting his obvious notoriety, they argued, he should be cited to appear only after a well-defined period of respite for self-defense. The first citation (3 August 1519) in the case had come to no term, since two weeks later (23 August) jurisdiction in the process had been turned over to Cajetan's tribunal. Luther had indeed responded, but Cajetan had given no definitive judgment in the case. He had the right, therefore, to another respite before final verdict and condemnation. The bull with its *monitio evangelica* was promulgated in Germany (21-29 September) and became operative on 27 November. Luther reacted with utmost contempt.[24] On 3 January 1521 he was solemnly excommunicated by the bull *Decet Romanum Pontificem* which finally brought the legal process to a close.

Essentially Luther's process concerned an altercation between an exempt religious and episcopal authority. The original issue (abuse of indulgences) in the case was not of first rate importance; in the stress and strain of the subsequent dialectic it grew and took on a new dimension (ecclesiastical authority and its competence). Luther was denounced to Rome by archbishop Albrecht almost as a matter of course and without a deep appreciation of the theological and religious questions involved, certainly without full awareness of their ultimate consequences. The case against Luther, if indeed there was a case in the late autumn of 1517 because of the provisional nature of his protest, should have been handled (at least in the initial stages) by the Augustinian superiors in Saxony, by the local ordinary and by competent theologians and lawyers. It was not. The attempt of Albrecht to procure a *processus inhibitorius* against Luther's activity constituted a threat to academic freedom; he was professor at the new university of Witten-

24. In the months after the publication of *Exsurge Domine* Luther authored three of his most fundamental works against the Catholic tradition: *The Babylonian Captivity of the Church, The Freedom of a Christian Man,* and *An Address to the Christian Nobility of the German Nation.* At the end of the year, within a few weeks of the publication of *Decet Romanum Pontificem,* he burnt the papal bull in public.

berg and his protest (the ninety-five theses), as an invitation to a disputation, was academic in character. The case, as it developed far from Germany in Rome, was managed by men who were not well informed on the issues in question; it rested on a legal method that was effete and which only served to polarize an insignificant issue out of all proportion.

THE SCOPE OF AUTHORITY
OF EPISCOPAL CONFERENCES

By Frederick R. McManus

The purpose of this chapter is to consider the present and future authority of the episcopal conferences. This is done in the light of the American experience and the conciliar and postconciliar determinations of the competence of such conferences. It would be possible to go far afield, for example: (a) into an exploration of specific areas of competence—but such observations will here be limited to examples;[1] (b) into questions of procedure—although these

1. In point of fact, when it deals with "non-binding" decisions of the episcopal conferences, the conciliar decree on the subject, *Christus Dominus* (October 28, 1965), speaks as broadly as anyone might desire: the conferences are to promote "that greater good which the Church offers mankind, especially through forms and programs of the apostolate which are fittingly adapted to the circumstances of the age" (n. 38, 1). It is only when (canonically) binding decisions are at issue that conflicts over the present and future competence of conferences become serious.

are significant enough and require refinement and development;[2] (c) into the complexities of interritual and international or supranational conferences.[3] Rather than develop such points, it is more than enough to indicate here the scope of competence of episcopal conferences and then to raise some of the issues related to the extension or diminution of this competence.

2. Whatever may be said of the two-thirds rule applicable in the case of binding decisions of the conferences (below), certainly the determination of this two-thirds on the basis of the entire (voting) membership (*ibid.*, 38, 4) — rather than on the basis of the voting members who are actually present and cast valid votes, according to canonical (canon 101, §1, n. 1) and usual parliamentary procedure — is an excessive requirement. In effect it gives (or can give, if observed) an extraordinary weight to those absent or otherwise impeded. There are indications that this inhibiting rule will have to be reconsidered.

3. *Christus Dominus* is fundamentally open on the question of supranational and international conferences and positively encourages contacts between national conferences (n. 38, 5). The apostolic letter *Ecclesiae sanctae* (August 5, 1966: AAS 58 [1966] 757-787) takes a different point of view: the statutes of supranational and international conferences are to be enacted by the Apostolic See (I, 41, §4) rather than enacted by the conferences and merely reviewed or confirmed (*recognoscenda*) by the Apostolic See (*Christus Dominus*, n. 38, 3). Moreover, *Ecclesiae sanctae* introduces a new limitation, namely, prior reference of *actiones* or *rationes* of an international character to the Apostolic See (I, 41, §4) and it gives a grudging enumeration ("*Rationes inter Conferentias Episcopales ... haberi poterunt ....*") of interconference communications (I, 41, §5). The tone and intent have changed. For a commentary on these sections of the papal document, see K. Mörsdorf, "Decree on the Bishops' Pastoral Office in the Church," in H. Vorgrimler, ed., *Commentary on the Documents of Vatican II*, II (New York: Herder and Herder; London: Burns and Oates, 1968), 290-295. The author appears to resolve conflicts in favor of *Ecclesiae sanctae* rather than *Christus Dominus*.

THE ROLE AND AUTHORITY OF EPISCOPAL CONFERENCES

It might be difficult to document[4] the continued hesitation felt in some parts of the Church concerning the role and authority of episcopal conferences. This feeling certainly persists, although hardly in the extreme form encountered during the Second Vatican Council. At that time it was suggested, to offer an example, that a juridically binding authority of conferences "would seem to contradict the monarchical nature of the residential episcopate, which monarchical nature appears to be of divine law."[5]

Such opposition to episcopal conferences was and is largely based upon a fear that the jurisdictional authority of the diocesan bishop (otherwise greatly enlarged by the Council)[6] will be diminished by the conference. Perhaps this kind of hesitation should be dismissed out of hand: we have recovered an understanding of authority as service. If in the most profound sense the bishops are the members of the servant class in the Church, the diocesan bishops should be the last to be concerned over a loss of authority or power to an episcopal conference.

Alternatively, any fear of the conference's authority should be dissipated by a sense of the Spirit of God at work in the Church. The strongest supporters of the developing episcopal conferences are the first to recognize the human and serious risks in episcopal conferences. The genuine

4. Apart from the papal documents referred to below.

5. Vatican Council II, *Emendationes a Concilii Patribus scripto exhibitae super schema Decreti de Episcopis ac de Dioecesium Regimine* (1963), p. 36.

6. E.g., *Christus Dominus*, n. 8, 28.

danger lies not in diluting diocesan episcopal authority but in compromising the ultimate authority which is Christ's alone and which resides in the whole communion of Christian people.

Yet the attitude and atmosphere of misgiving over any supradiocesan authority need to be attended to and answered. There are anomalies in such a position. For example, some suggest that the supradiocesan authority (other than the primatial authority) is a novelty in the Church. This ignores seventeen centuries of particular synods, patriarchal, primatial, and metropolitan.

A more common feeling is that the episcopal conference is or may become an unwarranted entity interposed between the chief bishop and the individual diocesan bishop. The latter anomaly is compounded by the fact that there are other entities or ecclesiastical offices and officers similarly interposed between the pope and the diocesan bishop. For some reason these are not considered a threat by those ordinarily fearful of the conferences.[7]

Perhaps the most effective response to difficulties of this sort is the entirely positive doctrinal affirmation in the Dogmatic Constitution on the Church. There the collegial union of the bishops is said to be "apparent also [that is, in addition to acts of the entire *collegium*] in the mutual relations of the individual bishops with particular churches and with

7. For example, it is most unlikely that there would be unfavorable reaction, on the part of those who see the conferences as a potential barrier between the diocesan bishop and the pope, to the increased authority of papal representatives, legates, etc. in the motu proprio *Sollicitudo Omnium Ecclesiarum* (June 24, 1969). See art. IV-IX, compared with canon 267 of the Code of Canon Law.

the universal Church."[8] Applications of the principle are then made by the conciliar Fathers, and the section concludes with the succinct statement:

> By divine Providence it has come about that various churches established in different places have in the course of time coalesced into several groups, organically united, which, preserving the unity of faith and the unique divine constitution of the universal Church, enjoy their own discipline, their own liturgical usage, and their own theological and spiritual heritage. Some of these churches, notably the ancient patriarchal churches, like parent stems [matrices] of the faith, have begotten other, daughter churches. With these they are connected down to our own time by a close bond of charity in the sacramental life and in their mutual respect for rights and duties. This variety of local churches with one common inspiration is particularly splendid evidence of the catholicity of the undivided Church. In like manner the Episcopal Conferences [Coetus Episcopales] of today are able to render a manifold and fruitful assistance, so that the collegial sense [collegialis affectus] may be concretely applied.[9]

8. Vatican Council II, dogmatic constitution, *Lumen Gentium*, November 21, 1964, n. 23.

9. *Ibid.* The relationship of the parts of the quoted paragraph of n. 23 is obscured in the J. Gallagher translation (W. M. Abbott, ed., *The Documents of Vatican II* [New York: Herder and Herder, Association Press, 1966], p. 46) from which the quotation is adapted. The Gallagher translation breaks the unity of thought dividing the paragraph before the mention of the episcopal conferences. This incorrectly weakens the comparison of the episcopal conferences with the "rites" and with the patriarchal churches.

This text, even more than the longer, *ex professo* treatment of episcopal conferences in *Christus Dominus,* fixes such bodies in the ecclesial structure both historically and doctrinally. The text chooses the best precedent[10] for the association or grouping of a number of local churches on a scale of major significance, namely, the patriarchal churches.[11] The conferences of bishops are understood as a relatively new canonical institute in the Church, but are explicitly called a sign of the "collegial sense" so crucial to Chapter III of *Lumen Gentium.*

It may be that *affectus collegialis* does not do justice to the manifestation of episcopal collegiality on the particular or regional level.[12] We can dismiss the quibbles over the meaning of collegiality. The term itself may mean the common action of all the bishops or of some of the bishops or, for that matter, of the local bishop with his *presbyterium* and people. It may refer, properly and canonically, to the

10. It is obvious that other examples could have been given, especially the particular synods or councils of almost every age. Another example, on a smaller scale, is the metropolitan structure, which also groups local churches together. When *Lumen Gentium* recites the tradition for the collegiality of the entire *collegium,* it adduces "the practice, introduced in ancient times, of summoning several bishops" to participate in episcopal consecration (n. 22).

11. The comparison can be carried further: the president of the episcopal conference, although elected for a term, has a quasi-patriarchal office. He exercises authority only synodally, as do patriarchs. He should enjoy precedence over cardinals, as should patriarchs. Cf. Peter K. Medawar, "The Rights of the Eastern Church," in Maximos IV Saigh, ed., *The Eastern Churches and Catholic Unity* (New York: Herder and Herder, 1963), pp. 148-150. The comparison is weaker, historically and sociologically, in the case of episcopal conferences which are on the scale of traditional ecclesiastical provinces.

12. Cf. K. Mörsdorf, *art. cit.,* p. 284.

corporate action of any *collegium* in the Church.[13] Collegial power or collegial action is attributed by the Council to the whole body of bishops;[14] it is then attributed, in the perhaps attenuated expression *affectus collegialis*, to the episcopal conferences.

It is evident that the conciliar commissions (the Doctrinal Commission and especially the Commission on Bishops and the Government of Dioceses) were not anxious to open up anew the issue of "strict" episcopal collegiality in relation to the conferences. On the one hand, both in *Lumen Gentium* and in *Christus Dominus*, the assertion of a collegiality to be exercised in the conferences in the same sense as the collective action of the entire *collegium* or *coetus*

13. Cf. *Notificationes* made by the Secretary General of the Council in the 123rd general congregation, November 16, 1964, published ("Ex Actis Ss. Oecumenici Concilii Vaticani II") at the end of the constitution *Lumen Gentium*. In the *nota explicativa praevia*, the first point made is that *collegium* is not employed (in reference to the *Ordo, Corpus, Coetus* or *Collegium Episcoporum* as a whole) in the strictly juridical sense as of a *coetus* of equals. Thus it might be more properly used of a body such as an episcopal conference than of the entire body of bishops! But this is only to offer a debater's argument. The Second Vatican Council, especially in Chapter III of *Lumen Gentium*, was concerned with the doctrine of the collegiality of the entire order of bishops in the Church; in n. 23 the Council *also* attributes collegiality or *affectus collegialis* to a limited body of bishops, namely, the episcopal conference.

Perhaps it is not out of place to mention the formal authorship of the celebrated or notorius *nota explicativa praevia*. Whatever its origin or development, its formal author was the doctrinal commission of the Council. It was communicated to the other members of the Council (actually for a second time) by Paul VI, the *"Superior Auctoritas"* referred to in the *Notificationes*.

14. *Lumen Gentium*, n. 22; cf. *Christus Dominus*, n. 4. As pointed out already, n. 23 of *Lumen Gentium* begins by speaking of the "collegial union" which also exists in the mutual relations of the individual bishops with the particular churches and the Universal Church.

of bishops is avoided.[15] On the other hand, nowhere is there a denial that the particular *coetus* or conferences of bishops manifest collegiality the same as or analogous to that of the entire episcopate, although on a limited territorial scale.

The fact is that, although the conflict over episcopal collegiality still raged at the time, only 77 out of 2226 conciliar Fathers voted in the negative when the paragraph quoted above was put to a distinct vote (September 1964).[16] The statement in n. 23 of *Lumen Gentium* should be seen as an assertion of the providential goodness of episcopal conferences. It demands that the roots for the conferences, as for patriarchal and other particular synods, be sought in the nature of the Church rather than in transitory concessions of the canon law.[17] The doctrinal basis for the conferences is carefully explained by Mörsdorf:

15. Vatican Council II, *Schema Decreti de Pastorali Episcoporum Munere in Ecclesia, Textus Recognitus et Modi* (1965), p. 118.

16. Vatican Council II, *Schema Constitutionis Dogmaticae de Ecclesia, Modi*, III, Caput III (1964), p. 3. No *modus* was offered contrary to this inclusion of episcopal conferences in the doctrine of n. 23 or to the use of the term *collegialis affectus* with reference to the conferences (*ibid.*, pp. 41-42). This was at the point, only two months before the promulgation of *Lumen Gentium*, when one *modus* would "not admit the existence of the college of bishops" (*ibid.*, p. 35).

17. It is a weakness of the Code of Canon Law to misplace particular synodal action in the title, "*De suprema potestate deque iis qui eiusdem sunt ecclesiastico iure participes*" (Book II, part I, title VII). This placement reduces the authority of patriarchs and metropolitans, councils and synods, to ecclesiastical law, as if these had no basis in the divine constitution of the Church, in particular, in the communion of local churches. At the same time the placement suggests that particular collegial and synodal life in the Church developed from above ("the supreme authority") rather than from below, namely, out of the relationship of particular churches, in each of which particular churches the *Ecclesia* is first and fully realized (see *Lumen Gentium*, n. 26).

The synods of dioceses grew from below, from the sense of communion based on the common mission of the apostles through Jesus Christ. Thus synods were not arbitrarily established, but followed from the communion that is of the essence of the Church. . . .

Since the purpose of synods is seen in the context of *communio,* they cannot be misrepresented as being without a theological basis and merely serving a practical end.[18]

The failure of the Second Vatican Council to pursue this question formally was due to a number of causes which need not be considered here. Certainly there was an awareness of the issue, but this seemed to be coupled with a wish to avoid the conciliar crisis which might arise for those who found every expression of collegiality unpalatable. For example, in reference to the very first declaration of the Council concerning episcopal conferences,[19] the conciliar Commission on the Liturgy explained that the expression *ex potestate [coetuum episcoporum] a iure concessa* was chosen so as not to prejudice the doctrinal question: "By saying *a iure concessa,* we intend to make no judgment concerning the theological foundation of this power [of the conferences]."[20] In other words, the authority of the episcopal conferences, however specified or developed in canon law, may be properly rooted—and, we may now say, should

18. *Art. cit.,* p. 282.
19. Vatican Council II, constitution *Sacrosanctum Concilium* (on the liturgy), December 4, 1963, art. 22, §2.
20. *Schema Constitutiones de Sacra Liturgia, Emendationes,* IV (1962), 7.

be rooted—in the Church's nature as a communion of churches.

We may regret that the constitution *Lumen Gentium* did not develop a more adequate doctrine of the local church or of the Universal Church as a communion of individual churches.[21] The latter point is made at the beginning of n. 23 of *Lumen Gentium*, before the passage already quoted:[22] "In and from such individual churches there comes into being the one and only Catholic Church." In fact this doctrine, though barely expressed in the actual constitution, is a major key to the ecclesiological development that produced *Lumen Gentium*:

> On the one hand there is the ecclesiology of the Universal Church, visibly signified by a visible organ of this universal unity, the pope, and in the case of ecumenical councils, by the episcopal college brought together by the pope; on the other, there is the eucharistic ecclesiology or communion of local churches. The term *collegium*, collegial communion, signifies, first of all, then, unity of faith and sacrament in the life of the Spirit, existing in the life of the Spirit, existing in the bosom of the church assembled about its priests and bishop; the

21. But see the constitution *Sacrosanctum Concilium*, art. 26, 41. *Lumen Gentium*, n. 26, says: "This Church of Christ is truly present in all legitimate local congregations of the faithful, which, united with their pastors, are also called churches in the New Testament [cf. Acts 8:1; 14:22-23; 20:17, and *passim*]." Cf. K. Rahner, "Chapter III, The Hierarchical Structure of the Church, with Special Reference to the Episcopate, Articles 18-27," in H. Vorgrimler, *op. cit.*, I (1967), 216-217.

22. Above, at note 9.

brotherhood of these local churches, their union in charity, is a larger manifestation of this collegiality.[23]

It is only a step from understanding the Church as a communion of churches to a proper appreciation of every limited, particular, or regional manifestation of this communion (the *collegialis affectus*) as rooted in the Church's inner life and nature. To state the obvious, at least the presumption favors the role and scope of episcopal conferences, since these must be viewed as a fresh statement of the synodal aspect of the church community.

Nevertheless the canonical determination of the institute or structure itself is not divine. And the episcopal conferences, prior to the Second Vatican Council, had little recognition in the written law of the Latin Church. The meager references to such conferences, and then only at the provincial level,[24] are well known.[25] What is less well known is that, immediately prior to the Council, at least

23. C. Moeller, "History of Lumen Gentium's Structure and Ideas," in J. Miller, ed., *Vatican II: An Interfaith Appraisal* (Notre Dame, Ind.: University of Notre Dame Press, 1966), p. 132.

24. There was nothing in the law of the Code to prohibit or inhibit the coalescence of provincial episcopal conferences, even with their very limited authority, into regional or national conferences. This possibility underlies the very broad expression *"competentes varii generis territoriales Episcoporum coetus legitime constitutos"* in *Sacrosanctum Concilium* (art. 22, §2). See *Schema Constitutionis de Sacra Liturgia, Emendationes, IV,* p. 7: "This holds not only for conferences properly so called, but also of a plenary or provincial council, in fact, according to circumstances, of the assembly of bishops of several regions."

25. Canons 292; 1507, §1 (authority of provincial conferences [*conventus*] to determine certain *taxae*); 1909, §1 (their authority in the case of judicial fees).

two slight areas of jurisdictional competence had been acknowledged in the conferences at the national level: to
change the color of liturgical vesture, with only a consultation of the Apostolic See required;[26] to establish certain
ritual changes in the baptism of adults and to approve
vernacular translations of this rite, the latter without reference to the Apostolic See.[27]

These very small indications in the pre-conciliar written
law offer a striking contrast to the way in which, since the
middle of the nineteenth century, the canonical institute
of the episcopal conference had developed or was developing. It was of course no less canonical because of its origin
in customary usage. In fact the process illustrates how the
custom of the Church may be a superior, and certainly more
significant, side of the canon law than the written enactments.

THE AMERICAN EXPERIENCE

This treatment of the scope of episcopal conferences and
their authority is to be related to the American experience.
It is therefore necessary to begin by noting that the conference of bishops of the United States came upon the scene
very late, well into the twentieth century. Earlier developments elsewhere have been summed up as follows:

26. S.R.C., *Novus Rubricarum Breviarii ac Missalis Romani Codex*,
July 26, 1969, n. 117.
27. S.R.C., *Ordo Baptismi Adultorum per Gradus Catechumenatus
Dispositus, Normae*, n. 3, 5-6.

The place of origin seems to be the city of Mechlin (Mechelen) in Belgium. Here, beginning in 1830, the Belgian bishops started to meet annually in the archiepiscopal house. Soon, however, the same phenomenon appeared in many other countries. In 1848, the bishops of Germany met for the first time, in Würzburg; since 1869, they met annually in Fulda. The bishops of Bavaria had an annual meeting in Freising, beginning with the year 1850. Austrian bishops met in Vienna from 1849 on. In Italy, regional meetings were held, especially meetings of the bishops of Umbria, from 1849 on. The Irish bishops had their first meeting in Dublin in 1854. Pope Leo XIII strongly promoted these meetings of the bishops of an entire country: in Spain, in Portugal, in Austria, in Hungary, in Brazil. During his reign, Propaganda issued instructions for similar meetings in China and in India. The eastern churches of the Armenian and of the Greek-Melchite rites also introduced the use of these assemblies. The Congregation for Bishops and for Regulars issued the first rules for such meetings for Austria and for Latin America. The experience and the praxis in Austria were of great moment in this rapid development.[28]

28. P. Huizing, "The Structure of Episcopal Conferences," *The Jurist,* 28 (1968) 163-164. Appended to this article (pp. 175-176) is a bibliography on various aspects of episcopal conferences. Among the articles listed, see especially P. Fransen, "Die Bischofskonferenz — Kernproblem des Konzils," *Orientierung,* 27 (1963) 119-123; 128-134; J. Hamer "Les conferences episcopales, exercise de la collegialite," *Nouvelle Revue Theologique,* 85 (1963) 966-969.

The conference of bishops of the United States assembled for the first time in September 1919, at the call of the archbishops of the country. Meeting in Washington at The Catholic University of America, the episcopate issued its first national pastoral letter since the Third Plenary Council of Baltimore in 1884.[29] Significantly it was signed: "Given at Washington, in Conference, on the 26th day of September, in the year of our Lord, 1919. In his own name and in the name of the Hierarchy. James Cardinal Gibbons, Archbishop of Baltimore."[30]

In this pastoral letter the American bishops announced the formation of the National Catholic Welfare Council (later Conference) in succession to a similar organization which had been set up during World War I, the National Catholic War Council.[31] This development has its importance for two reasons: because of the extraordinary accomplishments of the N.C.W.C. in later years and because the growth of the N.C.W.C. agencies or instrumentalities of the episcopate confused and even inhibited the development of the episcopal conference as such.

There is, however, a prehistory to the American episcopal conference which deserves mention. The immediate predecessor of the conference of bishops was the annual meeting of the metropolitans of the country. Assembling without the authority of an episcopal conference, much less the authority of a council, this gathering represented some continuity with the several national synodal assemblies of the nine-

29. P. Guilday, ed., *The National Pastorals of the American Hierarchy* (*1792-1919*) (1923; reprinted Westminster, Maryland, 1954), p. 265.

30. *Ibid.*, p. 340.

31. *Ibid.*, p. 296.

teenth century. These assemblies were the seven provincial councils of Baltimore, held while the province of Baltimore was coextensive with the United States,[32] and the three plenary councils of Baltimore (1852, 1866, 1884). They demonstrated the collegial character of the episcopate in a period when it would hardly have been clearly expressed in this way. Even prior to these councils, just after the establishment of the province of Baltimore,[33] there was an important meeting of the bishops with Archbishop John Carroll.

This meeting, held in 1810, is interesting as a forerunner to the episcopal conference. It was most certainly not a provincial council; in fact plans were laid at the 1810 meeting for the first provincial council in 1812 (which did not take place until 1829). Yet the bishops who assembled in 1810 (Leonard Neale, coadjutor of Baltimore, Michael Egan of Philadelphia, John Cheverus of Boston, and Benedict Flaget of Bardstown, together with the archbishop; the see of New York was vacant) passed a series of resolutions or ordinances "which were made obligatory on all the congregations of the Province of Baltimore."[34] These *acta* were regularly prefixed to the decrees of the later provincial synods.[35] In this 1810 meeting we have a provincial episcopal conference with sufficient collegial feeling, if not synodal form, to enact disciplinary laws binding all the five dioceses.

32. 1829, 1833, 1837, 1840, 1843, 1846, 1849.

33. April 8, 1808.

34. Guilday, *A History of the Councils of Baltimore* (1791-1884) (New York, 1932), p. 74.

35. *Concilia Provincialia Baltimori Habita ab anno 1829 usque ad annum 1849* (ed. altera, Baltimore, 1851), pp. 26-28. The ordinances are entitled *"Quidem ex articulis Ecclesiasticae Disciplinae quos Illme ac Revmi DD. Archiepiscopus Baltimorensis et Episcopi Americae Foederatae, communi consensu, anno 1810 sanxerunt."*

This was done, moreover, in the absence of the Ordinary of one of the sees, and a titular bishop was the first signatory after the metropolitan.[36]

A final item of prehistory may be added, this time in reference to a conciliar gathering in the strictest sense. It illustrates the existence of an authentic collegial sense in the nineteenth century American episcopate. The quotation is from one of Bishop John England's[37] pleas for the holding of the provincial synod overdue since 1812:

> The deranged and unsettled state of the American church can be reduced to order and peace and permanent system only by provincial synods of the American hierarchy. That much as I would value even the temporary quiet and highly as I would obey a Papal legate, I solemnly and earnestly deprecate and am adverse to this extraordinary mode of doing what I think can be done by the proper and ordinary mode of a provincial synod. Because the usual mode of a synod is more congenial to the practice of the Church. Because the usual mode of a synod is more congenial to the old canons of the Church. Because the usual mode of a synod has been prescribed by the last general council. Because the usual mode of a synod has been found most beneficial in those places in which it has been followed. Because the usual mode of a synod has been preferred by most holy prelates whose example is most precious and useful in the Church. Because the usual mode of a synod is

36. *Ibid.*, p. 28. Perhaps this may be considered a precedent; the twentieth-century American episcopal conference, unlike others, was not limited to diocesan bishops.

37. Bishop of Charleston from 1820 to 1842.

more in accordance with the spirit of our national institutions, and because it is the mode which will best please
the flock and insure their support to its resolutions.
Whereas placing the power in the hands of an individual
appears to be an encroachment upon the rights of diocesan bishops, and an attempt to reduce them to the level
of Vicars-Apostolic. It destroys what Cardinal Bellar-
mine calls the republican form of Church government. . . ."[38]

The spirit of Bishop England's argument strikes a responsive chord in twentieth century ecclesiology, as it was
indeed a sound, traditional position. Until the third plenary council of Baltimore in 1884 the record of the American
church did include rather frequent national councils. Then
there was a lapse and the entire episcopate did not gather
formally until the meeting of 1919.

It is sometimes difficult to disentangle the relationship
between the body of bishops who constituted the episcopal
conference and the National Catholic Welfare Conference.[39]
The formal motion to establish the Conference, then called
"Council," appeared to identify it with the episcopate or
hierarchy: "It is the sense of this meeting that an organization be formed *of the Hierarchy* to be known as the National Catholic Welfare Council and its duties and powers

38. Letter to Archbishop Ambrose Marechal of Baltimore, June 25,
1827, quoted in Guilday, *Councils of Baltimore*, pp. 83-84. As already
noted, the provincial synod was finally held in 1829.

39. For information on the beginnings of the N.C.W.C., see "The
September Meeting of the American Hierarchy," *Ecclesiastical Review*,
61 (1919), 7-19; for an account of the development of the N.C.W.C., see
F. T. Hurley, "National Catholic Welfare Conference," *New Catholic
Encyclopedia* (New York: McGraw-Hill, 1967), pp. 225-229.

be indicated by those present."[40] It was clear from the beginning that the membership of the N.C.W.C. included the entire hierarchy of bishops of the United States:

> Every bishop, residential or titular, who serves or has served the Church in the United States, its territories or possessions, has active and passive voice in the Conference.[41]

Or, as later expressed in reference to the civil incorporation of the Conference:

> Every bishop, residential or titular, who serves or has served the Church in the United States, is an ex officio member of the National Catholic Welfare Conference, Inc. by reason of his appointment as bishop. By vote of the bishops in annual meeting assembled, individual bishops become members of the legal corporation, N.C.W.C., Inc.[42]

On the other hand, the first announcement to the Catholic community of the United States spoke of the N.C.W.C. in terms of the agencies grouped together and, in particular, of the several departments constituted under the organization:

40. Extract from minutes of 1919 meeting; italics added. *The National Catholic Welfare Conference, Its Organization, Departments and Functions* (Washington, 1942 [privately printed]), p. 37.

41. *Ibid.,* p. 7.

42. *The National Catholic Welfare Conference Normae* (Washington, 1960 [privately printed]), pp. 4-5.

We have accordingly grouped together, under the National Catholic Welfare Council, the various agencies by which the cause of religion is furthered.[43]

The N.C.W.C. was officially described as "the executive agency of the Catholic Bishops of the United States";[44] it was thus, or appeared to be, distinct from the "Annual Meeting of the Hierarchy," although the same assembly was itself the National Catholic Welfare Conference. And the actual work of the collective concern of the bishops was to be through the departments set up from the beginning (education, social welfare, press and literature, societies and lay activities, missions).[45]

A celebrated controversy marked the first years of the N.C.W.C. and was resolved only in 1922 by the long delayed approval of the organization by the Holy See. This illustrates the fundamental problem. The specter of diminished episcopal authority in the local churches brought the N.C.W.C. close to papal suppression, and the terms of the 1922 compromise indicate the issues:

3. . . . As the decisions of the bishops at these meetings have nothing in common with conciliar legislation, which is governed by a prescription of the Sacred Canons (Cod. Can. 281, seq.), they will not have the force of law since, as from the beginning, it has been clearly understood the meetings are held merely for friendly conference about measures of a common public interest

43. Guilday, *National Pastorals*, p. 296.
44. *Normae*, p. 4.
45. Guilday, *loc. cit.*

for the safeguarding of the Church's work in the United States.

4. . . . All questions should deal with those topics proposed by His Holiness, Pope Benedict XV, in the Brief, "*Communes*," dated the 10th of April, 1919.

8. . . . Whereas the name, the National Catholic Welfare Council, is open to some misunderstandings, and in fact has not been acceptable to all, it may be well for the bishops to consider whether it would not be wise to choose some other name, as for instance, "The National Catholic Welfare Committee." Meanwhile, all should know that this organization, however named, is *not to be identified with the Catholic hierarchy itself* in the United States.

9. . . . But care must be taken:

. . . (b) that no infringement of canonical authority of any Ordinary in the government of his diocese be made by any agent or committee thus established. . . .[46]

The negative tone of this document from the Holy See, which supplemented the canonical approbation of the assembly and N.C.W.C.,[47] is reflected in a constant insistence upon the voluntary character of the conference:

The annual meeting of the hierarchy is not a council or legislative assembly, as is contemplated by the Sacred

46. S. Consistorial Congregation, instructions, July 4, 1922: J. T. Ellis, ed., *Documents of American Catholic History* (Milwaukee: Bruce, 1962), pp. 607-609; italics added.

47. S. Consistorial Congregation, decree, June 22, 1922: Ellis, *Documents*, p. 607.

Canons, and, therefore, the resolutions of the bishops at its meetings do not have the force of law.[48]

The formal limitation of the body's activity to the areas mentioned by Benedict XV in 1919—literally, "social questions" and "educational problems"[49]—was inevitably amplified in the course of time. But the resentments and fears of a supradiocesan authority remained. The bishops at their annual meeting and in the activities they sponsored did not feel free for many years to enter directly into such matters as doctrine, worship, or canonical discipline and structures.

The paradox is this. The N.C.W.C., as agency, secretariat, and instrument of the episcopal conference, prospered and became a model for many other such organizations because of its departments and their concrete achievements. Yet, because of the limitations and inhibitions mentioned above, the American experience contributed practically nothing to the ecclesial concept or the canonical figure of the episcopal conference. In the practical order, the N.C.W.C. was an actual exercise of collegiality by a national episcopate, but the extreme effort to divorce this action from a canonically visible structure and to avoid the identification of the episcopal hierarchy with the N.C.W.C. meant that an American doctrine or theory of episcopal conferences was almost non-existent at the time of the Second Vatican Council.

THE COUNCIL

During the second period of the Second Vatican Council (fall, 1963) the schema for the decree on the pastoral office

48. *Normae*, p. 3.
49. Letter, *Communes*, April 10, 1919: *AAS*, 11 (1919) 171-174.

of bishops in the Church[50] was debated in some nine general congregations.[51] The next stage of the decree was debated at three general congregations in the fall of 1964.[52] To complete the chronology, the emended and re-emended schema was finally approved at the general congregation of October 6, 1965, by 2167 votes to 14; the decree was enacted and promulgated at the public session of October 28, 1965, during the fourth and final period of the Council. When the section dealing with the structure and authority of conferences (n. 38) was directly voted upon (November 6, 1964), only 71 out of 2021 votes were negative.

The fourth paragraph of n. 38 of this decree, *Christus Dominus*, defines the authority of episcopal conferences to make decisions which have the force of binding juridically (*vim . . . iuridice obligandi*) as follows: "only in those cases in which either the common law shall prescribe this or the particular mandate of the Apostolic See, given at its own initiative or at the petition of the conference itself, shall establish this."[53]

The definitive text of this section does not reflect as substantial a change in the course of the conciliar process as might be expected. The passage in question was emended in order to make the basis of voting the entire membership of the body ("two-thirds of the votes of the prelates who pertain to the conference with deliberative vote"), as al-

50. Originally called the decree on bishops and the government of dioceses.

51. November 5-15, 1963.

52. September 18-22, 1964.

53. ". . . *in casibus dumtaxat in quibus aut ius commune id praescripserit aut peculiare Apostolicae Sedis mandatum, motu proprio aut ad petitionem ipsius Conferentiae datum, id statuerit.*"

ready mentioned.[54] An earlier version had described the *vim iuridice obligandi* in different terms: "oblige the individual bishops even juridically."[55] Happily this notion, that the real issue is restraint upon the bishop, rather than norm for the community, was suppressed.

The enumeration of matters in which binding decisions could be made by the conferences was another change. The 1963 version had read:

(a) when it is a question of particular matters which either according to the common law or by special mandate of the Apostolic See have been committed to the national conference of bishops to be considered and resolved;

(b) when it is a question of declarations of major significance to be made in the name of the national conference of bishops;

(c) when it is a question of matters to be treated with the civil government, which affect the entire nation;

(d) when the gravity of the matter requires a common mode of action by all the bishops and at the same time at least two-thirds of the prelates present with a deliberative vote judge that the decision itself is to be supported with juridical force for all.[56]

After the rather thorough revision of this version, the definitive text did remain entirely open to the extension of

54. Cf. *Schema Decreti de Pastorali Episcoporum Munere in Ecclesia, Textus Emendatus* (1964), p. 87, for this textual change. See above at note 2.

55. Cf. *Schemata . . . , Schema Decreti de Episcopis ac de Dioecesium Regimine* (April 22, 1963), p. 16.

56. *Ibid.*

authority through the common law or special mandates. Nevertheless it is evident that the text was severely limited as a result of the conciliar debate and process. And the heart of the question of episcopal conferences is their capacity to make binding decisions with juridical weight or, as it is put more commonly, their legislative authority.[57]

The divergent feelings of the Second Vatican Council on this issue may be conveniently summarized in the positions taken by three American cardinals, all now deceased: Spellman of New York, Meyer of Chicago, and Ritter of St. Louis.

Cardinal Spellman held to the minority position, which was fearful of any encroachment upon the papal authority.[58] He therefore stated that the conferences should have no juridical authority:

> . . . It would not be good to give the conferences the power of deciding matters with a juridic obligation for each bishop.
>
> It is necessary for bishops to remain completely free in the government of their dioceses although morally —not, indeed, juridically—it would be fitting that in matters that pertain to the whole nation they agree with the rest of the bishops.[59]

57. Perhaps it is well to say, once for all, that the question was *not* whether the conferences should be juridical or canonical institutes. It was whether these canonical institutes should have, among other kinds of authority, the power to make juridically binding decisions. The Council chose the latter, attributing or acknowledging such power, even though in limited areas. The conferences are lawmaking bodies, but only within the terms of n. 38 of *Christus Dominus.*

58. Intervention of November 11, 1963, in V. A. Yzermans, *American Participation in the Second Vatican Council* (New York: Sheed and Ward, 1967), pp. 382-383.

59. Intervention of November 13, 1963, in Yzermans, pp. 386-387. See

Cardinal Meyer took the middle position, which was substantially in support of the compromise ultimately written into the conciliar decree. His proposal was framed to permit the conferences to make decisions with juridical force only

> when there may be questions of particular matters which will have been entrusted to the national episcopal conference for discussion and decision, whether in virtue of common law, or by special commission of the Supreme Pontiff or of the Ecumenical Council.[60]

Finally the intervention of Cardinal Ritter totally rejected any fear of the episcopal conference as an encroachment upon the individual bishop's authority or as a barrier between the pope and the bishops. Supporting the substance of the schema (in its broadest expression of the authority of conferences), he urged the constitution of "national episcopal conferences having juridical status and strength."[61]

The preoccupation of the bishops from all parts of the world was with the question of juridic authority of the episcopal conferences. Perhaps this is the reason for a notable

also the interventions of Cardinal McIntyre of Los Angeles, November 5, 1963 (*ibid.*, pp. 379-380) and November 12, 1963 (*ibid.*, p. 383): "However, the introduction of a judicial element is not necessary; in fact it is also useless!"

---

60. Intervention of November 12, 1963, in Yzermans, p. 384. Perhaps the reference to "Supreme Pontiff" rather than "Apostolic See" reflects the desire of some conciliar Fathers that the pope should deal directly and even personally with the episcopal conferences, without the intervention of curial officials or legates.

61. Intervention of November 12, 1963, in Yzermans, pp. 385-386.

gap, at least upon reconsideration, in the submissions of the American and other English-speaking bishops. A substantial and significant contribution to this debate was possible from the Anglo-American legal, political, and cultural tradition. If episcopal conferences are a sound development from every theological, ecclesiological, and canonical viewpoint, their discussion in the general council would have profited from the Anglo-American parliamentary tradition and experience, from the concepts of constitutional responsibility, from the ways in which the conflicts in representing a constituency may be resolved, from the theory of balance of powers, and the like.

This defect is not mentioned as criticism, but it was a regrettable omission. Those who had an authentic civil tradition of parliaments and congresses had the greatest reason to support and refine the institute of episcopal conferences. It was the time to recall Bishop England's position, in favor of what we would now call the synodal or collegial principle as "more in accordance with the spirit of our National institutions."[62]

CHRISTUS DOMINUS

It would be worthwhile to study in detail the entire development of the section of *Christus Dominus* which limits the obligatory force of decisions of episcopal conferences to (a) cases prescribed in the common law, (b) cases determined by special mandate of the Apostolic See, whether at

62. Above, at note 36.

its own initiative or upon petition of the conference.[63] The following observations, however, are confined to the text itself.

(1) Ordinarily the above specification of authority is taken as referring to an exercise of the legislative power. This power was formerly confined at the national level, at least by the written law, to regional or plenary councils. Yet Bonet has pointed out that a threefold division may be made among the decisions of episcopal conferences, that there are three aspects to their canonical role:

(a) decisions of legislative value . . . ;

(b) decisions which, without becoming law in the proper sense, are nonetheless juridically binding;

(c) pastoral or disciplinary agreements without strictly juridical binding force.[64]

This division offered by Bonet is limited to disciplinary decisions affecting church order in one way or another. It does not consider, for example, the area of doctrinal declaration and witness through statements and pronouncements as a part of the episcopal conference's function as official *magisterium.* Such a function may in fact be of far greater significance. But this threefold division can be crucial to a

63. *Christus Dominus,* n. 38, 4.

64. M. Bonet, "The Episcopal Conference," *Concilium,* 8 (1965) 53. It is worth recording that Bonet, who died in 1969, was chairman of the juridical subcommittee of the Conciliar Commission on the Liturgy. This subcommittee formulated the first expression of the role of episcopal conferences during Vatican II. Cf. *Sacrosanctum Concilium,* art. 22, §2; 36. In a similar vein, see P. Huizing, *art. cit.,* pp. 174-175.

proper understanding of the disciplinary authority of conferences.

The making of law, in the strict sense of the canon law for the people of their own churches, and the making of other juridically obligatory decisions—with both of which n. 38, 4, of *Christus Dominus* is concerned—may be much less significant than the pastoral and disciplinary determinations which have "only" morally binding force. The tendency of this paper is evident enough. It is to propose an enlargement of the scope of legislative authority of the conferences. But this proposal is in no way directed at the increase of laws or the notion that the creation of new laws and fresh legal systems is an end in itself.

We are caught in a paradox. The signs of these times in the Church point to a diminution of the quantity of laws. They point to simplification and to increase only in laws which protect rights. There is even an antinomian position in regard to the ecclesiastical law which, even if it becomes excessive to the point of absurdity, should deter us from any great faith in the contemporary effectiveness of laws piled upon laws.

Yet the legislative authority of episcopal conferences or their right to make juridically obligatory decisions is an inescapable test of their efficacy. It will be urged later that the conferences should have whatever legislative authority is appropriate or necessary at their level in the ecclesial structure. At this point it is enough to say that conferences are judged as a force in the Church, perhaps because of the juridical mentality with which we are saddled, on the basis of that kind of authority.

(2) Because it was drawn up in the framework of particular councils, n. 38 of *Christus Dominus* speaks of a Roman *recognitio* of these juridically binding decisions of episcopal conferences.[65] It is difficult to find an English verb which will convey enough and not too much of this *recognitio:* to review or examine or inspect, to evaluate or approve or accept or confirm. *Recognitio* is a second consideration of the matter, the law, or the decision, by a superior authority in the Church, but it is a reconsideration which does not make the law or decision that of the superior authority.[66]

In the case of most episcopal conferences the immediately superior authority is the Apostolic See of Rome. There is thus every precedent in the recent history of the Latin Church for the requirement of this *recognitio.* The review or confirmation of conciliar (now conference) decisions is, however, neither essential nor in any sense constitutive. It is a means, and not necessarily the best means, by which the Roman See may act as arbiter and recourse among the churches.[67]

65. Logically *Christus Dominus* first (n. 36) urges the development of the traditional form of councils, which are in practical desuetude. The *acta* and decrees of plenary (and provincial) councils require Roman *recognitio* (canon 291, §1); the constitutions or decrees of diocesan synods do not (canon 362).

66. Since it is a procedural point, this is somewhat beside the central issue. The background and commentaries on canon 291 should be consulted.

67. The Constitution on the Liturgy succeeds in keeping the distinctions clear between (a) what is the right of episcopal conferences (however much the positive law demands Roman confirmation) and (b) what is reserved to the primatial see and hence requires the latter's consent to the "petition" of the episcopal conferences. See *Sacrosanctum Concilium*, art. 36 compared with art. 40; also art. 63. The distinction is not preserved elsewhere very carefully.

(3) The heart of n. 38, 4, refers to the scope or extent of the authority of episcopal conferences. It may be interpreted in one of two ways.

First, it is certainly intended to express, and does express, the strictest limitation upon the competence of conferences. This is the meaning of *dumtaxat;* the language is the product of debate and compromise, already mentioned, by which the text was pared down to its present limits. Thus it is correct and legitimate to say that episcopal conferences are severely limited in their juridically effective authority.

Yet the other side of the coin, the second and just as legitimate interpretation, is this: the Council's decree is open to any development; no least limitation is placed by the Council upon the developing authority of conferences.

The scope of this binding authority may be, and has already been, enlarged by the common law, whether this common law is enacted by the ecumenical council or by the primatial see or indeed by customary usage. *Christus Dominus* placed no limits on this enlargement.

The scope of this binding authority may be, and has already been, enlarged—without the need for common legislation or custom—by the special mandate of the primatial see. And, to make this last process simpler and clearer, the Fathers of Vatican II added something that would have been certain otherwise, namely, that this mandate may be at the initiative of the Roman See (a directive that a conference decide an issue with juridical effect) or in response to a request from the conference. *Christus Dominus* placed no limits on this enlargement.

Thus it is correct to say that episcopal conferences do not have competence to receive recourse from administrative decisions of bishops or appeals from judicial sentences;

to transfer the incardination of clergy from one diocese to another;[68] to set up a system of exemption of religious to the authority of the conference; to amend, suppress, or replace the common law *de processibus* or *de poenis et delictis;* to alter the discipline, as opposed to the rite, of the sacraments; to canonize saints.

But each such denial of the authority now enjoyed by the episcopal conferences should be qualified by the phrase "without application to the Apostolic See." Such is the patent sense of *Christus Dominus.* It is the reason why we suggest that n. 38, 4, for all that it is a grudging and limited concession, is completely open to any development which is agreed upon by the Roman pontiff and the episcopal conferences. It is open to any such development whether the conferences act together or in small groups of conferences or individually.

EVOLUTION IN THE SCOPE OF AUTHORITY

At the present moment the episcopal conference may lawfully act, with force obliging the clergy and laity of its jurisdiction, only in specified matters. The enlargement of those specified areas is both possible and likely. It is thus misleading to say that the conferences are limited to this or that matter. One should indicate both the evolution of the common law concerning their scope of authority and also the potential application to the Apostolic See for greater competence—in harmony with or beyond the common law or even, by dispensation, contrary to the common law.

68. But see Vatican Council II, decree *Presbyterorum Ordinis,* December 7, 1965, n. 10; *Ecclesiae sanctae,* I, 2.

That this increased scope of authority is a likely future development is conjecture. That it has developed beyond expectation, especially in the cases enumerated in the common law, is a fact. The Council itself, the legitimate author of the common law,[69] made its own enumeration of canonical matters within the scope of conferences, beginning with the Constitution on the Liturgy (which thus anticipated *Christus Dominus*).[70]

69. It is not out of place to relate that, in one conciliar commission, certain cardinal members had repeatedly to be reminded that the ecumenical council was indeed *supra Codicem* or to repeat the canard that the minority theologians, although espousing the doctrine of a *fons duplex* of revelation, held to one theological source, the *Codex Iuris Canonici*.

70. For a list of instances of liturgical legislation, see F. R. McManus, "The Juridical Power of the Bishop," *Concilium*, 2 (1964) 46-47. The right of episcopal conferences in liturgical matters, according to *Sacrosanctum Concilium*, embraces liturgical adaptations (n. 37-40), in particular the creation of new national rituals (cf. n. 63b); nor is the establishment of a new ritus in the sense of the several major liturgical rites of East and West excluded (cf. n. 4). Some episcopal conferences have taken these possibilities very seriously. For example, see *Rituel pour la célébration du mariage à l'usage des diocèses de France* (Paris: Brepols, 1969). This rite was approved by the French episcopal conference on April 14, 1969 (the *Ordo Celebrandi Matrimonium* of the Roman Ritual was authorized March 19) and confirmed by the Congregation for Divine Worship on June 2. The French ritual accepts most of the structure of the marriage service of the Roman Ritual, but rejects some of the texts of the latter and offers alternatives to almost every text it chooses to employ.

Sacrosanctum Concilium consistently uses the expression *auctoritas territorialis* with cross reference to its art. 22, §2, in order to describe any collegial episcopal authority higher than the diocesan bishop; this authority may be a council or a simple conference. According to the intent of *Sacrosanctum Concilium*, the authority may even be at the level of an ecclesiastical province (above, note 24), but see Paul VI, motu proprio *Sacram Liturgiam*, January 25, 1964, n. X: *AAS* 56 (1964) 139-144; S.R.C., instruction *Inter Oecumenici*, September 26, 1964: *AAS* 56 (1964) 877-900.

Examples may be offered from two conciliar decrees, which were formally implemented in the motu proprio *Ecclesiae sanctae* of August 5, 1966: from *Christus Dominus:* the right to care for special groups not susceptible to the usual pastoral ministry;[71] to examine questions of the boundaries of dioceses;[72] to examine questions of the boundaries of ecclesiastical provinces and regions;[73] from *Presbyterorum Ordinis:*[74] the right to see to the establishment of institutes for the financial security of the clergy, health and other insurance.[75]

An index to the conciliar documents will reveal the frequency with which n. 38, 4, of *Christus Dominus* was immediately applied in the new common law. More significant is the fact that almost no papal legislative act since the Council has failed to specify or augment these areas of competence. The principal examples in *Christus Dominus* and *Presbyterorum Ordinis* were mentioned above so that their subsequent elaboration would illustrate the point concerning the post-conciliar common law.

The references in the conciliar decrees to the distribution of the clergy do not mention directly the role of the

71. N. 18; this concern or care is expressed in *Christus Dominus* "through the voluntary agreement and united efforts" of the episcopal conference. It becomes, in *Ecclesiae sanctae* (I, 9), a commission of everything pertinent to "the study and moderation of their spiritual care" to "a priest delegated for this or a special commission established for this" by the conference. (In *Christus Dominus* the reference is to all kinds of special groups; in *Ecclesiae sanctae,* to migrants and pilgrims. See also S. C. pro Clericis, general directory [for the pastoral ministry *quoad "Turismum"*], April 30, 1969, II, 2: *AAS,* 61 [1969] 370).

72. N. 24; see *Ecclesiae sanctae,* I, 12.

73. N. 41; see *Ecclesiae sanctae,* I, 42.

74. On the ministry and life of presbyters, December 7, 1965.

75. N. 21; see *Ecclesiae sanctae,* I, 8.

episcopal conferences.[76] In the motu proprio *Ecclesiae sanctae* they are "to enact ordinances and to publish norms for bishops [*ordinationes statuere et normas pro Episcopis edere*]." [77]

The absence of an explicitly conciliar mention of the conferences in the matter of ecclesiastical property is corrected in *Ecclesiae sanctae:* they are competent "to enact appropriate ordinances . . . [*opportunas statuere ordinationes*]" to impose assessments (*subsidia*) on dioceses in favor of the apostolate or charity or of churches in need.[78]

The conciliar decrees, as noted above,[79] speak of a limited role of episcopal conferences in relation to the material welfare of the clergy; *Ecclesiae sanctae* says that they are to establish norms (*normae statuantur*), for individual dioceses or for several dioceses together or for the whole territory, for the proper support of the clergy and to see to the establishment of diocesan institutes for the holding of funds for this purpose.[80]

The failure of *Christus Dominus* to speak of the conferences in reference to the naming of bishops is partially remedied. Whatever the method employed, the conferences have the right to consider candidates and to propose names to the Apostolic See.[81] Again *Christus Dominus* speaks of

76. *Christus Dominus,* n. 6; *Presbyterorum Ordinis,* n. 10.

77. I, 2. Here, as elsewhere in *Ecclesiae sanctae,* the episcopal conferences are properly treated as parallel to patriarchal synods: "Synodorum Patriarchialium et Episcopalium Conferentiarum erit . . . ."

78. I, 5.

79. At note 75.

80. I, 8.

81. *Ecclesiae sanctae,* I, 10. This concession must also be classed among restrictive developments (below). It had the apparent purpose of asserting the right of the Roman pontiff to name and institute bishops, whereas the Council had spoken of this right in general terms as belonging

the resignation of bishops without reference to the conferences;[82] *Ecclesiae sanctae* attributes to the episcopal conference the right to determine, through a general norm for the territory, the terms of support for retired bishops.[83]

These examples should be enough to illustrate the development in the common law, but the picture is onesided without reference to other instances of restriction and curial trepidation about the growing canonical role of conferences. The formal treatment of episcopal conferences in *Ecclesiae sanctae* is an example already mentioned, especially in the matter of supranational conferences and the relations of conferences with each other.[84] Perhaps the first postconciliar example was the effort, less than two months after the promulgation of the Constitution on the Liturgy, to emasculate the competence of conferences in relation to vernacular translations of liturgical texts. This effort would have been more serious except for numerous changes introduced in the papal document after its original publication in *L'Osservatore Romano.*[85]

to "the competent ecclesiastical authority" (*Christus Dominus,* n. 20). For a recent study of the nineteenth-century tradition in the United States for the naming of bishops, so different from present practice, see J. T. Ellis, "On Selecting Catholic Bishops for the United States," *The Critic,* 7, n. 6 (June-July, 1969) 43-55. Six different methods were employed between 1789 and 1833 (*ibid.,* p. 45), including the acknowledgement of some *ius eligendi,* now almost a dead letter in the Latin Code (cf. canon 329, §3).

82. N. 21.
83. I, 11.
84. N. 41, especially §4, 5. See above, note 3.
85. Paul VI, motu proprio *Sacram Liturgiam,* January 25, 1964: *AAS* 56 (1964) 139-144. Cf. F. R. McManus, *Sacramental Liturgy* (New York: Herder and Herder, 1967), pp. 51-54.

Again, in spite of the formal and deliberate exclusion of papal nuncios and delegates from *de iure* membership in conferences by action of the Council,[86] there was a later attempt to interject such representatives.[87] This direction has taken new shape in the recent definition of the office of papal representatives. The latter are given a formal role —both as intermediaries and on their own responsibility— in the alteration of ecclesiastical jurisdictions "while the faculty of the episcopal conferences of formulating wishes and proposals . . . and the discipline of the Eastern Churches remain unchanged."[88] While not members of the episcopal conferences, they are to be "present at opening session of every general assembly, apart from any further participation in other acts of the conference upon invitation of the bishops themselves or by explicit order of the Holy See."[89] "These

86. *Christus Dominus*, n. 38, 2.

87. S. C. Consist., *Archetypon Statuti Conferentiae Episcoporum* [n.d.], art. 8: "Licet Legatus Romani Pontificis ob peculiare quod in territorio obit officium, ad Episcoporum Conferentiae de iure non pertineat, convenit tamen ut ad fraternum instaurandum cum universa loci sacra Hierarchia colloquium, in primum saltem congressionem cuiuslibet sessionis Conferentiae idem invitet.

"Liquet praeterea Legatum Romani Pontificis aliis Conferentiae congressionibus posse interesse vel de peculiari Sanctae Sedis mandato vel ipsa Conferentia invitante."

Art. 12: "Agendorum rerum libellus conficitur a Consilio permanenti (ubi hoc deest, a Praeside Conferentiae); verum tamen antequam ad Episcopos Conferentiae mittatur, evidentes ob causas, opportune Legato Romani Pontificis exhibeatur."

Attention is drawn to the last point; if it were adopted in the statutes of episcopal conferences, it would mean a prior Roman intervention in their work even greater than in the case of plenary councils (cf. canon 289).

88. Paul VI, motu proprio, *Sollicitudo Omnium Ecclesiarum,* June 24, 1969, art. VII: *AAS* 61 (1969) 473-484. Cf. *Christus Dominus*, n. 22-24; 39-41; *Ecclesiae Sanctae*, n. 12, 42.

89. *Ibid.*, art. VIII, 2. See above, note 87.

papal representatives will further be informed, in adequate time, of the assembly's agenda and will receive copies of the transcript for [their] own information and to send them to the Holy See."[90]

Without multiplying examples, one can see a contrasting pattern: limitations and hesitations on the part of the Roman See, reflected in the very announcement of the topic for the 1969 *Synodus Episcoporum*, and the inevitable enlargement of the authority of competences. The enlargement is as much a matter of current history and social and political influences as of canonical doctrine. The inevitability of the development is clear from the quantity of new recognitions and acknowledgments of the competence of conferences in papal documents. Sometimes this takes unlikely paths, dealing with "binding decisions" far different from the legislative authority, for example, the right of conferences to confer confessional jurisdiction for the sake of tourists[91] or to set up judicial tribunals for the causes of saints.[92] The instances of such increased competence may be significant or insignificant in themselves; the accumulation is great and seems inevitably to become greater.[93]

90. *Ibid.*

91. S. C. pro Clericis, general directory [for the pastoral ministry *quoad* "*Turismum*"], April 30, 1969, II, 2: *AAS*, 61 (1969) 370: "Conferentiae Episcopales insuper invitantur consulere pro viribus ut praesertim frequentioris Turismi tempore, facultatem sacras confessiones excipiendi extendant Sacerdotibus omnibus iam in sua Dioecesi eadem gaudentibus, dum in toto territorio nationali iter agunt, vel etiam, specificis in casibus, quando exteras regiones peragant."

92. Paul VI, motu proprio *Sanctitas clarior,* March 19, 1969: *AAS* 61 (1969) 149-153.

93. A major breakthrough is the concession by the Holy See of simplified procedural norms for matrimonial cases in the United States, at the petition of the National Conference of Catholic Bishops (letter from

LEGISLATIVE COMPETENCE: TWO POSITIONS

This summary description or illustration brings us to the basic questions: should the scope of authority of episcopal conferences continue to be enlarged by bits and pieces? Or has the time come for a sharper definition of principle than was possible in *Christus Dominus?* Even in the present, not very satisfactory, policy of concessions to conferences by new decrees of the primatial see, we should advert to the point of theological and canonical doctrine made at the beginning: Much as the episcopal conferences are dependent upon the written common law (or upon the slow growth of custom) for the concrete applications of their competence, the basis of that competence is not in concessions from superior authority but in the communion of the particular churches which the members of the conference head.

Two representative opinions may be cited in connection with the future evolution of episcopal conferences:

Mörsdorf speaks of the likely development of a "general competence" for the conferences, while he recognizes the

---

the Prefect of the Council for the Public Affairs of the Church, April 28, 1970, prot. n. 3320/70). In virtue of this the American episcopal conference may, for example, "permit the competent ecclesiastical Tribunal to derogate from this norm [of a collegiate Tribunal] for a specified period of time so that a case may be handled by a single judge" (Norm 3). The instances of this canonical extension of authority could be multiplied, whether for individual conferences as in this case or for all episcopal conferences. A final example of the latter may be added: according to the motu proprio *Matrimonia mixta* of April 29, 1970, to determine the manner of making the *cautiones* (n. 7), the norms for licit dispensation from canonical form in mixed marriages (n. 9), and regulations for recording such marriages (n. 10); they need only "inform the Apostolic See of all decisions which, within their competence, they make concerning mixed marriages" (n. 12).

advantages of lawmaking on the occasion of solemn synods or regional and plenary councils:

> The synods of particular churches have general legislative and other legal powers in their territories, whereas the episcopal conference has so far been given only particular powers of this kind. True, these individual faculties have now become very numerous and it may perhaps be expected that the episcopal conference will receive a general competence in the near future, yet the more solemn synod has certain advantages.[94]

His balanced judgment is in harmony with the pattern described above:

> On the whole it cannot be overlooked that the present [conciliar] directions aim at limiting the powers of the episcopal conferences as hierarchical institutions. But it is doubtful whether this system can be carried through at all. For the constant increase of individual competencies in the post-conciliar legislation which might continue indefinitely can hardly be combined with the modern desire for clear, brief and intelligible legislation. Hence it is to be expected that the reform of canon law will unify the competencies of the episcopal conferences and make them of more general application.[95]

Huizing, on the other hand, would remove legislative authority from the conferences—reserving this to formal

94. *Art. cit.*, p. 283.
95. *Ibid.*, p. 291.

particular councils—while he recognizes their general competence to make non-legislative, obligatory decisions. It is his position that laws in the strict sense should be made only by councils; he assumes that "it will not be so difficult for the bishops to extend the conference into a synod or to convoke a synod. This will be even easier if the previous authorization of the Roman See [canon 281] will no longer be required."[96] He seeks both to restrict and to enlarge the authority of conferences:

It has to be stated also that the lack of legislative power in the episcopal conferences all through their development did not cause serious harm. The difficulty was rather that at times one or two bishops refused to accommodate themselves to the desires of all the others. There is now a reasonable solution for this problem without conferring formal legislative power on the episcopal conferences. It would be enough that a decision approved by two-thirds of the members be binding for all.

. . . . The power of the conferences consists not in proper legislative powers but in a power to decide issues before them in such a way that all the members are bound by the decision. Such a power to decide should not be restricted to various determined cases. To the synods the proper legislative power will be reserved [in this proposal]. . . .[97]

These two positions agree in extending the scope of binding decisions of episcopal conferences to "all issues

96. *Art. cit.,* p. 174.
97. *Ibid.,* pp. 174-175.

within the limits of the common law," that is, a "general competence" not restricted by petty concessions and niggling distinctions. The Huizing proposal, however, besides retreating from the decree of the ecumenical council, creates a new indecisiveness hardly palatable in our age. What is to be considered apt for legislation? What is to be left in the gray area of non-legislative binding decisions? His position has other weaknesses as well: (1) too ready an assumption that conferences could become synods or councils without formality; (2) a failure to see the need or at least the potential of extra-synodal legislation, just as appropriate on the national level as in the diocese; (3) the uncertainty that the primatial see will lessen its intervention in particular councils; (4) most serious of all in its psychological and indeed political effects, the perilous stretching of the tender strands of accepted subsidiarity and decentralization in the ecclesial society.

The great advantage of Huizing's proposal is that it moves away from the juridical concept of the Church. It acknowledges that the canon law, in the strict sense of particular legislation, is neither an end in itself nor a panacea for the troubles of the Church.

CONCLUSION

The answers which this paper offers, as a result of the summary recital of facts and reflections above, are the following:

1. The episcopal conferences should first be recognized in law as possessing the general competence of a particular synod, national or regional or plenary as it may be called.

This should not require the present formalities of (2) the previous *venia* of the Roman pontiff, (b) the presidency of a legate of the pope, and (c) the authority of the legate over the agenda.[98]

This would in fact permit an episcopal conference to pass from its ordinary decision to those decisions (relatively few, it is to be hoped) which demand the form or sanction of the canon law. It should mean also that the conference itself, without necessarily conceding a deliberative vote to persons other than the present canonical membership, would become as open to the necessary participation of specialists, consultants, and representatives of clergy and laity as a particular council.[99]

Such a clear, decisive step would eliminate the current underbrush of multiplying concessions. It would place the conferences on a sure footing as a hierarchical institution very similar to the traditional patriarchal synods. They would possess a competence not restricted except by the common law—and even this restriction can be lifted by leave of the superior ecclesiastical authority.

Doubts and hesitations, whether those expressed in the conciliar debate or later manifested in curial actions, should be allayed by a procedural safeguard—either the one essential to the constitution of the Church, which is the right of recourse to the primatial see, or the present requirement of a two-thirds majority, at least as a temporary expedient. The need for confirmation of laws, whether by the next

98. Can. 281, 289.

99. Cf. Can. 282, §3; 286, §3. It is hard to understand Huizing's reasoning (*art. cit.*, p. 174) about the advantages of a conference which excludes all but bishops.

higher authority or by the primatial see, is an unnecessary formality but one which can surely continue to alleviate anxieties. In fact one or other of these possibilities should suffice to prevent any undue imposition by a conference upon a minority, however small.

2. Once the troubling matter of legislative and similar competence has been resolved, the principle of ecclesiastical subsidiarity needs to be applied fully to the episcopal conferences—chiefly at the national level, but with analogous application at every other level: provincial, regional, and supranational. The sharpest canonical definition of this may be found in n. 8 of *Christus Dominus,* which speaks of the bishop of an individual church.

All the ordinary, proper, and immediate power which is required for the exercise of their pastoral office belongs per se to the bishops, as successors of the apostles, in the dioceses entrusted to them, the power which the Roman pontiff has, by virtue of his office, to reserve cases to himself or to another authority remaining intact always and in everything.[100]

The implications of this statement of *Christus Dominus,* central to the position of the Second Vatican Council on

100. N. 8a. The contribution of a major intervention by the late Cardinal Ritter to this section of *Christus Dominus* should be recorded (November 7, 1963: Yzermans, pp. 381-382). The philosophical contradiction between *omnis potestas* (of the bishop) and reservation *semper in omnibus* (of the pope) is certainly open to discussion, but the conciliar accomplishment was to reverse irrevocably the presumption that the bishop possesses only the jurisdictional powers conceded to him by the Roman pontiff.

the office of the diocesan bishop, have not begun to be realized. They have in fact been confused with the related declaration, insignificant by comparison, that bishops may dispense from the general law except in reserved cases.[101] Here, however, the suggestion is that the principle be applied, in acknowledgment of the Church's nature as a communion of individual churches, to the episcopal conferences.

The analogy is by no means perfect. In one case it is the pastoral office of the diocesan bishop, in the other the authority of a body or assembly of bishops. Yet the principle of subsidiary action, as we have come to call it, is similar. In the case of the episcopal conferences, the principle may be expressed by saying that these bodies should have all the pastoral authority needed for the exercise of their function, unless there has been some special reservation by a superior authority (whether that of the primatial see or, for example, that of a supranational or international conference) and provided, of course, that the formalities or procedures designed to protect minority rights are satisfied.

The Second Vatican Council happily chose to speak of hierarchical communion and pastoral care and solicitude rather than of jurisdiction. Nor is the present suggestion intended to descend to a new and more complex juridicism. It may well be that the episcopal conference will find little need to become involved in the classical divisions of legislative, judicial, and executive or administrative power. It is desirable, however, that the inherent collegial function and potential of these bodies be recognized without equivocation, especially as regards their presumptive authority vis-a-

101. N. 8b.

vis the primatial see—if only so that they can get on with their work, having available to them the means, in canonical terms, to improve ecclesiastical institutes if these stand in the way of the Church's mission.

The recognition of such a principle, however formulated, demands both political wisdom and faith in the Spirit's action in the community. The political wisdom is that we try to profit from the lessons of constitutionalism, federalism, representation, and the like, without slavishly adopting any feature of political systems. The confidence in divine help should support the community in its release from excessive centralization and in what may appear to be a greater surrender of the autonomy of the local or individual church.

The purpose of episcopal conferences is not only the common good, looked on as the fulfillment of needs common to the whole territory, but the good of the individual particular churches. This may well require in the episcopal conference, as in the particular synods from their earliest history, the right to intervene to correct abuses in the individual churches. *Christus Dominus* makes the point in reference to the synods or councils as it introduces the whole question of "bishops cooperating for the common good of many churches":

From the very first centuries of the Church bishops, as rulers of individual churches, were deeply moved by the communion of fraternal charity and zeal for the universal mission entrusted to the apostles. And so they pooled their abilities and their wills for the common good *and for the welfare of the individual churches.* Thus came into being synods, provincial councils, and plenary councils in which bishops established for various churches the way to be followed in teaching the truths of faith and ordering ecclesiastical discipline.[102]

The fulfillment of the analogy between synods and conferences and now this presumptive authority of the latter, according to a logical subsidiarity in the Church, can form the basis of future development for the good of the Christian people. But a third point needs to be made.

3. A theme of this paper has been to dismiss the fears that episcopal conferences encroach upon the authority of individual bishops. Another and more reasonable fear, that the conferences themselves should seek exclusively or even largely juridical solutions to problems, has been mentioned often enough. It is also necessary to indicate that the conferences must now respect the principles of collegiality and subsidiarity in their own operation.

First, there is the collaboration of the entire community at the level of the respective episcopal conference. This is not easy to achieve, but it is necessary if communion and community are to be more than a matter of the association of bishops. That these bodies are episcopal conferences does not make them any less ecclesial bodies and in the *Ecclesia* the community comes first, not the order of bishops.

Next, the conference must respect the divisions and the subdivisions, the *portiones* of the flock, especially the dioceses. N. 8 of *Christus Dominus* speaks of limitations upon the pastoral authority of bishops solely in terms of reservation of particular cases by the Roman pontiff. This

102. N. 36. Italics added.

is incomplete. Another limitation upon the exercise of the pastoral office of the individual bishop is his need to act collegially with the presbyterium and the rest of the clergy, with the whole of the Christian people, and indeed to respect the subsidiary rights, integrity, and relative autonomy of individual congregations and communities. Similarly, if the principle of *Christus Dominus* is applied analogously to the episcopal conference, the latter must respect, and proclaim its respect for, the individual local churches which it unites.

ECUMENICAL CONSIDERATIONS

If one needs to make a supporting argument for the stronger role of the episcopal conference in today's Church and today's world, it is to be found in ecumenical considerations. If the subsidiarity and the collegiality which the episcopal conferences should enshrine are not thus strengthened, if there is not genuine decentralization, it is hard to see how any church or ecclesial community can ever accept full communion with the Roman See and the churches in communion with it. The point was made explicitly in the conciliar debate, like so many other points touching ecclesial structures, by one of the Greek Melkite bishops, Archbishop Elias Zoghby:

In our day, when the Catholic Church is trying to become more accessible to the communion of Eastern Orthodoxy and is preparing for ecumenical dialogue, the only form of Church government which the Second Vatican Council can propose to the churches of the East is synodal governments, i.e., government by genuine bishops' conferences with real power. To speak of conferences which would be purely consultative would forestall the possibility of dialogue.[103]

It is not directly pertinent to the present topic to consider whether the synodal government of the Eastern Churches now in full communion has been or is respected by the Roman Church. At least the Second Vatican Council is unequivocal: the rights of the churches to their own rule is asserted repeatedly.[104] More to the point is the fresh confirmation of the Roman position on ecclesial unity:

> . . . This sacred Synod confirms what previous councils and Roman pontiffs have proclaimed: in order to restore communion and unity or preserve them, one must "impose no burden beyond what is indispensable" (Acts 15:28).[105]

The issue can be put in this way. If the churches of the West now in communion with the Roman See cannot recover their synodal form of government, both in the local churches and in the communion of several or many local churches at the various possible levels of episcopal conferences, the credibility of non-Catholic Christians will be stretched out of existence. The conciliar documents are

103. *L'Église Grecque Melkite au Concile* (Beyrouth: Dar Al-Kalima, 1967), p. 209; trans., *Council Speeches of Vatican II* (Glen Rock, N.J.: Paulist Press, 1964), pp. 126-127.
104. Decree *Orientalium Ecclesiarum* (November 21, 1964), n. 3-6, 9; decree *Unitatis redintegratio* (November 21, 1964), n. 16.
105. *Unitatis redintegratio,* n. 18.

sufficient to the purpose, or at least they open the way to the collegial developments necessary for ecumenical progress in the area of church government. This kind of collegial growth is a good instance of what we can learn from the unbroken traditions of other Christian churches.

A complicating factor, pertinent to the question of episcopal conferences, is the failure in the West to distinguish properly between the primatial and patriarchal offices of the Roman bishop. The pope's role as Western patriarch can be the explanation, if not always the justification, for intervention in the affairs of the particular churches of the West. In dealing with the restoration of the patriarchal office and the creation of new patriarchates,[106] the Second Vatican Council undoubtedly had in mind directly and perhaps exclusively the Eastern situation, but the application to the West is obvious. The Western patriarchate already has its natural divisions and subdivisions. The sooner these are recognized as having a canonical status parallel to the old patriarchates —but with the new terminology and the new forms of conferences and presidents—the sooner the inner nature of the Church will be clarified and the tensions tearing it in all directions may be alleviated.

A conclusion to these observations and suggestions has to be repetitious. The one Church is a communion of charity. Its hierarchical structure makes it realizable in each local community and is the key to the communion of churches. The institutional structure is quite secondary to life and mission; just as with laws and discipline, the need for a complex institutional structure may be greater or less tomorrow. But these structures, including that of the episcopal

106. Cf. *Orientalium Ecclesiarum*, n. 4, 9.

conference, must authentically reflect the community of mission and activity, the collegial nature of every assembling of God's people, and respect for the right and dignity of each such coming together. This is really the purpose of clarifying and solidifying the role and competence of the episcopal conference today.

PAPAL DIPLOMACY
AND THE CONTEMPORARY CHURCH

By James Hennesey, S.J.

Four years ago I wrote an article in which I suggested that the Church's understanding of itself in the Second Vatican Council, with the stress laid there on episcopal collegiality, ecumenism and religious liberty, boded ill for the future prospects of Church-State relationships built on an institution-to-institution basis. I implied that one logical casualty of changing ecclesiological emphases would be papal diplomacy.[1] Response was disappointingly slim. A dear friend and colleague hinted that the last such persecutor of the papal diplomatic establishment had been Adolf Hitler.[2] A graduate student in the midwest was impatient with my gradualist approach; he predicted that apostolic

1. James Hennesey, S.J., "U.S. Representative at the Vatican?" *America*, December 4, 1965, pp. 707-711.
2. Robert A. Graham, S.J., "Another Point of View," *America*, December 4, 1965, pp. 710-711.

nuncios and delegates would disappear automatically, once proper national episcopal conferences were functioning.[3] Finally, but somewhat belatedly, I became a star attraction in a staff report of the Baptist Joint Committee on Public Affairs.[4] Meanwhile the exchange of diplomatic representatives between the Holy See and sovereign states has continued to increase at a rapid rate. In 1870, the last year of the Papal States, there were only 17 diplomatic missions in Rome. By 1914 the total was down to 14. At Pope John XXIII's accession in 1959 there were 36 accredited ambassadors and ministers. The count rose to 52 by 1965 and 69 in 1969.[5] The picture is hardly that of a dying institution.

There are several ways in which to discuss papal diplomacy. One question is whether the pope should maintain diplomatic ties with secular governments. In this case, the pope accredits a nuncio, a pro-nuncio or an internuncio to the government in question. The papal representative becomes a member of the diplomatic corps in the capital to which he is sent. He deals with whatever business may occur

3. *America*, January 15, 1966, p. 61.

4. "Diplomatic Relations with the Vatican," Staff Report, Baptist Joint Committee on Public Affairs, Washington, D.C., April 1968, p. 8.

5. A good historical survey is found in Robert A. Graham, S.J., *Vatican Diplomacy: A Study of Church and State on the International Plane* (Princeton, 1959). Another standard reference work is Igino Cardinale, *Le Saint-Siège et la diplomatie: Apercu historique, juridique et pratique de la diplomatie pontificale* (Paris, 1962). Diplomatic representatives to and from the Holy See, as well as the list of Apostolic Delegates, are reported annually in the *Annuario Pontificio*, published by the Vatican Press. On October 15, 1969, Canada became the sixty-ninth nation to establish diplomatic relations with the Holy See. Canadian Prime Minister Pierre Elliott Trudeau stated that the step was being taken because the Vatican was an important center for diplomatic contact and the gathering of information. (Jay Walz, "Canada and the Vatican Establish Diplomatic Ties," *The New York Times*, October 16, 1969).

between the papal government and the one to which he is accredited. He also has the added responsibility of dealing with the Catholic Church in the country. He channels purely ecclesiastical business to and from Rome, he reports to Rome on local church conditions and he plays a part in the selection of bishops. If there is a concordat between the Holy See and his host country, the nuncio deals with matters that may arise in connection with it. He is, then, a fully-accredited diplomat, but with a mission to the church and its bishops as well as to the secular government of the country in which he resides. Following normal diplomatic practice, this type of relationship is usually reciprocal. When the pope sends a diplomatic representative to a secular government, that government sends an ambassador or a minister to represent it at the Vatican. His function is to handle any and all business that may occur between his home government and the Holy See. Inevitably he becomes involved in Church affairs. These *are* the business that occurs between governments and the Holy See.[6]

There is another type of papal representative, the apostolic delegate. His position is, by definition, non-diplomatic.

6. Nuncios rank with ambassadors. Internuncios rank with ministers. Since the 1815 Congress of Vienna international protocol has recognized the right of a nuncio to be dean of the diplomatic corps in the country to which he is accredited, regardless of his seniority among his ambassadorial colleagues. At the present time some nations do not recognize this right. Since 1965 the title "pro-nuncio" has been used by the Holy See to designate the head of a nunciature, ranking as an ambassador, in a nation that does not acknowledge the papal representative's automatic right to the deanship. Also, while reciprocity is the normal rule, there are exceptions. The United Kingdom has a minister at the Holy See, but the Holy See maintains no diplomatic representative in London, where its agent is an apostolic delegate who has no formal diplomatic role. There is a nuncio in Bern, but no Swiss ambassador at the Vatican.

He is not accredited to a secular government, but he is the representative of the pope to a given area. This may include an entire national territory (as, for example, the United States), or it may include several nations (as, for example, West Africa). The delegate deals with local church affairs. If he has any dealings with secular governments they must be unofficial. There is no reciprocity. The nation in which an apostolic delegate resides does not normally send an agent to the Holy See.

PAPAL DIPLOMACY AS A WHOLE

In this paper we shall be concerned with papal diplomacy as a whole. This includes not only the technical diplomatic relationship which arises with the reciprocal accreditation of nuncios and ambassadors, but also the larger question of the Holy See's relationships with the Catholic Church in its various local settings throughout the world. In the past much of the discussion has focused on the relatively narrow question of formal diplomatic relations between the Holy See and a given nation. It was this preoccupation that gave rise to the question I asked in *America* in 1965: "U.S. Representative at the Vatican?" But I would like to suggest that in the wake of Vatican II, with its emphasis on the collegial nature of the Church, the focus has shifted. We have not only to ask whether the Holy See should engage in formal government-to-government relationships with national states; we must, and more importantly, ask what is the nature of the papal relationship to the Catholic churches of the world, and then we must ask what structure ought be built upon that relationship.

It will perhaps be helpful at this point to summarize briefly the history of the development of papal representation. The first nuncios seem to have been appointed in the middle of the 15th century. Under Pope Gregory XIII (1572-1585) it became common for the chief Catholic powers to receive permanent nuncios and to reciprocate with their own diplomatic missions in Rome. Not until the French Revolution were relations established with non-Catholic powers, while the 1815 Congress of Vienna really marked the inauguration of modern papal diplomacy.[7] With the growth of Roman centralization in the 19th and 20th centuries, papal representation abroad grew apace. The initial diplomatic exchange was with Europe, but as the Church became for the first time in its history truly universal in physical extent, with indigenous churches on every inhabited continent, more and more nations in the Americas, Asia and Africa have sent diplomatic missions to the Holy See and have had nunciatures established in their own capitals. Where this was not done, apostolic delegates have been despatched.[8] Like so many other things ecclesiastical which early take on a veneer of the ageless, the papal diplomatic corps is a relatively new feature in an ancient Church, a response to the specific demands of certain periods in the Church's history. The roots of the idea of worldwide papal

7. See Graham, *Vatican Diplomacy,* and Cardinale. The most recent international confirmation of the status and rights of papal diplomats was in the 1961 Convention of Vienna. (Cardinale, pp. 111-113).

8. The best introduction to this period of the Church's history is Roger Aubert, *Le Pontificat de Pie IX (1846-1878)* (2nd ed.; Paris, 1963). For the situation prior to the great centralization of the 19th century, see James Hennesey, S.J., "National Traditions and the First Vatican Council," *Archivum Historiae Pontificiae,* 7 (1969), 491-512.

representation are in the early modern period; its flowering has been a much more recent phenomenon.

The most recent document to touch upon papal diplomatic practice is the apostolic letter *motu proprio Sollicitudo Omnium Ecclesiarum* (June 24, 1969), on "The Duties of Representatives of the Roman Pontiff."[9] A study of *Sollicitudo* shows that it is much more than a simple description of the roles of papal diplomatic functionaries. It adopts a philosophy of the Church that needs careful comparison with the ecclesiology of Vatican II. This ecclesiological question is far more radical to our subject than any considerations of mere politics or history. We shall come to *Sollicitudo* in a moment. But first there are some other background materials.

Perhaps the most comprehensive recent defense of the Vatican's international diplomatic involvement was made in a speech delivered at the 250th anniversary of the Pontifical Ecclesiastical Academy on April 25, 1951, by Monsignor Giovanni Battista Montini.[10] After admitting the objections that could be raised to papal diplomatic activity, the future pope argued that these disadvantages were far outweighed by the opportunities afforded the Holy See of participation in the world of international diplomacy. On January 12, 1970, responding to the New Year's greetings of the diplomatic corps accredited to the Holy See, Pope Paul VI once more re-emphasized his conviction of the value of papal

9. The full text of *Sollicitudo* is in *L'Osservatore Romano* [English ed.], July 17, 1969; and in *Acta Apostolicae Sedis,* 61 (August 8, 1969), 473-484.

10. Cardinale, pp. 183-197, reprints a large part of this speech under the chapter heading, "La diplomatie pontificale: répresentation du Christ." See also Graham, *Vatican Diplomacy,* pp. 31-32.

diplomatic activity. He placed first among its merits that it enabled the Holy See to take action through official governmental channels for the achievement of peace. He also alluded to the other role of his representatives when he declared that they contribute to the good of the Church by helping local churches strengthen their bonds with Rome.[11] There is no doubt at all of the firmness of the pope's convictions about the value of his representation abroad, whether that representation is technically diplomatic or through apostolic delegates. He sees the institution as providing an entree for his peace efforts and he also sees it as a force binding local churches more closely to the central government. These ideas are spelled out in *Sollicitudo Omnium Ecclesiarum* also. But there are, and have been, other forces at work in the complicated world of a developing ecclesiology, and some of them should be heard. I would like to present two examples of differing approaches, one of them contemporary, the other an historical note on the American experience. Then we shall finish with an analysis of *Sollicitudo*.

CRITICISM OF THE PRESENT APPROACH

A relatively mild critic of the present papal approach to international representation, but who has borne the brunt of considerable criticism is the Cardinal Archbishop of Malines-Brussels, Leo Jozef Suenens.[12] The Belgian primate's

11. "Co-operating for the Common Good," *L'Osservatore Romano* [English ed.,] January 22, 1970, pp. 2-3.

12. For the interview in which Suenens expressed his mind on papal diplomacy, see "Unity in the Church in a New Perspective. An Interview with Cardinal Suenens," *The Tablet* (London), May 17, 1969, pp. 484-

comments on the papal diplomatic enterprise, in an interview in the spring of 1969 were hardly radical, which is not surprising, since he lives within a system where papal diplomacy is part of the accepted way of life. I happened to be in Rome in December, 1961, when the reorganization of Belgium's primatial Archdiocese of Malines and the promotion of Bishop Suenens to head it under the new name of Malines-Brussels were announced. I also happened to be in Brussels a month later and read there an official notice to the effect that the recent papal dispositions in the matter of the archdiocese and its new bishop had no effect until they had been ratified by the Belgian Parliament.[13] In any event, the problem for Suenens is that papal nuncios (he does not advert to apostolic delegates) combine the diplomatic role of ambassador of the Vatican State with the religious "watching brief" of a "de-centralized member of the Curia, whose task it is to watch over, on the spot, the carrying out of canonical regulations, and to supervise the bishops."[14] The Belgian cardinal would turn the ambassadorial function over to laymen. He does not ask the more important questions:

493; and "Suenens: Toward Unity and Freedom in the Church," *The National Catholic Reporter,* May 28, 1969, reprint, p. 8. For a discussion of some of the controversy surrounding Suenens' interview, see Robert C. Doty, "Address by Pontiff Viewed as Rebuke to Belgian Prelate," *The New York Times,* June 24, 1969. This *Times* report on the promulgation of *Sollicitudo Omnium Ecclesiarum* suggested that the following words of Pope Paul were "a clear allusion to attacks such as those by Cardinal Suenens": "We cannot be insensible to the criticisms, not all accurate and not all just, nor always respectful or opportune, that are directed from various sources against this Apostolic See, under the more easily vulnerable name of the Roman Curia."

13. The *Annuario Pontificio* gives the dates for these events as December, 1961, but that was not quite how it happened.

14. *The Tablet, loc. cit.*, p. 492.

must the ambassadorial function exist at all? Or the religious function? And he misses the point by suggesting that papal nuncios might seriously be considered as representing the minuscule state of Vatican City.[15] They represent the Holy See, something quite different, a unique entity in international law and one which insists on recognition as such.[16] Any discussion of papal diplomacy as if it were Vatican City diplomacy simply ignores the issues. One question that must be answered is whether the Church, precisely as church, should in the latter half of the twentieth century maintain official diplomatic relationships with national states. Also to be answered in the same historical context is the further question: is worldwide papal representation essential, or even useful, to the harmonious relationship of pope and bishops? The questions are political, historical, ecclesiological. The answers to them must be consistent with the Church's understanding of itself in the present post-conciliar epoch.

U.S. - VATICAN RELATIONS

The issues have been clearer in the American history of this Roman-local relationship. There is evidence along the

15. Graham, *Vatican Diplomacy*, pp. 238-239, makes it clear that possession of the temporal power in Vatican City is not the basis for papal diplomacy. Cardinale, *op. cit.*, pp. 63-81, distinguishes the Holy See ("the juridical personification of the Church, as the state is of the nation") from the Vatican State.

16. Robert A. Graham, S.J., "Papal Diplomacy," *The New Catholic Encyclopedia*, 4, 882, writes: "The Holy See's status in the world community arises fundamentally from the Roman Pontiff's position as a religious leader. He is the head of an enduring institution (*societas perfecta*) sovereignly independent."

two lines: that of diplomatic relations and that of papal-episcopal relations.

The United States maintained consular relations with the Papal States from 1797-1870 and a legation in papal Rome from 1848-1868, when Congress refused further appropriations for it. The ostensible reason for the closure was the mission's political insignificance; unfortunately the congressional debates were tinged with religious bigotry. But more important was that even the most conservative contemporary American Catholics were delighted at the end of the legation. As William Madden has put it, "these Catholics realized that despite precautions the presence of an American representative at the Vatican, with direct access to the Holy Father, remained an almost direct invitation to interference in internal American church affairs."[17]

Reciprocity during the twenty years of the Roman legation was apparently never seriously considered by the United States, and both the American government and Catholic American bishops reacted coolly to the idea when it was broached during the 1853 visit to these shores of the

17. The standard sources are Leo Francis Stock, *Consular Relations between the United States and the Papal States, 1797-1870* (Washington, 1945); and *United States Ministers to the Papal States: Instructions and Dispatches, 1848-1868* (Washington, 1933). A recent treatment is in William O. Madden, S.J., "American Catholic Support for the Papal Army, 1866-1868," unpublished doctoral dissertation, Pontifical Gregorian University, Rome, 1967, pp. 54-68. The quotation is from p. 68. Among Madden's witnesses to the non-necessity of the Roman legation are William McCloskey, Rector of the American College and later Bishop of Louisville, Robert Seton, arch-conservative and very "Roman" grandson of Blessed Elizabeth Ann Seton, and James A. McMaster, lay editor of the New York *Freeman's Journal* and self-appointed voice of extreme rightwing orthodoxy in America.

new papal nuncio to Brazil, Gaetano Bedini.[18] The question
of United States-Vatican ties would come up again during
the years of World War II, when Presidents Roosevelt and
Truman maintained a personal representative with ambassadorial rank and, in his absence, a chargé d'affaires in the
Vatican. The authorized biography of the late Cardinal Spellman indicates that as early as 1932 that prelate was working
for the establishment of such relations, through Joseph P.
Kennedy and others.[19]

The involvement of Cardinal Spellman in the Roosevelt-
Pius XII dealings suggests that there have been American
Catholic leaders who saw advantages in such a relationship
between the head of their Church and the head of their
nation. Archbishop John T. McNicholas, then Chairman of
the Board of the National Catholic Welfare Conference, was
another. He argued in 1948 that the United States might
send a representative to the pope as head of Vatican City.[20]

18. James F. Connolly, *The Visit of Archbishop Gaetano Bedini to
the United States of America, 1853-1854* (Rome, 1960).

19. Myron C. Taylor, *Wartime Correspondence between President
Roosevelt and Pope Pius XII* (New York, 1947) outlines these diplomatic
dealings. Taylor served both Roosevelt and Truman as Personal Repre-
sentatives at the Vatican. See also, by the American chargé d'affaires who
remained in Vatican City throughout the war, Harold H. Tittman, Jr.,
"Vatican Mission," *Social Order*, 10 (1960), 113-117. Spellman's involvement is described in Robert I. Gannon, S.J., *The Cardinal Spellman Story*
(Garden City, 1962), pp. 153-175. Numerous documents on this era of
Papal-American relations have been published in *Actes et documents du
Saint-Siège relatifs à la seconde guerre mondiale*, particularly to date
in volume five (Vatican City, 1969).

20. Graham, *Vatican Diplomacy*, pp. 344-347. Commenting on the archbishop's suggestion, Graham reiterates the fact that the only real basis
for diplomatic relations with the pope is with him as "head of the
Catholic Church, at least in his aspect of world moral authority."

But opposed to this line of thought is a strong and consistent American Catholic tradition of opposition both to formal diplomatic ties between the Holy See and the civil government and to the stable presence in the midst of the American church of Roman representatives. This tradition was expressed very baldly in 1784 by John Carroll, who six years later became the first Catholic bishop in the United States:

> . . . the Catholic clergy and laity here know that the only connection they ought to have with Rome is to acknowledge the pope as spiritual head of the Church; that no Congregation existing in his States shall be allowed to exercise any share of his spiritual authority here; that no Bishop Vicar Apostolical shall be admitted, and, if we are to have a bishop, he shall not be *in partibus* (a refined Roman political contrivance), but an ordinary national bishop, in whose appointment Rome shall have no share. . . .[21]

What Carroll had to say of "vicars apostolical" applied equally to other foreign prelates. The American church developed a strong conciliar and collegial tradition in the nineteenth century.[22] The bishops sought to have Baltimore declared the primatial see and were turned down in 1852 by

21. John Carroll to Charles Plowden, April 10, 1784, in Thomas Hughes, S.J., *History of the Society of Jesus in North America, Colonial and Federal* (London, 1917), Documents, I, II, 619-620.

22. For development of this theme, see James Hennesey, S.J., "Papacy and Episcopacy in 18th and 19th Century American Catholic Thought," *Records of the American Catholic Historical Society*, 77 (1966), 175-189; "The Baltimore Council of 1866: An American Syllabus," *ibid.*, 76 (1965), 157-172; and "Councils of Baltimore," *The New Catholic Encyclopedia* (New York, 1967), II, 38-43.

Roman authorities who were wary of the idea that the American church should have a "national character."[23] A decade and a half later the same warning was sounded in an *Instructio* sent to the American hierarchy by the Sacred Congregation of Propaganda, which cautioned them against the danger of creating a "national" church in the United States.[24] During the 1880's the American bishops successfully resisted Rome's wish to send an Italian legate to preside at the 1884 Third Plenary Council of Baltimore.[25] But the bishops were unsuccessful in their later efforts to prevent establishment of a permanent apostolic delegation in Washington in 1893. Most eloquent in opposition was Bishop John Lancaster Spalding of Peoria, who spoke of "the fixed and strongly-rooted desire, which exists through the whole English-speaking world to manage as far as possible one's own affairs." American Catholics, he declared, "are devoted to the Church; they recognize in the pope Christ's Vicar, and gladly receive from him the doctrines of faith and morals; but for the rest, they ask him to interfere as little as may be." As for the actual Delegate, Archbishop Francesco Satolli, Spalding felt that it was impossible "for an Italian to enter by an inner line of thought into American character or

23. John Tracy Ellis, "The Centennial of the First Plenary Council of Baltimore," in *Perspectives in American Catholicism* (Baltimore, 1963), pp. 157-159, reports on the primacy and other similar questions. The title of primate for the holder of the premier see had been requested in May, 1849 by unanimous agreement of the American bishops.

24. *Concilii plenarii Baltimorensis II, in ecclesia metropolitana Baltimorensi a die VII ad diem XXI octobris MDCCCLXVI habiti, et a Sede Apostolica recogniti, acta et decreta* (Baltimore, 1868), pp. xxiv-xxviii.

25. John Tracy Ellis, *The Life of James Cardinal Gibbons, Archbishop of Baltimore 1834-1921* (2 vols.; Milwaukee, 1952), I, 204-218. The idea was proposed to, and rejected by, Gibbons as early as 1880 and it was not dropped until 1883.

into the vital principles which underlie and mould American institutions."[26]

John Tracy Ellis has done a study of the coming of the Delegate in his monumental *Life of Cardinal Gibbons*. He points out at the beginning the problems that are caused when information does not flow freely between Rome and national churches. The creation of the Washington apostolic delegation finally came about, he notes, after an impasse had developed between the Romans, who wanted a nunciature here, and the Americans, who thought that the purpose could be best served by assignment of a resident American prelate in Rome who would serve as a channel for United States affairs.[27]

There is a preponderant weight of historical evidence that American Catholics have not favored diplomatic ties with the Holy See. The nineteenth century American Catholic tradition combined an intense loyalty to the pope with the desire "to manage one's own affairs" described by Bishop Spalding. The data is interesting; it looks to be irrelevant,

---

26. Taken from the *New World* (Chicago), December 21, 1892, and quoted in David Francis Sweeney, O.F.M., *The Life of John Lancaster Spalding, First Bishop of Peoria, 1840-1916* (New York, 1965), pp. 213; 215. The appointment of the first apostolic delegate in Washington was largely engineered by liberals in the American hierarchy of the time, notably Archbishop John Ireland of St. Paul and Monsignor Denis O'Connell, who thought they saw an opportunity of furthering their own views against those of more conservative churchmen. In Rome, Pope Leo XIII and Cardinal Secretary of State Mariano Rampolla del Tindaro saw creation of the Washington delegation as another step in the general rapprochement they hoped to achieve with republican governments. The best recent treatment is by Gerald P. Fogarty, S.J., "Denis J O'Connell: Americanist Agent to the Vatican, 1885-1903," Unpublished Ph.D. dissertation, Yale University, 1969, pp. 187-228.

27. Ellis, *Life of Gibbons*, I, 595-652.

at least in the political sphere. The continuing interest, for example, of the Nixon Administration in ties with the Vatican and the annually increasing number of diplomats being accredited to the Holy See both suggest that neither past American practice nor American constitutional theory will be normative. The pragmatic answer on papal diplomacy is clear enough: it is going to be around for a long time. The European Church-State experience is still dominant.

THE QUESTION OF COLLEGIALITY

To our other question, then. A development that ultimately found expression in Vatican II's dogmatic constitution on the Church was that of a collegial understanding of Church government. And this is the really key question: that of the nature and structure of the Church itself. It is one thing to ask if the Holy See properly operates as a special-type government among governments. It is fundamental to ask what is the nature of the relationship between the bishop of Rome and his church and the other bishops of the world and their churches, and then to judge structures in terms of that answer.

This is also an area in which the American tradition, at least as we have seen it from Carroll to Spalding, has something to say. But once more that tradition with its emphasis on collegiality and the legitimate autonomy of a national church seems irrelevant. The reason for this is that in 1970 the meaning of Vatican II's declaration on the collegiality of the episcopate seems less clear than when it was first proclaimed.

We are at the basic tension that must be resolved, or at least recognized and understood, before the more practical *pros* and *cons* can be argued. *Sollicitudo Omnium Ecclesiarum*, the June, 1969 apostolic letter on representatives of the Roman Pontiff, provides a clear context for the investigation, and it is time now to study it in some detail.

Pope Paul's stance is clear from the opening lines of the *motu proprio*. He declares his need, which none will deny, to be "informed about the state and condition of each church" throughout the Catholic world.[28] But before this he establishes the whole foundation of his subsequent argument:

> The care of all the churches, to which We have been called by the hidden design of God, and for which We must one day give an account, requires that, as Vicar of Christ, We should be adequately present in all parts of the world. . . .

The emphasis on the papal role as Vicar of Christ involves a reminder of the pope's power as ruler in the universal Church. But we miss here something of the context of Vatican II, where the title is used in chapter III of the Dogmatic Constitution on the Church:

> . . . this Council has decided to declare and proclaim before all men its teaching concerning bishops, the successors of the apostles, who together with the successor

28. The English text published in *L'Osservatore Romano* [English edition], July 17, 1969, has been followed. Further references will be to *SOE*, with the pagination from *L'Osservatore*. The text begins on p. 2.

of Peter, the Vicar of Christ and the visible Head of the whole Church, govern the house of the living God."[29]

There is no suggestion here, or elsewhere in *Sollicitudo Omnium Ecclesiarum,* that the Second Vatican Council has nuanced the papal governing power by emphasizing directly the fact that "bishops govern the particular churches entrusted to them as vicars and ambassadors of Christ."[30] The plain fact is that we have here a papal document written nearly four years after the solemn promulgation of *Lumen Gentium* and dealing with relationships between Rome and local churches that takes virtually no account of the doctrine of collegiality. Pope Paul has in this instance chosen to take his stand firmly in the "paternal" rather than in the "fraternal" tradition of the Church.[31]

Sollicitudo's second paragraph begins: "For the Bishop of Rome, by reason of his office, 'has full, supreme and universal power, which he can always freely exercise.' "[32] The footnote reference is to n. 22 of *Lumen Gentium,* and the text is indeed found there, but as a repetition of Vatican I's canon on the subject.[33] The section in question was inserted

29. Dogmatic Constitution on the Church, *Lumen Gentium,* III, n. 18, in: Walter M. Abbott, S.J. (ed.), *The Documents of Vatican II* (New York, 1966), p. 38.

30. *Ibid.,* n. 27; p. 51.

31. The terms are borrowed from the excellent study of the liberal tradition in the Church by the distinguished English historian Meriol Trevor, *Prophets and Guardians: Renewal and Tradition in the Church* (Garden City, 1969).

32. *SOE,* p. 2. Footnotes are on p. 12 of the July 17, 1969 *L'Osservatore Romano.*

33. Abbott, p. 43; Henricus Denzinger, *Enchiridion Symbolorum, definitionum et declarationum de rebus fidei et morum* (ed. Adolfus Schönmetzer, S.J., ed. 34; Freiburg, 1967), n. 3064; John F. Clarkson et al. (eds.), *The Church Teaches* (St. Louis, 1955), n. 211.

at Vatican II to conciliate the teaching of the two Vatican Councils. But the clear main thrust of n. 22 of *Lumen Gentium* is to enunciate the doctrine of collegiality. It is, to say the least, odd to find excerpts from this later and deliberately more comprehensive teaching being used to reaffirm the monarchical approach of Vatican I. This *is* especially true when the excerpts are in fact quotations from the earlier council and noted as such.

THE NATURE OF PAPAL POWER

The same pattern continues. There is one direct reference to Vatican I: for the statement that papal power is "ordinary and immediate." But then comes a reference to *Lumen Gentium*, to the effect that the pope "as the successor of Peter . . . is the perpetual and visible source and foundation of the unity both of bishops and of the whole company of the faithful." Once more, *Sollicitudo* quotes Vatican II quoting Vatican I. And the context and use of the statement reflect the thrust of the 19th, not the 20th century, council.[34] The next reference is similarly handled. The papal role in keeping the episcopate "one and undivided" is referred to n. 18 of *Lumen Gentium;* it occurs there as a quotation from the prologue to *Pastor Aeternus,* the dogmatic constitution on primacy and infallibility of Vatican I.[35] The final paragraph in this section of the papal *motu proprio* includes two scriptural references (Mt 16:18; Lk 22:32) which are also to be

34. Abbott, p. 44; Denzinger-Schönmetzer, n. 3051; Clarkson, n. 201.
35. Abbott, p. 38; Denzinger-Schönmetzer, n. 3051; Clarkson, n. 201.

found in chapter four of *Pastor Aeternus,* which deals with the infallible teaching authority of the pope.[36]

The texts about which we have been talking, and which are put forth in *Sollicitudo* as the basis for papal legations, diplomatic or otherwise, are the very ones about which Gérard Philips has written:

> A perusal of the text [of chapter three of *Lumen Gentium*] shows that it is full of additions designed to block at the start every attack on the primacy of the pope. The overloading of the text with all these soothing precautions makes it somewhat prolix and hinders the style—as can easily be seen if one puts the reassuring clauses in brackets. These redactional touches succeeded in lessening the misgivings of many Western bishops, but weakened the text in the eyes of the Eastern Churches, who needed to be convinced that the Catholic Church really accepted and revered the divine institution of the episcopacy.[37]

Karl Rahner has commented on the same subject:

> Regrets were often expressed in the discussion of this section [n. 22 of *Lumen Gentium*] that the doctrine of the primacy, which no one doubted, was inculcated too often in this article in repetitions inspired by overanxiety, even in contexts where it was not called for by the subject-matter.[38]

36. Denzinger-Schönmetzer, nn. 3066, 3070; Clarkson, nn. 213, 216.

37. Gérard Philips, "Dogmatic Constitution on the Church: History of the Constitution," in Herbert Vorgrimler *et al.* (eds.), *Commentary on the Documents of Vatican II,* I (New York, 1967), 129.

38. Karl Rahner, S.J., "Dogmatic Constitution on the Church: Articles 18-27," *ibid.,* p. 96.

The net result of the selective process followed in composing the introduction to *Sollicitudo Omnium Ecclesiarum* is that the insights of Vatican II into the relationship of pope and bishops, Rome and local churches, are set aside. A century's theological development which came to fruition in *Lumen Gentium* is ignored in favor of an older and partial ecclesiology.

Sollicitudo is framed as an explicit and deliberate response to the request made by the Fathers of Vatican II in n. 9 of *Christus Dominus*, the decree on the pastoral office of bishops in the Church, that, "in view of the pastoral role proper to bishops, the office of legates of the Roman Pontiff be more precisely determined."[39] As the late Archbishop Paul Hallinan pointed out, the whole decree *Christus Dominus* was intended as a pastoral and practical statement on the episcopal role in the Church following upon the theology of the episcopate enunciated in chapter three of *Lumen Gentium*.[40] Practical reorganizations and redefinitions consequent on these documents would be expected to rely heavily on a collegial understanding of the functions of pope and bishops in the Church. *Sollicitudo* nowhere uses the term "collegiality," but instead relies on a description of the way in which the contemporary papal mission requires "an intense exchange of relations" between pope and bishops. Several modalities are suggested: the episcopal visits *ad limina apostolorum,* the pope's own travels to various parts of the

39. SOE, p. 2. For the text in *Christus Dominus*, see Abbott, p. 402. The call for redefinition of the role of legates of the Roman Pontiff follows directly upon the Council's strong expression of desire that the Roman Curia be reorganized and adapted to the needs of the times and of various regions and rites.

40. Paul J. Hallinan, "Bishops," in Abbott, p. 389.

world, a larger international representation in the Roman Curia, the advisory Synod of Bishops, and the despatch of temporary or permanent papal representatives. The primary function of these last is to unite the local churches and Rome. This is seen as operating in two ways: by facilitating a two-way informational channel through which Rome learns of developments in the several "ecclesial communities" and through which those local communities learn of the actions of the various Curial offices in their regard, and by providing a "support and safeguard" to local bishops, priests, religious and faithful, who would find a pontifical representative such "since he represents a superior authority which is an advantage for all." [41] The primary emphasis throughout the *motu proprio* is on the mission of the pope's legates to the local churches, but section ten treats of what has been described previously as "a right inherent in Our very spiritual mission and supported by centuries-old development of historical events," the sending of papal diplomatic representatives "to the supreme authorities of nations in which the Catholic Church is established or is in some way present." Section eleven deals with papal representation and international bodies. [42] The whole is conceived on the model of two perfect societies engaged in dialogue about their common subject: man. [43] While reference is made to the opening paragraphs of Vatican II's pastoral constitution on the Church in the Modern World, *Gaudium et Spes*, [44] there

41. *SOE,* pp. 2-3.
42. *SOE,* pp. 3 (n. X), 2, 12 (n. XI).
43. *SOE,* p. 2.
44. *Ibid.* The reference is to nn. 1-3 of *Gaudium et Spes* (Abbott, pp. 199-201).

is once more a divergence of emphasis from the conciliar documents. Commenting on *Gaudium et Spes,* Donald Campion has written:

> The most distinctive note in the text, many already agree, is that of the Church putting itself consciously at the service of the family of man. It may well be that in generations to come men will read this as a highly significant step toward a rethinking of conventional ecclesiological images, e.g., that of the Church viewed as a 'perfect society' standing over against the perfect society of the *Civitas.*[45]

Sollicitudo Omnium Ecclesiarum prefers to speak in terms of what from the Middle Ages until the promulgation of *Gaudium et Spes* in 1965 was certainly the classical doctrine on the interrelation of Church and society.

There are two other parts of the apostolic letter on Pontifical representatives that must be mentioned: sections six and seven, which deal with the nomination of bishops and the establishment or suppression of dioceses, and sections eight and nine, which mark out the competence of papal representatives vis-à-vis episcopal conferences and conferences of major superiors of religious institutes of men and

45. Donald R. Campion, S.J., "The Church Today," in Abbott, pp. 185-186. For an outline of the history of the theological development away from the "perfect society" approach originally taken by Vatican II's theological preparatory commission to the "profoundly different outlook on the relations between the spiritual and the "temporal" eventually framed in *Gaudium et Spes,* see Yves Congar, O.P., "The Role of the Church in the Modern World," in Vorgrimler, V (New York, 1969), pp. 202-223, particularly pp. 207-216.

women. In its decree on the appropriate renewal of religious life, *Perfectae Caritatis,* the Second Vatican Council suggested that conferences of religious superiors might profitably co-ordinate their apostolic efforts with those of the episcopal conferences.[46] *Sollicitudo* gives the pontifical representative a role. He is

> called to give advice and assistance to the major superiors residing in the territory of his mission, for the purpose of promoting and consolidating the Conferences of Religious Men and Religious Women and to co-ordinate their apostolate, educational, welfare and social activity, in agreement with the directive norms of the Holy See and with the local Conference of Bishops.
>
> He will therefore be present at the opening session of the Conferences of Religious Men and Religious Women and will take part in those acts which, by agreement with the major superiors, may demand his presence.
>
> He will also be informed, in adequate time, of the agenda of the meeting and will receive copies of the documents in order to take cognizance of them and to forward them to the Sacred Congregation concerned.[47]

There is here an obviously strong emphasis on the role of the representative of the Roman central authority of the Church which raises the further question of the role that would be left to episcopal conferences in regard to the religious within the territory.

46. Abbott, p. 480 (*Perfectae Caritatis,* n. 23).
47. *SOE,* p. 3 (n. IX).

EPISCOPAL CONFERENCES

When we come to the episcopal conferences themselves, the pontifical representative's role is slightly less emphatic:

> . . . the Pontifical Representative will always bear in mind the extreme importance of their task, and consequent need to maintain close relations with them and to offer them every possible help.

He is not a member of the conference, but he is to be present at the opening session of every conference meeting and he may participate in the sessions "upon invitation of the bishops themselves, or by explicit order of the Holy See." He is also to receive copies of the agenda and a transcript of the proceedings, for his own and the Holy See's information.[48] And, despite the competence of national episcopal conferences in the matter, the pope's agent retains a considerable role in the selection of new bishops and in matters connected with the erection, division and suppression of dioceses.[49]

Thus far *Sollicitudo Omnium Ecclesiarum.* To put it into perspective it may help to recall the intervention that probably triggered inclusion of the brief reference to papal legates in *Christus Dominus,* to which Pope Paul alluded as one reason for publication of the apostolic letter. The incident occurred at the Second Vatican Council's 49th general congregation on October 16, 1963, during discussion of the *schema* on the Church. Bishop Joachim Ammann, O.S.B.,

48. *SOE,* p. 3 (n. VIII).
49. *SOE,* p. 3 (nn. VI, VII).

Swiss-born and formerly a missionary in present-day Tanzania, noted that the two concepts of collegiality of the bishops and dependence on the Holy See demanded that the bonds between Rome and the world episcopate be tightened. Pope Paul's *exordium* to *Sollicitudo* echoes the same sentiment. But Bishop Ammann's conclusion was different. He asked whether this union necessitated the presence of papal representatives throughout the world. He suggested that these representatives were seen as "shadows hiding the genuine face of the Church . . . imitating the secular powers . . . mixing in international politics." And he concluded: "It is time to put the representation of the Holy See in various countries in the hands of patriarchs and bishops designated by their respective national conferences," who would have "a better knowledge of the language, the history, and the social, political and religious life of their respective countries."[50] Nothing eventually was said on the matter in *Lumen Gentium;* it was left, as we have seen, for *Christus Dominus* and then for *Sollicitudo Omnium Ecclesiarum,* where its treatment has been in the manner just described.

CONCLUSIONS

What conclusions can we draw? There is no doubt of Pope Paul VI's deep conviction that in papal diplomacy he has an effective instrument for the good of the Church and of the Church's mission in the world. On the sheerly diplomatic plane this judgment is shared by the sixty-nine nations

---

50. Floyd Anderson (ed.), *Council Daybook Vatican II,* 1 (Washington, 1965), 187; Henri Fesquet, *The Drama of Vatican II* (tr. Bernard Murchland, New York, 1967), pp. 168-169.

that maintain missions at the Vatican and by many other professional diplomats. Papal diplomacy, moreover, has a firm basis in international law. But these are not the basic questions. Papal diplomatic activity may or may not be a valuable instrument. Addressing the diplomats accredited to the Holy See on January 12, 1970, the pope referred to the use that his predecessors Pius XII and John XXIII made of their diplomatic position in quest of peace.[51] Others have felt that papal involvement in diplomatic activity compromises the pope's role as a moral and religious leader. There are solid reasons why good and loyal Catholics have questioned the wisdom of a worldwide papal representation. Some of these reservations have been voiced recently by Cardinal Suenens. Others we have seen in the context of the history of one church, that of the United States. In any case, a definition of the Holy See's role in the modern world and a judgment on the instrumentalities it employs cannot be made to depend on solely pragmatic grounds. If there are to be papal representatives around the world, diplomatic or non-diplomatic, their function must be understood in terms of the Church's present understanding of itself, in terms of an ecclesiological development that has reached at least to the teaching of *Lumen Gentium,* if not beyond. *Sollicitudo Omnium Ecclesiarum,* based as it is on an ecclesiology that is all but nominally pre-Vatican II, does not provide the answers we need. The questions still remain.

---

51. *L'Osservatore Romano* [English ed.], January 22, 1970, pp. 2-3.

SUBSIDIARITY, ORDER AND FREEDOM IN THE CHURCH

By William W. Bassett

The order of the Christian Churches is a reality of major significance for ecumenical study at this time. Ecclesiastical discipline and administrative procedures reflect and perpetuate in a practical way an essential aspect of common faith experiences as they have been lived in greatly divergent cultural traditions. With the increase of theological consensus in dialogue, Church order comes more clearly into focus because of the serious obstacles to Christian unity raised by the historical development of ecclesial ministries and canonical systems. Because of an insistent ecumenical concern, therefore, we must now ask more directly than we have been able to in the past whether a coincidence of belief in the nature and mission of the Church will allow the continuance of a viable plurality of Church orders. Put another way, does Church unity postulate of necessity a fundamental administrative uniformity,

To see more clearly the validity of this question, we must further define Church order by distinguishing within it elements of structural concern upon three different levels. Upon the basic doctrinal level that directly embodies the rudiments of Christian faith itself, there are questions concerning the nature of the Church as a community, its ministries and offices. Upon another level, which we shall term the level of pastoral and liturgical practice, there are further questions, such as bear upon the ways in which the Christian mission of preaching, healing and sanctifying is fulfilled. On this level, for example, there is the perplexity found in the varying response of the Churches to the problems of divorce and remarriage, or the usages of liturgy in the elements of worship and sacramental ritual. It is not so certain that these two levels are clearly distinct. Without doubt they are closely interrelated. Yet upon a third level an even wider divergence among Christian communities is evident. This is in the various polities or internal administrative systems of the Churches, e.g., organizational procedures of personnel management, property acquisition and holding, financing methods, systems planning, etc. Church order, therefore, includes structural and procedural factors that are multilevelled and contain problems of more or less radical doctrinal importance.

Institutions and institutionalization in ecclesiastical life, while rudimentarily reflecting aspects of doctrine and belief, therefore, embody also pragmatic sets of rules, decisional processes and systems models that perpetuate workable solutions to past problems of community mission, viability and continuity. The problems of Church order for Christian unity thus are extremely complex. They are too intricate for a simple answer to be given at this time to the question we have posed.

While literature develops in studies of ministry, pastoral practice, liturgy and the sociology of religion, the underlying canonical question of Church order has yet to be adequately articulated. To specify the dimensions of this question from a Roman Catholic point of view, I believe, is very important. This specification shall be attempted in elaborating the considerations which follow.

THE FUNDAMENTAL CANONICAL CONCERN

Within the Roman Catholic Church the three levels of order described above have tended to coalesce in a jurisdictional issue, which itself may be ultimately doctrinal. For if the pope has full ordinary, immediate and direct jurisdiction over the Church,[1] he retains a residual right to take an initiative to alter or determine any matter of persons or communities of Christians regarding the legitimation of ministries, pastoral practices, the liturgy or even the management of properties.[2] The magisterial role of the papacy, the teaching office, therefore, is not the only, or apparently even the most important, ecclesiological obstacle to Christian unity. The jurisdictional principle substantiating a residual

1. The Code of Canon Law, canon 218; const. *Aeterni Patris,* First Vatican Council, Denz. 1826-1827; const. *Lumen Gentium,* n. 22, Second Vatican Council; Schema *Lex Fundamentalis Ecclesiae,* canon 33. (Cf. note 7 infra.)

2. The Code of Canon Law, canons 220, 247, 248, 257, 329, 1257, 1431, 1518, 1556, 1557, etc. *Lex Fundamentalis Ecclesiae,* canons 33-35, 40, §3, 41, 78, §2, 80.

right to total control of the Church is a more serious question. What does acceptance of the papal office as "spokesman for the Church" or as a "center of visible unity and charity" mean? In canon law this is not what the papal office is in actuality. The absolutizing of structures within the Catholic Church is less a result of expediency than it is of principle. For example, does the pope have the right to reserve the adjudication of all marriage cases to a procedure he alone may decide? All episcopal elections? All property transactions? From a theoretical point of view one must question the possibility of unravelling the strands that were historically interwoven into the mantle of both pope and patriarch now worn by the bishop of Rome.

To pose the canonical question on a lower echelon, do those who urge the acceptance of the episcopal office in a reunited Church wish also the present canonical mode of the exercise of the episcopal office? Or yet more basically, in canonical principle all the baptized are subject to the positive law of the Roman Catholic Church in obedience to its legitimately constituted authorities.[3] Is this a question of belief or one of Church polity? The ecumenical movement today forces us to confront these issues directly and honestly. They cannot be dismissed as non-problems.

But the same issues must also be faced within the Catholic Church itself in an effort to isolate the elements of ideology from those of faith in the institutional crisis through which the Church is now passing. For the sudden emergence of a new problematic, social transformation, changing needs and the abandonment of previously secure cultural assump-

3. The Code of Canon Law, canons 12 and 87; *Lex Fundamentalis Ecclesiae*, canon 6.

tions have precipitated an almost cataclysmic crisis of order and institution within the Church. Whether this crisis is called one of authority or one of relevancy is relatively unimportant. What is important at this time is a critical discernment of the essential from the accidental, what is believed to be of God's design in Church order from the product of human wisdom and cultural adaptation.

In the present critical time of transition the Church is undergoing the fifth major cultural transformation in its history. Without settling the difficult historical question of periodization, we might say generally that the first brought the embryonic forms of Christian community from the Hebraic *kahal* into the Greek world. The beginning of the Constantinian era in which the privileges and prerogatives of the Roman state religion were subsumed into Christianity was the second transformation. The vast and profound effects of the Hildebrandine reform in the eleventh century and the sixteenth century Reformation live on to remind us of the third and fourth great transformations in Church order that have brought us to our present situation of discord and division. The Church is now undergoing a fifth social and religious revolution which calls into question even more radically the accepted structural forms and ecclesiastical law. It is vital at this time to see the correct issues in this questioning as they bear upon the projected embodiment of Christ's redemptive act in communities for our time and our world.

An analysis of order in the Roman Catholic Church, therefore, not in terms of rules or even institutions, but rather as a clarification of the basic theories of social dynamics, the organizational principles and jurisprudential assumptions which underlie the present system, is imperative. Only upon such a profound analysis can we be secure in saying that this system must change drastically and that it can do so fully within the faith commitment of Catholic ecclesiology. Can an administrative system developed to secure a primary and pervasive aspiration for harmony be restructured to reflect the principle of freedom and charismatic spontaneity in Church order? A Church reunited and renewed must aspire to a structural unity that will enable it to become among men the guardian of justice, the monitor of freedom and a living witness to the integrity of the person.

PERSONAL FREEDOM AS AN OPERATIVE PRINCIPLE OF CHANGE

The freedom of persons in the Church must become an effective principle of renewal in ecclesiastical order both for ecumenical and cultural imperatives. The ordering function in the Catholic community in the past has been normally attributed to authority, law and the organs of ecclesiastical administration. These factors, not freedom, were said to be primary; in fact, they were so basic that they have been identified traditionally with the social order of the Church itself. In assuring the conditions of interpersonal coexistence and cooperation law and authority are still thought of as essential pre-conditions to individual freedom. What is left to the individual, on the other hand, after socially necessary restrictions have been made, is freedom, the ordered scope of self-determination and initiative. Thus, freedom seems to be the result, not a component of ecclesiastical order. Indeed, it has been said, this relationship of order and freedom is the only possible one in the Church.

The element of truth in this orientation of freedom and authority is only partial, however, for the theory itself rests upon an inadequate interpretation of the role of social authority in the Church as an instrument to guarantee freedom and the finality of Christian freedom itself.[4] For in reality the Church consists not just in the coexistence of individuals, with their freedom guaranteed, but in the cooperation of all for the purpose of achieving the greatest possible self-fulfillment of all. This self-fulfillment is freedom, is maturity in Christ; it is, thus, the primary end and principle of the ecclesiastical order. "When Christ freed us," St. Paul says, "he meant us to remain free" (Gal. 5:1). Authority in the Church, be it that of popes or bishops, serves not a primary function. It serves only a subsidiary function. Law in the Christian community is a helping instrument to reveal the implications of love. It gives practical guidance to the life of persons called to holiness together. The ends, responsibilities, functions and authorities of the community of the Church and communities within the Church are ordered to

4. We understand freedom in a substantive sense, in the words of Christian Bay, as the capacity, the opportunity and the incentive to develop and express one's potentialities (*The Structure of Freedom* [New York, 1965], p. 15). "The growth and realization of man's individuality is an end," Erich Fromm says, "that can never be subordinated to purposes which are supposed to have greater dignity" (*Fear and Freedom* [London, 1960], pp. 149-150). The most thorough study of the meanings of freedom is that of Mortimer Adler, *The Idea of Freedom* (2 vols.; New York, 1961-1962). Note also should be taken of the very important research developments of the Canon Law Society of America, *The Case for Freedom: Human Rights in the Church*, ed. James A. Coriden (Washington, 1969). I am also indebted to the study of Johannes Messner, "Freedom as a Principle of Social Order," *The Modern Schoolman*, XXVIII (1951), 97-110.

the freedom and fulfillment of persons. It cannot be otherwise, nor can the priority of ends again be inverted.

Since the social good of Christians is diversified in kind and pluralistic in structure according to individual needs and aspirations, the right of free association, pluriformity in living the Christian experience, and the integrity of individual response to grace are primary values. Self-responsibility and self-determination are radical Christian rights. The rights and duties of authority, though more comprehensive, coexist within a galaxy of the equally elemental rights of individuals in themselves and in community.

Thus it seems manifest that the Church's social authority functions in ordering law and administrative decisions to the intrinsic purpose of Christian self-determination and freedom. It renders cooperation and fulfillment possible by eliminating adverse human elements that radically foil the self-fulfillment of persons in Christ by restricting them to ignoble, passive, subservient roles and depriving them of an active and constructive part in shaping the life of the community of the Church. The principle of freedom postulates the subsidiary role of authority in the Church and is fully compatible with the divinely constituted Church order. It is a view of authority as a service for the building up of persons within the Body of Christ.

The jurisdictional dilemma posed by the principle of subordination in Roman Catholic canon law can be transcended, therefore, by the development of equally valid principles of freedom and subsidiarity. Thus a change in Church order may be made possible by the acceptance of a view of Christian leadership that is pastoral and diaconal. Residual rights of intervention may cede to the effective limitations placed upon a role of ministering primarily to the freedom and good of persons in the community of those who follow the Lord in faith and love.

THE PRESENT PRINCIPLES OF ORDER IN THE CATHOLIC CHURCH

The basic principles of Catholic Church order are derived only partially from scriptural revelation. The New Testament may supply evidence to substantiate belief in a continuing charismatic community with ultimate hierarchical authority vested in the episcopate.[5] A more immediate source of administrative principles, however, is acknowledged to be the diverse human models of government that have served the processes of adaptation and imitation through history. These latter factors bear tangibly upon the mode in which ecclesiastically authority is exercised in the present. Thus there should be distinguished in discussing Church order in canon law an evangelical service of authority, a Gospel model of a holy guiding body to direct and sanctify the faithful, and a culturally conditioned apparatus of practical procedures that is human, consensual, and capable of great change in contemporary determination.

The Catholic Church as an ancient and perduring society has been profoundly influenced in its organizational profile

5. The Second Vatican Council, the Constitution *Lumen Gentium*, n. 20. In this reference consult Hans Küng, *The Church* (New York, 1968), pp. 388-481; Rudolf Schnackenberg, *God's Rule and Kingdom* (New York, 1963); Eduard Schweizer, *Church Order in the New Testament* (London, 1963); and Myles Bourke, "Reflections on Church Order in the New Testament," *The Catholic Biblical Quarterly*, XXX (1969), 493-511.

by the acculturation process.[6] From the simplicity of feeble beginnings basic developmental factors in societal growth led to the modifications that time brought in role expectations of the holders of office, institutions such as the religious congregations and traditional class distinctions among the faithful. A vast panoply of ceremonial and symbolic acts and expressions reflects this influence of history. These are too evident in ecclesiastical life to need recounting here.

What must not be forgotten, however, is that the influence of time and culturally conditioned thought patterns upon the community of the Catholic Church is much more profound than mere symbol. Intimately tied to the strands of Church life and activity are basic assumptions concerning the nature of person, community, law and government. These in turn rest upon conclusions derived from the premises of historical organizational theories of personal and societal interaction.

This system and the principles upon which it is built have remained virtually intact as a consistent and exclusive governmental construction for perhaps a millenium. Though anachronistic and now recognized to be intolerably burdensome upon persons in the Church, they could not have been effectively challenged in the past without involving a total rejection of Catholicism or refuge in smaller communities through the process of religious exemption. Yet this must not continue to be necessary. For love of the Church we must honestly admit that in the light of the Gospel and the human experience the continuing governance of the Church

6. Arthur Mirgeler, *Mutations of Western Christianity* (New York, 1961), particularly pp. 130-151; Edmund Hill, "Authority in the Church: Development of Institutions," *The Clergy Review*, L (1965), 674-685.

according to the present system and its principles is theologically destructive and will lead to the great denigration of the personal dignity of large segments of the faithful. Let it be perfectly clear that a crisis of order or authority is not necessarily a crisis of faith. It may be the prelude to a reintegration of creative energies in the Church and the birth of a new style of living.

The medieval institutionalization of Church order has placed bishops into a position where their role is largely that of administrators and ceremonial functionaries. Priests and religious cannot command the integrity of their personal lives; they are totally vulnerable to the whim of their superiors in a condition of life approaching bondage. The laity cannot be fully active and responsible for the Church; they are to be consulted at most only where decisions are made touching upon the area of their secular competency.

The feudal style of life projected by ecclesiastical administrators in the Catholic Church was unchanged substantially by the disciplinary reforms of the Council of Trent. Indeed, the absolutist theories of authority by divine right popular in the immediately post-tridentine era added a rigidity and triumphalism to the system that since led to its virtual adulation by generations of canon lawyers. In spite of much theological speculation about the nature of the Church as a pilgrim people, even now almost five years after the Second Vatican Council the recent development by the Commission for the Revision of Canon Law of a *Lex Fundamentalis Ecclesiae* reveals no serious contemplation of imminent change.[7] Yet notwithstanding apologetic pro-

7. This schema is the first product of the Commission. It has been prepared for the consultation of the episcopate as a constitutional law

testations to the contrary, I shall maintain that the conciliar emphasis upon the primacy of the person in the Church, his dignity and responsibility before God and man, is so significantly new a factor in ecclesiastical administrative theory that it must have radical consequences in the renewal of Church order. Unless these consequences are organically developed and realized in practice, the crisis within the Church will be compounded to tragedy and the hope of the ecumenical movement dashed in a new era of pride and intransigence.

The administrative system of the Church today continues to favor role over person and cast individuals into the static categorization of vocational levels of aptitude and right. Legal methodology in canon law is deductive and conceptualist,[8] thus eliminating continuing flexibility and development, as law is seen to be the terse statement of sacred mandates from above rather than the result of a practical decisional process within access of the community of Christians itself. Real communities are rarely possible on either parochial or diocesan levels, as an in-built administrative bias prefers the juridical ordering of territorial and group units of a tightly structured and controlled world organization. The measure of initiative allowed to the faithful in worship, religious life and community determination is jealously monitored. The disposition of goods and monies remains arbitrary and secret. An appointee system of pro-

for the Church, a juridical expression of a Catholic ecclesiology as the basis for the revision of a new code of canon law. It is dated May 24, 1969.

---

8. Cf. my article "Law and the Gift of the Spirit," *Thought*, XLIV (1969), 165-184; also Stephan Kuttner, "The Code of Canon Law in Historical Perspective," *The Jurist*, XXVIII (1968), 129-148.

motion to ecclesiastical office is practically ubiquitous, removing the element of accountability to the community. And procedures to adequately secure the rights of all the faithful in conflict situations are either totally lacking, alarmingly deficient or simply not thought to be important. Decisions continue to be made that deeply affect the lives and dispositions of most of the faithful, not only without hearing them, but without any compulsion to acknowledge that they have a right to be heard. The ancient order of the Church where frequent councils gathered the clergy and laity in mutual consultation and support, an authentic *sensus ecclesiae*, is today virtually nonexistent.[9] These facts are not only the result of burgeoning growth and unwieldly size. They reflect a medieval theory of law and government

---

9. The synodal structures and deliberative processes were essential to the administration of the ancient Church. More than 75 councils met in the fourth century, at least 10 of which were at Rome, and most of them took place in the last quarter of the century. In the fifth century about 20 councils were held at Rome. The series of African councils of which we have record began with the Council of Carthage in 348-49, and after 394 others followed in quick succession. From 394 to 426 at least 24 councils met at the African capital. In the fourth century the universal Church was directed by decisions made in councils in Nicea (325), Sardica (343), Gangra (340, 370), Antioch (332), Elvira (305), Arles (314), Ancyra (314), Neo-Caesarea (314, 325), Laodicea (340, 380), Achtichat (365), and Constantinople (381, 382, 394). The two great councils of the East in the fifth century, Ephesus (431) and Chalcedon (451) made significant laws regarding Church order. And the important series of councils held in Gaul from the middle of the fifth century, at a time when the barbarian invasions had paralyzed conciliar activity in Africa and Spain, must not be forgotten: Riez (439), Orange (441), Vaison (442), Angers (453), Tours (461), Arles (463), Vaunes (465), Bourges (472), Vienne (471, 475), etc. Record of these councils can be found in such standard collections as Mansi, Hardouin, etc. An excellent study of the synodal structure of the pre-Nicene Church is that of Hans Grotz, *Die Hauptkirchen des Ostens von den Anfängen bis zum Konzil von Nikaia* (325) (Rome, 1964).

in which the faithful are seen as the passive subjects of authority placed within the discretionary disposition of superiors by a divine law that determines the hierocratic ordering of human societies.

The Church in the West emerged from the middle ages transformed from the rather loosely knit communion of patristic times to a rigidly organized feudal kingdom, the Christendom. With not too much exaggeration J. N. Figgis wrote in his important study, *Political Thought from Gerson to Grotius*: "In the Middle Ages the Church was not a state, it was the state." Rome moved away from a coordinating role and a concept of authority as resting in the smaller church communities, ecumenically linked, to what the canonists developed from the vicarious theories of power, a hierarchic "descending" theory of government, claiming that all world power, ecclesiastical and temporal, was transmitted through one man, the pope, *medius constitutus inter Deum et hominem* (Innocent III), to the Body of Christ.

Facilitating this transformation and reflecting upon its social implications, the canonists of the Hildebrandine reform cast the basic principles of ecclesiastical administration that continue to be operative today.[10] These principles were strengthened by the theoretical elaborations of the com-

10. There are many good studies of the development of legal and canonical theories in the early Middle Ages. Among those consulted are Walter Ullmann's two books, *The Individual and Society in the Middle Ages* (London, 1967) and *Principles of Government and Politics in the Middle Ages* (London, 1961); Gerd Tellenbach, *Church, State and Christian Society at the Time of the Investiture Controversy* (Oxford, 1966); Marc Bloch, *Feudal Society* (Chicago, 1962); J. P. Whitney, *Hildebrandine Essays* (Cambridge, 1932); F. Kempf, in *Sacerdozio e Regno da Gregorio VII a Bonifacio VIII* (Rome, 1954); and John A. Watt, *The Theory of Papal Monarchy in the Thirteenth Century* (London, 1965).

mentators upon Gratian's *Decretum*, the Decretists, and upon the later papal decretals, the Decretalists.[11] Following the demise of the strong conciliarist movements of the fifteenth century[12] curial canonists prevailed through the Counter-Reformation. Ultramontane sympathies were further strengthened by the defeat of Gallicanism, Febronianism and Josephinism until their implicit confirmation in the era of papal absolutism following the First Vatican Council.[13] The effect upon the organizational profile of the Church has been of inexorable centralization and pervasive jurisdictional ideology.

The juristic argument for papal authority rested not on any charismatic gift, nor on sacramental orders, nor on personal initiative, but on a juridical right. Utilizing the force of Roman law to buttress the Petrine promise of Matthew 16:18, according to the legal principle "the heir continues the deceased" *(Haereditas est successio in universum ius)*, the canonists developed a theory of total papal dominion. The pope claimed the sole right of delegation of all human authority. The words of Christ, *Data est mihi omnis potestas*, applied to his vicar on earth, led ultimately by logical extension to the high papalism of Innocent IV, who could

11. For a good basic delineation of this development and its agents see Ronald Cox, *A Study of the Juridic Status of Laymen in the Writing of the Medieval Canonists* (Washington, 1959).

12. See Brian Tierney's *The Foundations of Conciliar Theory: The Contribution of the Medieval Canonists from Gratian to the Great Schism* (Cambridge, 1955), and "Collegiality in the Middle Ages," *Concilium*, VII (1965), n. 1, 4-9.

13. See Robert McNally's *Reform of the Church: Crisis and Criticism in Historical Perspective* (New York, 1963), pp. 103-140, and "The Tridentine Church: A Study in Ecclesiology," in *Law for Liberty: The Role of Law in the Church Today*, ed. J. Biechler (Baltimore, 1967), pp. 69-76.

claim from this that *omnis creatura vicario Creatoris subdita est.* The sacred authority of the popes, essentially superior to the powers of this world, was exercised through the echelons of episcopal and priestly orders, in whose ranks alone men were empowered to mediate the interpretation of terrestrial realities. Ministry in the Church came to entail a professionalism not the least awesome by its mastery of complicated ritual, cultic language and canonical formalities. Through the clerks, the popes after Gregory VII exercised the *cura totius Christianitatis,* the care of all Christianity. Thus a theoretical base was given to the dominant clericalisation of the Church.

However extravagant were the claims, and however thorough was the ecclesiastical institutionalisation of Hildebrand, these were overtopped, in the words of Alberic Stacpoole,[14] in the great era of the canonists, between the succession of Innocent III and the untimely death of Boniface VIII. As Hildebrand had acted, so the canonists formulated. The famous *Dictatus Papae,* the general statement of papal policies and prerogatives, was elaborated into a tight and consistent theory of papal monarchy by the middle of the thirteenth century.

The canonists recognized four basic principles, the fundamental assumptions of the science of Church law:

First, the unitary nature of society, with the papacy at the head of the *corpus mysticum* on earth, as the principle of unity. This was rooted in the Greek philosophical concept of order, the Roman imperial concept of law, and the Augustinian concept of the *civitas Dei;*

14. "The Institutionalisation of the Church in the Middle Ages," *The Ampleforth Journal,* LXXIII (1968), 343.

Second, the duality of power, where kingship had jurisdiction in the temporal order, and the priesthood, the *sacerdotium*, in the spiritual. This was extended in the guise of *libertas ecclesiae* into temporal matters, the clerical privileges of forum and the canon, tithes, immunities from secular exactions, and so forth;

Third, the cooperation of powers, the so-called *duplex ordo jurisdictionis*, where the clerical order might requisition the secular at will for ecclesiastical purposes;

Fourth, the superiority of the spiritual order, the *imperium sacerdotii* over matters spiritual and temporal. Of this superiority Hugh of St. Victor and Innocent III after him claimed its preeminence *in dignitate, in institutione, in auctoritate, in tempore.*

From the titles of *vicarius Christi* and *pontifex maximus*, and the juridical right to the *plenitudo potestatis* were drawn a specific papal office, *judex ordinariorum omnium*, i.e. that the pope was an omnicompetent court of first instance for the whole of Christendom, the direct bishop of every man, the confessor of every believer. Innocent IV and Boniface VIII after him claimed the *regimen unius personae* by divine right, to ensure the utility and make provision for the necessity of the people of God. The famous bull *Unam Sanctam* (1302) articulates this ultimate papal claim. It is addressed to the *discentes, id est, laici,* the now passive recipients of law, *minorennes* in total subjection to ecclesiastical authority.

In the sixteenth book of the Theodosian Code (438) and variously throughout the codification of the emperor Justinian (535) the clergy by civil statute had been given special privileges which raised them to a specific kind of dignity in the closed state and society of the later empire. The Christian ministry stepped into the role and position once occupied by the pagan priesthood. The episcopal office in Roman law was made equal to the civil magistracy, given its dignities and many of its powers.

The clergy were exempted from various kinds of taxes and from particularly onerous civic and municipal functions (*Cod.Th.* XVI, 2,2, of 333; XVI, 2,7, of 330). They were given a separate sphere of jurisdiction. It appeared that, since the clergy judged in the name of God, they themselves could not be judged by ordinary civil courts but only by their bishops or their peers. This was the prerogative of a constituted body and not a favor granted to individuals, and so this privilege of a separate clerical jurisdiction, the *privilegium fori,* recognized the total autonomy of the clerical society and its hierarchy (*Cod.Th.* XVI, 2,12, of 412).

Although the clergy were not yet dressed differently, the tonsure appeared after 360 in the East and in the second half of the fifth century in Rome. The obligations of continence, celibacy and various ascetical practices (Council of Carthage, c.19, of 297; Council of Elvira, c.33, of 305; Leo I, *Ep.*XIV, 4, etc.) further separated the clergy from the people. Later monastic insistence upon poverty and the movements of the canons regular in the Carolingian era to promote the common life made the clergy identifiably different. By the eighth century the clergy were the sole administrators of the sacraments, preachers, teachers of sacred doctrine and separated from the laity in community and in sanctuary.

From the late ninth and tenth century system of *Eigenkirchen* and *Eigenklostern* developed the system of benefices from Germanic law to enable the clergy to withdraw from secular occupations as a class apart and live off the revenues of the Church. The tithe system of the eleventh century strengthened this tendency and provided a source of revenue for the new system of papal taxation and annates.[15] A network of legations was used to shore up the Gregorian reform and became a regular part of papal government following the Investiture Controversy.[16] Manuscripts from the later middle ages are filled with complaints against the interference of wandering papal legates in churches almost throughout the whole of Europe. With the increasing number of reserved sees and the centralization of ecclesiastical government came an appointee system to eventually replace the traditional election of bishops *per clerum et populum*[17] and break down the intermediate system of cooptation into the episcopal college by co-consecration and notification of the metropolitans and neighboring bishops.[18] The canonical institute of dispensation, with consequent gradation of faculties and powers in the hierarchy, became prominent in the reign of Innocent III. At this time also the introduction of elementary Roman law studies in Bologna and Paris pro-

15. W. E. Lunt, *Papal Revenues in the Middle Ages* (2 vols.; New York, 1934).

16. Igino Cardinale, *Le Saint-Siège et la Diplomatie* (Tournai, 1962), pp. 26-27.

17. The most thorough study of elections in the Church in English is that of Anscar Parsons, *Canonical Elections* (Washington, 1939). Joseph O'Donoghue, in his *Elections in the Church* (Baltimore, 1967), depends for the historical analysis on Parsons. Note also J. Eidenschink, *The Election of Bishops in the Letters of Gregory the Great* (Washington, 1945), and R. L. Benson, *The Bishop-Elect, A Study in Medieval Ecclesiastical Office* (Princeton, 1968). John Tracy Ellis has a good article in contemporary perspective: "On the Selection of Bishops," *The Critic*, 7 (1969), 42-48.

18. Hans Küng, *Structures of the Church* (New York, 1964), pp. 237-238.

vided the principles of jurisprudence to change the character of Church canons to fit the secular model of law.[19]

Dioceses had already changed from communities of the faithful to administrative units of a world organization in the early thirteenth century when to the appointee system was added, in contradiction to the ancient canons, the regular practice of translating bishops from diocese to diocese.[20] Dioceses came to be measured as good, better and best, to be acquired for merit, honor or revenue. Canonists in these years compiled and commented upon the conciliar and papal decrees of previous centuries, applying the scholastic method to produce a uniform set of principles to regulate the life and government of the Church. Elaborating upon these principles they developed a jurisprudential system of ecclesiastical administration modeled upon the only viable political system then known, that of feudalism. The laity were relegated to a role of extreme passivity and the

19. Paul Fournier, "Un tournant de l'histoire du droit: 1060-1140," *Nouvelle revue historique du droit français et etranger*, 41 (1917), 129ff.

20. The canonical tradition forbidding a bishop to leave his diocese to take another is not only ancient but extremely strong. Pope Callistus (217-222) called such a bishop a "spiritual adulterer" (PL, XIII, 1192, para. 16). The same was repeated by St. Jerome (PL, CXXXVI, Letter 31, para. 14) and Pope Siricius (384-398) PL, XIII, 1192, para. 16). The Council of Sardica (343) absolutely forbade the translation of a bishop (Hardouin, *Acta Consiliorum*, I, 490). This reflects the law of the councils of Arles (314) (Hardouin, I, 266) and Antioch (341) (Turner, *Ecclesiae Occidentalis Monumenta*, II, 294:5). Later councils in the East and West repeated the ancient tradition of the wedding of a bishop to his people. Early medieval canonists, such as Hincmar of Rheims (808-882) (PL, CXXVI, 210), Burchard of Worms (965-1025) (PL, CL, cap. 72) and Yvo of Chartres (1014-1016) (*Decretum*, Bk. 5) upheld this tradition. The law is still maintained in the Oriental Churches. The Latin practice of recent centuries is a scandal, for it supposes the bishop to be primarily an appointed administrator, not the chosen leader of a Christian people.

clergy came to be disciplined upon the image of vassalage.[21]

In these years the procedures through which ecclesiastical authority is mediated in the life of the Church were fixed upon an elaborate hierarchical scheme. The papal court developed through a system of primitive consistorial consultation to the congregational form borrowed from the French monarchy in the reform of Sixtus V.[22] The apostolic constitution *Immensa* of 1588 confirmed in existence a princely power structure at the heart of the Church to continue the imperial court begun by Urban II in the late eleventh century. At the time of the Avignon captivity the papal court was the largest and richest Europe had seen.[23] At this time honorary titles and dignities were introduced into the Western Church, and the costumes of the courtly supernumeraries vied with those of the princes in color and sartorial splendor.[24] Canonists theorized upon a developing system of ecclesiastical appointments to distinguish the power of order, a sacramental role, from the power of

21. The liturgical rite of tonsure is modelled upon the oath and rite of fealty of a vassal to his lord. The present canon law still uses the Roman legal term for enslavement in reference to clerics, *mancipati sunt* (Canon 108/1).

22. For a good summary of the development of the papal curia under Pope Urban II, cf. Geofrey Barraclough, *The Medieval Papacy* (London, 1968), pp. 95-101. For the reform of Pope Sixtus V, cf. Bihlmeyer-Tüchle, *Church History* (Westminster, Md., 1966), III, 115-116.

23. G. Mollat, *The Popes at Avignon* (Edinburgh, 1963), pp. 279-318.

24. The title "monsignor" was derived from the usage of the French aristocracy. In 1630 Urban VIII gave to Cardinals the title "eminence." Pius IX gave bishops and abbots the prerogative of wearing the zuchetto at the First Vatican Council. Pius XI gave bishops the title "excellency" to put them on a par with the Italian senators after the Lateran Pact in 1929. See Gabriel LeBras, *Institutions ecclesiastiques de la Chretientè Medievale,* Coll. Fliche-Martin (Paris, 1959), and L. Cristiani, "Essai sur les origines du costume ecclésiastique," *Orientalia Christiana Periodica,* 13 (1947), 68-80.

jurisdiction, the power to rule in the Church. The meaning of jurisdiction was then borrowed from conceptualizations known from incipient studies in Roman and Germanic law.[25] To rule meant to be set above one's subjects. The pagan concept of *imperium* equated leadership with supremacy. The statement of ecclesiastical law ceased to be exhortatory, and became legally terse and concise. It was surrounded by a science of interpretation.

Office in the Church came to be decked with the trappings of privilege and honor. Episcopal thrones, jewelry and the heraldry of the feudal lords were the mark of the episcopal office.[26] On the eve of the Reformation bishops were no longer known among their people as those who presided at the Eucharist; they had private chapels constructed in their palaces. They no longer mediated God's forgiveness and assigned penance; they granted to priests and monks faculties to hear confessions and mete out indulgences. They no longer preached the word of God; instead, preaching

25. Gommarus Michiels, *De Potestate Ordinaria et Delegata* (Tournai, 1964), pp. 2-8; also 11-15. This meaning of jurisdiction still exists in canon law; cf. V. Tirado, *De Jurisdictionis Acceptatione in Iure Ecclesiastico* (Rome, 1940), pp. 180-184; and Victor de Reina, "Poder y sociedad en la Iglesia," *Revista Espanola de Derecho Canonico,* 19 (1964), 629-662.

26. Cf. H. J. McCloud, *Clerical Dress and Insignia of the Roman Catholic Church* (Milwaukee, 1947) and Bernard J. Ganter, *Clerical Attire: Historical Synopsis and Commentary* (Washington, 1955). E. Stommel's "Die bischöfliche Kathedra im christlichen altertum," in *Münchener theologische Zeitschrift* 3 (1952), 17-32; and Hermann Tüchle's "Baroque Christianity: Root of Triumphalism?" *Concilium,* 7 (1965), n. i, 72-76, are also interesting. The best available study of the medieval canonical theory of Church office is that of Donald Heintschel, *The Canonical Concept of an Ecclesiastical Office in the Decretum Gratiani* (Washington, 1954). The admonition of Origen, "Qui vocatur ad episcopatum non ad principatum vocatus, sed ad servitium totius Ecclesiae" (P.G. XIII, 239) seems to have been forgotten.

was delegated by faculty and appointment. Office in the Church was transformed to the distant role of administration and ceremony. The role of the bishop in the Church underwent an almost essential transformation from a patristic model of a father among his people to the administrator of Trent. Meanwhile the movement towards centralization undermined the freedom of conciliar and synodal forms of deliberation to break down almost completely the powers of self-determination of individual communities within the Church.

This world organization of tightly and uniformly modeled administrative units with identical courts, procedures, registries, titles and honors, promotion systems and job analyses runs now without account to the community of the faithful and independently of their ability to critically assess its value. For it is grounded upon an absolutist principle that has ceded to its agents the aura of divine right in the disposition of persons and goods in the Church. This system is the offspring of a clericalism that divided the Church into Gratian's two kinds of Christians.[27] It perpetuates a class distinction that makes meaningful cooperation between the faithful and their ministers very difficult.

From Roman law medieval canonists derived the concept of society as an all-embracing and comprehensive corporation.[28] Within the corporation of secular or Church so-

---

27. "Duo sunt genera Christianorum..." *Decretum*, VII, ch. xii, i. Canon 107 repeats: "Ex divina institutione sunt in Ecclesia clerici a laicis distincti...."; also *Lex Fundamentalis Ecclesiae*, canon 26.

28. A. Ehrhardt, "Das Corpus Christi und die Corporation im spätrömischen Recht," *Savigny Zeitschrift*, Roman. Abt., 70 (1953), 299-347 and 71 (1954), 255ff.; G. de Lagarde, "Individualisme et corporatisme au moyen âge," in *L'organization du moyen âge a la fin de l'Ancien Regime* (Louvain, 1937), II, 1-59.

ciety each man had a rank and a role, according to which he must relate to other members and the society as a whole. The individual was almost totally identified with his corporate role; and thus submerged in the exigencies of society.

St. Paul's teaching on baptism was refitted in the theories of the canonists to adapt incorporation into the Church to the Roman law conception of citizenship and subjection to the laws of the state.[29] The public order, the realm of *ius publicum ecclesiasticum,* controlled the activities of those who by baptism were given the privilege of personhood in the Church. Thus, the faithful in a new creation was made subject to a law and order *given* to him, not in any way made or determined by him. Fidelity, *fidelitas,* marked the closeness of man to God by the observance of those laws given through the theocratic monarchy set above the baptized.[30] Thus there emerged in the Catholic mind a divine pattern for the Church, based on the Pauline notion of subjection to higher authorities. The Church was the *congregatio fidelium,* in which faith was equated with obedience and the autonomy of the individual was submerged in the corporate whole.[31] Faith and obedience were the basic ingredients of the Christian life, and authority the principal

29. Cf. Ullmann, *The Individual and Society,* pp. 8-11. For a contemporary version of the same in commentary on canons 12 and 87, cf. D. Faltin, "De legibus quibus baptizati acatholici ritui orientali adscripti tenentur," *Apollinaris,* 35 (1965), 238-49; and Carlos M. Corral Salvador, "Incorporacion a la Iglesia por el Bautismo y sus consecuencias juridicas," *Revista Española de Derecho Canonico,* 19 (1964), 817-854, esp. 828ff. ("el bautizado queda constituido indeblemente *subditus ecclesiae*").

30. Cf. Ullmann, *The Individual and Society,* p. 7, and his *Principles of Government and Politics,* pp. 20ff.

31. Ullmann, *The Individual and Society,* pp. 10-11. This should be carefully compared with Congar, *Lay People in the Church,* pp. 22-48.

mark of the Church. Only in this way can the inequities of an applied system of justice be understood by the principle *unicuique suum*.[32]

Medieval society stressed the value of harmony and order, but in so doing divested the person of his individuality. No inferior could bring an accusation against a superior. He had no right of resistance. Transferred into the Church, there came to be no right of criticism of canon law or hierarchical decision.[33] The layman was a learner. Where primacy of office was uniquely honored the person with no public office was treated as a *persona minor*.[34] All power was conceived as being from above the person, as the administration of the Church grew ever closer in principle to the institute of guardianship in Roman law. By God's providence ecclesiastical office of itself was characterized by power over persons and the legal presumptions of knowledge and competence.[35] The faithful may request some equitable relief from the injustice of adverse decisions, but they have no right whatsoever to demand anything of their superiors. This hierarchical corporation was the all-inclusive milieu of the Christian life in the late Middle Ages.[36]

---

32. *Digesta,* I, 1, 10 (ed. Mommsen, p. 1): "Justitia est constans et perpetua voluntas ius suum cuique tribuere." Tellenbach, *op. cit.,* pp. 23-24; Ullmann, *The Individual and Society,* p. 15.

33. This is still the case in contemporary canon law; cf. canon 2344.

34. Canon 682 still considers the laity as passive and receptive, without deliberative voice in Church affairs. Cf. *Lex Fundamentalis Ecclesiae,* canon 29.

35. Cf. J. M. Cameron, *Images of Authority* (London, 1966); and Congar, "The Historical Development of Authority in the Church," in *Problems of Authority* (Baltimore, 1962), pp. 119-156.

36. Tellenbach, *op. cit.,* pp. 38-60.

In this static notion of human sociability obedience and compliance are virtues of paramount importance in the subjects of the law. Law, institution, unity and harmony prevail over the individual and his views. Extreme penalties were levied upon even minor infractions of that supreme dominion exercised with direct and immediate jurisdiction over the entire Church. The vocational stratification of civil society was mirrored in the administrative principles adopted by the Church. Rank and role were of extreme importance. The individual was merely the instrument of God to make the entire corporation grind on into the future with its divinely appointed mission. The law is supreme: *lex est anima totius corporis popularis*.[37] The *lex animata* in this system is the superior; following his will, the *mens legislatoris*, is the quest of virtue.[38] This accounts for the exaggerated importance of canon law in the Catholic Church.

The ecclesiastical administrative system of the Church today rests upon principles that reflect the same priority of values; the primacy of role over person, law over freedom, order over spontaneity, harmony over the creative dialectic, uniformity over pluralism and variety, obedience over love. Institutional values are protected by never admitting to error *(la bella figura)* or by the planned slowdown of change to an almost imperceptible creep *(pian piano)*. Office is given great privileges. The style of life of the holders of episcopal office is of those who are no longer brothers, but wealthy men set above the rank and file of the Church. The Church is not the pilgrim people of the theoreticians of the Second

37. *Monumenta Germanicae Historiae, Leges Visigothorum,* i, 2, 2. Note also the *Rex Pacificus,* Gregory IX's prologue to his *Decretals.*

38. L. Bender, *Legum Ecclesiasticarum Interpretatio et Suppletio* (Rome, 1961), pp. 14-15.

Vatican Council. It is still a world kingdom of absolutist control. This is the "system." It has no counterpart among Christian communities; indeed, it was rejected at the Reformation and is rejected today among our brothers in Christ.[39] It is a system of unfreedom. Beyond the justification of expediency, and this is a dubious Christian value, such a way of administration is not in keeping with the Gospel.

Lives are touched and molded, not by theories of baroque ecclesiastical fantasy, but by the way the Church appears to conduct its affairs among men today, by the way churchmen act. Catholic Church order in the practical polity of its procedures and life enshrines many of the structures of a social ideology that are no longer compatible with the self-understanding of civilized men. Though the primacy of the person has been continually stressed in papal social theory for application to secular society, it has made little impact upon the internal organization of the Church itself. Nowhere else is authority exercised today among Christians with such meager concern for the principle of its subsidiary functionality. Recent papal documents realigning the dicasteries of the Roman Curia and defining the role of papal representatives merely confirm the reluctance to decentralize or loosen the tight control over the faithful.[40]

39. J. Pelikan, *Spirit Versus Structure: Luther and the Institutions of the Church* (New York, 1968); Arthur Crabtree, "A Protestant Plea for a Pastoral Papacy," *Journal of Ecumenical Studies,* 6 (1969), 243-247; C. Braaten, "The Re-united Church of the Future," *Journal of Ecumenical Studies,* 4 (1967), 611-28; L. Vischer, "Reform of Canon Law: An Ecumenical Problem," *The Jurist,* XXVI (1966), 395-412.

40. Const. *Regimini Universae Ecclesiae,* 15 August 1967. AAS, 59 (1967), 885-928; and *Sollicitudo Omnium Ecclesiarum,* 24 June 1969. AAS, 61 (1969), 473-484.

THE SUBSIDIARY ROLE OF AUTHORITY IN A NEW CHURCH ORDER

A plurality of Church orders upon a pastoral and administrative level is possible in a reunited Church only by the application of the principle of subsidiarity. Prior to this time and as a prerequisite to further ecumenical progress the implications of subsidiarity must be fully explored within a new order in the Roman Catholic Church itself. This will require a new way of conceiving canon law and administrative theory, immediate structural changes and an extended period of experimentation to assess the result.

The principle of subsidiarity is an organizational rule of society. As a statement of the primacy of the person, that society exists for the person, not the person for society, the principle is clearly basic to Christian social ethics.[41] It belongs to the tradition of social doctrine emanating from the encyclical *Rerum Novarum* of Leo XIII in 1891. Pius XI forty years later in *Quadragesimo Anno* stated that "of its very nature the true aim of all social activity should be of help to the individual members of the social body but never to destroy or absorb them."[42]

Johannes Messner says, "No social authority, therefore, has a right to interfere with activities for individual and social ends as long as those responsible for those ends are able and willing to cope with them."[43] This is in keeping with the dignity of the person. The fulfillment of funda-

---

41. "Le principe: 'civitas propter cives, non cives propter civitatem' est un heritage antique de la tradition catholique et fut repris dans l'enseignement des Papes Leon XIII, Pie X, Pie XI, non de maniere occasionelle, mais en termes explicates, forts et precis" (Pius XII, Radio Message, 11 September 1956. AAS, 47 [1956], 679).

42. 15 May 1931. AAS 23 (1931), 177.

43. *Social Ethics* (St. Louis, 1949), p. 196.

mental rights and the pursuit of human perfection in freedom is the right and responsibility of each individual.

Society serves to aid the person, authority securing "the sum total of those conditions of social living whereby men are enabled more fully and more readily to achieve their own perfection."[44] In this way social authority is exercised in a way conducive to the common good of society and its members. This common good "is the good human life of the multitude, of a multitude of persons; it is their communion in good living. It is, therefore, common to both the whole and the parts into which it flows back and which in turn must benefit from it."[45]

Authority, therefore, does not replace nor should it interfere with the rights of persons. Its function is subsidiary: to aid the individual help himself. In this sense Messner is correct in saying: "The laws of subsidiary function and the law of the common good are in substance identical."[46] The law of subsidiary function prescribes that authority act for the common good in accord with the dignity of the human person by allowing men and lesser societies through social action to freely pursue their own perfection.[47]

In *Quadragesimo Anno* Pius XI stated the principle of subsidiarity as a principle of competency, restricting the competency of higher authorities in society only to what individuals and smaller communities need and cannot achieve for themselves:

44. John XXIII, *Mater et Magistra* (15 May 1961), *AAS* 52 (1961), 19.

45. J. Maritain, *The Person and the Common Good* (Notre Dame, 1966), p. 51.

46. *Op. cit.*, p. 196.

47. *Mater et Magistra*, n. 53; cf. also nn. 116 and 152.

This most serious principle remains fixed and unmoved in social philosophy: that which individual men can accomplish by their own initiative and their own industry cannot be taken from them and assigned to the community; in the same way, that which minor or lesser communities can do should not be assigned to a greater or higher community. To do so is a grave injury and disturbance of the social order; for social activity by its nature should supply help to the members of the social body, never destroy or absorb them.[48]

It is the very freedom and dignity of man, as Pope John XXIII stressed in *Pacem in Terris,* that sets constitutional limits upon the powers of authority.[49]

In 1946 Pope Pius XII, in addressing the newly appointed members of the College of Cardinals, said that the principle of subsidiarity "is valid for social life in all its organizations and also for the life of the Church, without prejudice to its hierarchical structure."[50]

WITHOUT PREJUDICE TO THE HIERARCHICAL STRUCTURE

The principle of subsidiarity is in harmony with the Gospel message of the freedom and dignity of man; it re-

48. *Op. cit.,* p. 203. In this reference consult Ewald Link, *Das Subsidiaritätsprinzip: Sein Wesen und Sein Bedeutung für die Sozialethik* (Freiburg, 1955), pp. 84ff.

49. 11 April 1963. *AAS* 55 (1963), 279; cf. also *ibid.,* p. 265.

50. ". . . che valgono per la vita sociali in tutti i suoi gradi, ed anche per la vita della Chiesa, senze pregiudizio della sua struttura gerarchia" (20 February 1946, *AAS* 38 [1946], 145).

flects the evangelical spirit of authority as service of love. It is, moreover, the organizational key to the restoration of the Church to the true *communio ecclesiarum* wherein men may be free and live the Christian experience in undoubted integrity. Rather than derogate from the value of the hierarchical structure divinely given to the Church, the application of subsidiary functionality will enhance and enrich its sanctifying potentialities. It will render practically possible a pastoral papacy and a pastoral episcopacy. It will be a defense against the cultural imperialism of the past and open the doors of the Church to the best of all human achievement. It will be an aid to divest *ministerium* from *imperium*.

The elements of Catholic belief relating to the essential structure of the Church are in no way incompatible with the principles of subsidiarity and freedom. To be assured of this, let us examine briefly some leading ecclesiological considerations.

(a) Hierarchy

The Church has a hierarchical structure, its guidance and rule having been entrusted by Christ to the Apostolic college and its successor, the body of bishops with the pope.[51] These have the power and mandate to preach the Gospel, administer the sacraments and give spiritual guidance.[52] The Church is not a democratic association established by men,[53] but a society established by God with a clear differentiation of organizational duties, rights and powers.

51. Const. *Lumen Gentium,* n. 20.
52. *Ibid.,* nn. 21-5.
53. Paul VI, *Ecclesiam Suam,* 6 August 1964. *AAS,* 56 (1964), 630-632.

The hierarchically constituted Church is directed by the immediate universal primacy of jurisdiction of the successor of Peter.[54]

Having said this, however, much remains yet unclear and variable in the circumstances of time and place where the Church is exposed to the determination of human freedom. Rahner observes, "Thus it is obvious that the permanent nature of the Church in her divinely bestowed constitution can emerge with varying degrees of clarity, purity and effectiveness in the historical phenomenon of the Church."[55]

By monarchical constitution is meant that the pope has full, direct, ordinary and general episcopal primacy of jurisdiction over the whole Church, not only in those things dealing with faith and morals, but also in those which pertain to the discipline and rule of the Church throughout the world. This is set forth explicitly in canon 218 of the Code of Canon Law.[56]

This does not mean, however, that the Pope can govern the Church arbitrarily or at whim. For the papal jurisdiction is carefully limited both by the divine right of the bishops and that of the charismatic community of the Church. Neither of these can the pope destroy or properly inhibit.

(b) The Bishops as Charismatic Leaders

"In the constitution of the Church," Rahner says, "the Spirit as Lord of the Church reserves to himself the power and the right to impart graces of inspiration to the Church

54. Denz. 3059-3064. First Vatican Council.
55. *Bishops: Their Status and Functions* (Baltimore, 1963), p. 15.
56. "1. Romanus Pontifex, Beati Petri in primatu successor, habet non solum primatum honoris, sed supremam et plenam potestatem iurisdictionis in universam Ecclesiam tum in rebus quae ad fidem et mores, tum in iis

without always and everywhere directing them through the official hierarchical organs of the Church."[57] It is extremely important to remember this in considering the bishops as identified with communities of God's People. All inspiration to guide the Church does not come from the top down; most frequently the movement is from the people up.

The bishops are representatives of Christ by divine institution, not merely indirectly as delegates of the pope. The pope is, indeed, the visible center of unity in the Church, but the bishops are themselves also channels of the inspiration of the Holy Spirit.[58] This role of particular bishops cannot be entirely institutionalized. The effect of this is not just so many dissident elements going in different directions, however, but the continuing enrichment of the Church unified in the representation of the episcopal college. The pope is head of the episcopal college and rules the Church with his brother bishops, never destroying or absorbing their charismatic role.[59]

---

quae ad disciplinam et regimen Ecclesiae per totum orbem diffusae pertinent. 2. Haec potestas est vere episcopalis, ordinaria et immediata tum in omnes tum in singulas ecclesias, tum in omnes et singulos pastores et fideles, a quavis humana auctoritate independens."

57. *The Episcopate and the Primacy* (New York, 1962), p. 16. Cf. also Rahner's *The Dynamic Element in the Church* (New York, 1964), pp. 42-83.

58. "What is to be completely avoided is the appearance that the hierarchical structure of the Church is an administrative apparatus with no intimate connection with the charismatic gifts of the Holy Spirit which are spread throughout the life of the Church" (Leo Joseph Cardinal Suenens, "The Charismatic Dimension in the Church," in *Council Speeches of Vatican II*, ed. H. Küng, Y. Congar, D. O'Hanlon [Glen Rock, N.J., 1964], p. 29). Cf. also H. Küng, "The Charismatic Structure of the Church," *Concilium*, 4 (1965), n. 1, 23-33.

59. Decree *Christus Dominus*, n. 8.

It is precisely in this concept of collegial inspiration and responsibility that unity and diversity become essential marks of the Church. Unity must be preserved, for we are all one in Christ, but the pluralism existing in the collegial body of bishops is also to be cherished. The infinite variety of gifts found among the members of the Mystical Body of Christ, as St. Paul recognized, are a precious grace of divine largesse to be served and fostered by the bishops.[60]

(c) The Source of Jurisdiction

The leading objection to the strict application of the principle of subsidiarity in the Catholic Church has not been based, however, upon the question of charismatic inspiration. It has been derived from the traditional canonical theory of jurisdiction. Greatly strengthened by the affirmation of the primacy of the pope in the First Vatican Council, proponents of this theory have dominated both canon law and ecclesiastical administration. All authority in the Church, they held, comes through the pope to the bishops and holders of office.[61] Since the principle of subsidiarity assumes innate rights and capacities in persons and communities beneath the supreme authority, they held the principle cannot be applied strictly to the Church. For in the Church lesser authorities are capacitated only by powers received by delegation from the pope. Perhaps this is what Pope Pius XII meant in adding the provision, "without prejudice to its hierarchical structure." In this theory the pope was not only the ultimate

---

60. Const. *Lumen Gentium*, n. 22.

61. D. Staffa, "De collegiali episcopatus ratione," *Revue de droit canonique*, 14 (1964), 100-205. Staffa's is the most thorough exposition of this integralist theory.

source of all authority, but he was uniquely responsible for all the Church and all the faithful. Thus, the fulfillment of this immense responsibility meant that through the Roman Congregations he had to be able to retain unquestioned control of all activities in the Church.

Notwithstanding a minority opinion in the past to the contrary, the Roman school of canon law traditionally taught the theory that all jurisdiction in the Church derives immediately from the pope. Charles Journet, writing shortly before the Council, said:

> . . . . When the Sovereign Pontiff, either of himself or through others, invests bishops, the proper jurisdiction they receive does not come to them directly from God, it comes directly from the Sovereign Pontiff to whom Christ gives it in a plenary manner . . . that is why the Sovereign must not be conceived as merely designating bishops who then receive directly from Christ their proper and ordinary authority, but as himself *conferring* the episcopal authority, having first received it from Christ in an eminent form.[62]

He does say, however, that jurisdiction belongs to the bishops by divine law and not merely ecclesiastical law.[63]

The various schools of thought regarding the derivation of episcopal jurisdiction were directly influenced by political events that had a profound effect upon the life of the Church. Febronianism and Gallicanism, for example, came to be identified with German and French theologians

62. *The Church of the Word Incarnate* (London, 1955), I, 404.
63. *Ibid.*, p. 405.

favoring the theory that jurisdiction comes with episcopal consecration immediately from Christ, and not from the pope.

The great Louvain canonist Zeger-Bernard van Espen (1646-1728) maintained firmly that the supreme authority in the government of the Church resides in the body of bishops, above the papal authority.[64] This theory was embraced in the eighteenth century by some of the highest ranking prelates of Germany and from there it spread through Europe. The auxiliary bishop of Trier, John Nicholas von Hontheim (1701-1790) published a book under the pseudonym, Justinus Febronius, entitled *De Statu Ecclesiae et Legitima Potestate Romani Pontificis*. In it he examined the "Gravamina Nationis Germanicae" in the light of their bearing on the general constitution of the Church. The principles of episcopalism of the French and Belgian ecclesiologists were applied to conditions in Germany following the Reformation. Some of these principles were: in order to win back separated Christians, there must be a restoration of the constitution of the early Church; the Roman primacy must be clearly defined; rights taken away from bishops and councils must be completely restored; the pope does not possess absolute monarchical powers; and the consent of the whole Church should be given to disciplinary laws.[65]

Agitation for support of episcopalism ended in Germany and Austria with the secularization of 1803, which terminated the civil jurisdiction of the prince-bishops. Episco-

64. G. LeClerc, *Zeger-Bernard van Espen (1646-1728) et l'Autorité Ecclesiastique* (Zurich, 1964).

65. *De Statu Ecclesiae et Legitima Potestate Romani Pontificis* (Bullioni, 1764), pp. 441-514.

palism then waned after the dogmatic definition of papal infallibility at Vatican I.

The effect of the theories of van Espen as a threat to papal authority, in Germany, France, Belgium and Austria, was to equate Catholic loyalty to the Roman notion of the derivation of episcopal jurisdiction. To claim anything but that jurisdiction came immediately from the Roman pontiff and mediately from Christ was to give ground to Gallicanism. But this was always a difficult thesis to hold. Theologically, it made the bishops delegates of the pope no matter how the canonical distinctions were drawn.[66]

One simply could not hold that bishops were mere delegates of the pope, however, even after the strong papal jurisdictional statements of Vatican I. The joint Declaration of the German Hierarchy in 1875 clearly asserted this. Seven points are clear in this statement:

(1) The pope *cannot* lay claim to the rights of the bishops or substitute his authority for theirs.

(2) Episcopal jurisdiction *is not* absorbed into papal jurisdiction.

(3) The decisions of the Vatican Council *did not* place the whole of episcopal authority in the hands of the pope.

(4) He *has not* in principle taken the place of each individual bishop.

(5) He *cannot* in relations with the Government, put himself in the bishops' place in any given moment.

(6) The bishops *have not* become the tools of the pope.

66. H. Küng, *The Council in Action* (New York, 1963), p. 229.

(7) They *are not,* in their relations with the Government, officials of a foreign sovereign.[67]

Pope Pius IX approved this statement as expressing "the true meaning of the Vatican decrees" and preventing the faithful from "forming a false idea of them.[68]

Even before the Second Vatican Council, therefore, there was a great deal of ambiguity. Strong theological views contrary to the Roman school were not suppressed. Rahner, for example, led a reaction in teaching:

> If the episcopal college is one and as such has a foundation in the Church, and if consecration as such brings a person directly into the college, then constitutional theology cannot recognize any purely 'absolute' ordination in the straightforward sense of the word: in every ordination to the sacramental power of order, there will be granted membership of the episcopal college—which is the holder, not only of the power of order, but irrevocably of pastoral authority.[69]

Wilhelm Bertrams said even more clearly:

> The episcopal office of governing in the Church is conferred upon a concrete subject through episcopal consecration. To exercise the office of governing in the

67. H. Küng, *The Council, Reform and Reunion* (New York, 1961), pp. 198-99.

68. *Ibid.,* p. 199.

69. *Bishops: Their Status and Functions,* p. 31.

Church, however, the divinely established and sacramentally conferred power of governing in the Church must be coordinated with the power of governing possessed by the other bishops. This coordination belongs to the Roman pontiff.[70]

The constitution *Lumen Gentium* of the Second Vatican Council clearly reversed the Roman school in its ecclesiological principles regarding the episcopacy, collegiality and the co-responsibility of the faithful. Christ gave a mission to the apostles, it says, that is to last until the end of time. This necessitates the appointment of successors to continue their ministry. Their duty is to the whole Church, to confirm and finish the work done by the apostles.[71] The primary responsibility of the bishop is to the universal Church and his is the chief office by which the apostolic commission is handed on. The office of the episcopacy is permanent and of divine institution, just as the Petrine office is a permanent part of the structure of the Church. The order of bishops has succeeded to the place of the apostles as shepherds of the Church.[72]

As the apostles were enriched with the power of the Holy Spirit, so are the bishops who receive the outpouring of the Spirit through the imposition of hands in episcopal consecration. It is through this consecration that the fullness of sacred orders is conferred.[73] Through ordination bishops

70. *The Papacy, the Episcopacy and Collegiality* (Westminster, Md., 1964), p. 54.
71. Const. *Lumen Gentium,* n. 20.
72. *Ibid.*
73. *Ibid.,* n. 21.

are made pastors of the flock and are entrusted with the high priesthood through which Christ preaches the Word, administers the sacraments and directs his people to sanctity.[74] The Council teaches that "episcopal consecration, together with the office of sanctifying, also confers the office of teaching and of governing which, however, of its very nature can be exercised only in hierarchical communion with the head and members of the college."[75] The Fathers of the Council continue that ancient tradition of both the East and the West, expressed especially in liturgical rites, that makes it clear that by consecration bishops receive the office to act in the place of Christ as teachers, shepherds and high priests of their people.[76]

The controversy concerning the origin of episcopal jurisdiction is thus settled. The role of the papacy is one of co-ordination, encouragement and support. It is not a source of authority, nor does it properly belong to the monarchical papacy to delegate authority in the Church in that which pertains to the direct activity of the pastoral ministry.

The meaning of the papal office of guidance is not to accomplish as much as possible of all the tasks of the Church by itself or through its administrative arm.[77] It must look instead to serving and aiding the full exercise of episcopal

74. *Ibid.*

75. *Ibid.*: "Episcopalis autem consecratio, cum munere sanctificandi, munera quoque confert docendi et regendi, quae tamen natura sua nonnisi in hierarchica communione cum Collegii Capite et membris exerceri possunt."

76. *Ibid.*

77. In this sense it cannot be said that the Roman Curia is an extension of the primacy. It is an institution of purely ecclesiastical determination. Cf. Y. Congar, *Report from Rome, II* (London, 1964), pp. 98-100.

duties and the rights of persons. It is, thus, clearly to be exercised within the limitations of the principle of subsidiarity.

> . . . the principle of subsidiarity requires that the Petrine office leave to the bishops, priests and people all that which can be carried out on their own responsibility, whereby bishops, priests and people do not require the cooperation of the Petrine office as such, and at the same time it promotes the greatest possible participation in the direction of the Church by bishops, priests and people.[78]

Papal legislation on minute points of discipline and the vast reservation of episcopal powers are not in accord with the true exercise of subsidiary functionality.

> According to the principle of subsidiarity, it is to be maintained, concerning actual legislation, that papal reservations are only to be established as the common good of the entire Church urgently requires them. Powers belonging to the bishops are not to be enumerated, for everything remains at the disposal of the local pastors, which has not been expressly withdrawn from them.[79]

The Second Vatican Council explicitly removed the only serious ecclesiological objection to the application of subsidiarity in the Church. As the *Nota Praevia* says, all previ-

---

78. H. Küng, *Structures of the Church*, p. 242.
79. M. Kaiser, "Das Prinzip der Subsidiarität in der Verfassung der Kirche," *Archiv für Kath. Kirchenrecht*, 33 (1964), 7.

ous teaching must be re-interpreted in the light of the teaching of *Lumen Gentium*.[80] This applies directly to the teaching of canonical administrative theories.

(d) Unity and Diversity

There is a tendency to attribute to the pope the strict responsibility or make him the sole proponent of unity or homogeneity in the Church. In this conception, the episcopacy represents the faction of pluralism and self-determination. By attributing these functions exclusively either to the pope or the bishops, these offices are set as much in opposition as one would oppose proponents of states' rights and strong federal power. This, however, is overly simplistic and quite radically incorrect. For both unity and diversity are marks of the Church to be cared for by all the faithful, bishops and pope.

The ministry of fostering and preserving the unity of faith and fellowship in the Church is the responsibility and prerogative not only of the successor of Peter but also of all his brother bishops both on a local and on a universal plane.[81] The presence of great variety which must exist in the Church is not properly the result of decentralization. It is brought about by the rights and exercise of supernatural gifts within the charismatic structure of the Christian com-

80. N. 2.: "Documenta recentiorum Summorum Pontificum circa iurisdictionem Episcoporum interpretanda sunt de hac necessaria determinatione potestatum."

81. Const. *Lumen Gentium*, n. 23. It is in union with the apostolic college that the bishop becomes a guarantee of union between the local and universal Church. "The sacrament of the *ordo episcoporum* begets the sacramental realization of the one Church of Christ in and through the local churches" (P. Anciaux, *The Episcopate in the Church* [Staten Island, N.Y., 1965], p. 85).

munity. The entire episcopal body, the pope and faithful, should foster these. "The episcopate of divine right should be the embodiment and guarantor of such a pluralism which will be more necessary in the future."[82] Pluralism is no more disunity than uniformity is unity.[83]

(e) The Local Church and the Church Universal

The Church even on a local level possesses a certain completeness of nature. It is not only a part of the whole, but it bears the faculties and characteristics of the whole Church.[84] In actuality the Universal Church is present in its concrete and particularized activity only. It is not an abstraction. In this sense, the Church as actual is said to be an "event."[85] The Church becomes an "event" in the most intense and actual way in the celebration of the Eucharist. Christ is present as Redeemer of his Body and Lord of the Church. In the Eucharist we are one with one another in Christ. This celebration must be localized. It takes place in a particular congregation united to a particular bishop in a given place.[86] The orientation of the Church, therefore, is toward local actualization.[87] Thus, we find in the New Testament a clear

82. Rahner, *The Episcopate and the Primacy*, p. 114.

83. J. Ratzinger, "Pastoral Implications of Episcopal Collegiality," *Concilium*, 1 (1965), n. 1, 20-33.

84. Const. *Lumen Gentium*, n. 26.

85. Rahner, *The Episcopate and the Primacy*, p. 25. See also J. A. Suoto, "Estructura juridica de la Iglesia particular: presupuestos," *Ius Canonicum*, 8 (1968), 121-202.

86. Const. *Lumen Gentium*, n. 26.

87. *Ibid.*: ". . . the Church of Christ is truly present in all legitimate local congregations of the faithful which united in their pastors, are themselves called churches of the New Testament. For in their locality these are the new people called by God, in the Holy Spirit and in much fulness (cf. I Thess. 1:5)."

identity between the individual community and the "church."

The primacy exists because the Church is to be a Church for the whole world and intended to be one. In so far as this one universal Church is to appear in particular places and achieve its full actualization in the celebration of the Eucharist, the episcopate exists by divine right. The rights and powers of the bishops must be sufficient to show forth the universal Church in the local church. Thus, unity and diversity, universality and particularity, by divine right anchor the axis between the primacy and the episcopacy in the Church.

(f) Human Means and Natural Principles

The administrative system and principles used by the hierarchy in the Church, as we have seen, are human means in their particularity. They reflect human sociability in the external organization of the faithful. The Church as institution acts through a human institutionalization that must be continually evaluated in the light of the human and the divine ends of the Church. Primary among these ends are freedom and service.

The Church is a universal human society, and this by divine institution.[88] If the Church, as Rahner says, is the tan-

---

88. W. Bertrams, "De Principio Subsidiaritatis in Iure Canonico," *Periodica*, 46 (1957), 29-43. "La volunta salvifica di Dio ha determinata nella Chiesa un'altra universale società a servizio della persona umana e dell'attuazione dei suoi fini religiosi" (Pius XII, Radio Message, 24 December 1942. *AAS* 35 [1943], 13). Cf. John C. Murray, "Freedom, Authority, Community," in *We, the People of God*, ed. J. Coriden (Huntington, Ind., 1968), pp. 145-157.

gible extension of the Incarnation,[89] then it is a Church of men and men's interpersonal activities and relationships. The Church in all its activities, in its powers of sacrament and jurisdiction, is a divinely ordered *subsidium* to enable men to attain their supernatural end in community.[90] Without any doubt, therefore, physical and moral persons, or communities, in the Church are possessed of rights. To their free implementation institutional factors are subsidiary.

Persons and communities should be able to express their proper individuality within the plenitude of the life of the Church. Overcentralization and tight control in matters of discipline and positive law are destructive of these values. More so is the subtle equation of *ministerium* and *imperium*. The fact that God works in the Church and has decreed its essential structure and purpose does not de-emphasize the dignity of the person in relation to the Christian community's common ends.

THE PRINCIPLE OF SUBSIDIARITY IN THE CONCILIAR DOCUMENTS

The documents of the Second Vatican Council, of course, do not contain a detailed blueprint for administrative reform

89. *The Episcopate and the Primacy*, p. 25.
90. Pius XII said as much in discussing the nature of the Church as an organic community in the encyclical *Mystici Corporis*: "Si totius et singulorum membrorum mutuam inter se rationem consideramus, in physico quolibet viventi corpore totius concretionis emolumento membra singula universa postremum unice destinantur, dum socialis quaelibet hominum compages, si modo ultimum utilitatis finem inspicimus, ad omnium et uniuscuiusque membri profectum, utpote personae sunt, postremum ordinatur" (*AAS* 35 [1943], 222).

in the Church. They do contain principles, however, from which practical conclusions must certainly be drawn. In the *Principia Quae Codicis Iuris Canonici Recognitionem Dirigant,* given to the bishops called to attend the Synod of Bishops in the fall of 1967, it is said that the reform of canon law must surely reflect the principle of subsidiarity according to the mind of the Second Vatican Council.[91] Though the principle of subsidiarity is mentioned *ex professo* only a few times in the council documents, the elements which demand the expression of subsidiarity are a major theme of their contents.

The Church affirmed in council a renewed awareness of the excellence of liberty, of personal responsibility and dignity. References to the dignity of the human person appear hundreds of times, and are sufficiently certain not to need documentation here. The greater responsibility and latitude for judgment given the bishops, however, should be shown as a clear indication of the importance of subsidiarity in re-organization. In these are implicit the rights and responsibilities of self-determination and freedom for persons and communities in the Church.

(a) The Constitution on the Sacred Liturgy

Canon 1257, which placed the entire regulation of the liturgy in the control of the Apostolic See, was reversed by the Council.[92] Individual bishops and the conferences of bishops are now primarily responsible for liturgical regula-

---

91. "Quae modo dicta sunt ad applicationem *principii subsidiaritatis* in iure canonico indubitanter pertinent" (p. 11). [emphasis added].

92. C. 1257: "Unius Apostolicae Sedis est tum sacram ordinare liturgiam, tum liturgicos approbare libros."

tion.[93] Only where the basic unity of rite is concerned or the common good of the Church is involved will the supreme authority in Rome retain control.[94]

In all matters which do not implicate the faith or the common good of all the faithful, the Council declared no desire to impose rigid uniformity.[95] The mode and circumstances of life, the genius and talents of local communities and nations should be expressed in the true spirit of the liturgy.[96] This means a wide range of local adaptation is possible. Within the local community the bishops should promote the liturgical apostolate, by encouraging pastoral action, study and necessary experimentation.[97] Specific details of competency in the area of the sacraments, sacramentals, the catechumenate and the life of worship of the local communities are well known.

(b) The Dogmatic Constitution on the Church

There are three specific references to the application of the principle of subsidiarity in the Church which have not been previously cited.

In Chapter II of the constitution, entitled "The People of God," the Council Fathers spoke of the universality of the vocation to belong to the new People of God.[98] Each member of the faithful contributes to the whole Church through his own special gift. Not only are there individuals with their

93. Const. *Sacrosanctum Concilium*, art. 22.
94. Art. 26.
95. Art. 37.
96. *Ibid.*
97. Arts. 44 and 45.
98. Const. *Lumen Gentium*, n. 13. Cf. H. Heimerl, "The Laity in the Constitution on the Church," *Concilium*, 3 (1966), n. 2, 68-72.

special gifts, but there are various ranks of those who exercise the sacred ministry and those in a special condition of state of life, for example, members who enter the religious life.

Within the Church there are particular churches which "retain their own traditions, without lessening the primacy of the Chair of Peter, which presides over the whole assembly of charity and protects legitimate differences, while at the same time assuring that such differences do not hinder unity but rather contribute toward it."[99]

This last statement expresses the function of higher authority with regard to the principle of subsidiarity. The "legitimate differences" and individual "traditions" are those which have evolved through local direction, and the principle of protecting these differences guarantees local control in all that does not hinder the unity of the Church.

In speaking of the pastoral office of the bishop the Fathers state that the bishop's power "is not destroyed by the supreme and universal power, but on the contrary it is affirmed, strengthened and vindicated by it."[100]

In discussing the role of the hierarchy in fostering religious life and safeguarding the role and effectiveness of various institutes, the Council taught that a restriction of the local authority or their power to rule themselves is justified only for the common good of the Church:

In order to provide more fully for the necessities of the entire flock of the Lord, any institute of perfection

99. *Ibid.*
100. *Ibid.*, n. 27. Cf. C. Hay, "The Ecclesiological Significance of the Decree on Ecumenism," *Journal of Ecumenical Studies,* 3 (1966), 343-353.

and its individual members may be removed from the jurisdiction of the local ordinaries by the supreme pontiff and subjected to himself alone. This is done in virtue of his primacy over the entire Church and in consideration of the common good. In like manner, these institutes may be freed from, or committed to, the charge of the proper patriarchal authority.[101]

(c) The Decree on the Oriental Catholic Churches

It is interesting to note that the reason given in this decree and in the Decree on Ecumenism for the autonomy of the individual churches and the right of self-regulation is traced to the service of the individual and his right to pursue his own perfection.

Since the spiritual heritage of the Eastern churches has contributed greatly to the universal Church, the Council "solemnly declares that the Churches of the East as much as those of the West have a full right and are duty bound to rule themselves, each in accordance with its own established disciplines, since all these are praiseworthy because of their venerable antiquity, more harmonious with the character of their faithful and more suited to the promotion of the good of souls."[102]

The dignity and the rights of the patriarchs and major archbishops of the Eastern churches are clearly recognized. The ancient traditions, liturgies and disciplinary laws of the East are said to be a treasure of the Church to be preserved. The intervention of the Roman Pontiff in the affairs of the

101. N. 45.

102. Decree *Orientalium Ecclesiarum*, n. 5.

Oriental churches is clearly restricted to cases of major importance only.[103]

(d) The Decree on Ecumenism

This decree, while looking beyond the purely internal structures of the Catholic Church, makes important observations on the freedom of the individual, his right to take responsibility for himself in spiritual matters and on the necessity for reform within the Church.

In discussing the principles of ecumenism, the Council Fathers caution that unity in essentials must be preserved but that everyone in the Church, according to his office, ought to be intent on preserving a proper freedom in the spiritual life, in discipline, in liturgical matters, and even in the theological elaboration of revealed truths. This course of action gives richer expression to the authentic catholicity and apostolicity of the Church.[104]

The history of the churches of the East has been one in which they have followed their own discipline. This has not been an obstacle to Church unity, but has contributed to the mission of the Church.[105] Legitimate pluralism redounds to the good of the whole Church. Even the differences in theological expression and the methods and approaches to understanding divine revelation have brought us nearer to appreciating the great mystery of salvation.

To remove all shadow of doubt, then, this holy Synod solemnly declares that the Churches of the East, while keeping in mind the necessary unity of the whole Church,

103. N. 9.
104. Decree *Unitatis Reintegratio*, n. 4.
105. N. 16.

have the power to govern themselves according to their own disciplines, since these are better suited to the character of their faithful and better adapted to foster the good of souls.[106]

(e) The Decree on the Pastoral Office of Bishops in the Church

Significantly, the opening words of this decree are the same as the opening words of the third chapter of the constitution *Lumen Gentium*. Much of what is contained there is reiterated and principles practically spelled out. Article 8 of the decree bears repetition, for it is upon this foundation that the entire re-orientation of canonical faculties in *De Episcoporum Muneribus* was based:

a) As successors of the apostles, bishops automatically enjoy in the dioceses entrusted to them all the ordinary, proper, and immediate authority required for the exercise of their pastoral office. But this authority never in any instance infringes upon the power which the Roman Pontiff has, by virtue of this office, of reserving cases to himself or to some other authority.

b) Except when it is a question of matters reserved to the supreme authority of the Church, the general law of the Church gives each diocesan bishop the faculty to grant dispensations in particular cases to the faithful over whom he exercises authority according to the norm of law, provided he judges it helpful for their spiritual welfare.

106. *Ibid.*

A radical reorganization of the Roman Curia was called for to adapt it to the needs of the times. "The Fathers also desire that, in view of the very nature of the pastoral office proper to bishops, the office of legates of the Roman pontiff be more precisely determined."[107]

The bishops were mandated to establish episcopal conferences, to set up commissions to determine diocesan boundaries and to study ways and means of choosing candidates for the episcopal office.

(f) The Decree on Priestly Formation

Here and in the Decree on the Life and Ministry of Priests the work of the Council was very sketchy and unsatisfactory. The first paragraph of the decree strongly urges the episcopal conferences to take responsibility for local adaptation. Despite this encouraging note, however, the Council Fathers failed to come to grips with the major problems of the clerical life. For example, the relationship between the exercise of the ministry of the Church and the permissible extension of higher authority into the privacy of the person of the minister was not discussed. The present structure of clerical life permits an unconscionable degree of control and manipulation. The time has arrived for an entire re-institutionalization of the life and ministry of priests.

Be this as it may, some consequences of subsidiary functionality are to be seen in the document. Canon 1357/4 for example, is abolished, as the regulation of seminaries is placed under the control of episcopal conferences.[108] Rome did retain the right, however, to approve their directives.

107. Decree *Christus Dominus,* n. 9.
108. Decree *Optatam Totius,* n. 7.

Various minor considerations related to the period of time between the reception of orders, the time of ordination and the post-ordination courses of study are left to the discretion of the bishops.

(g) The Decree on the Apostolate of the Laity

This decree does not directly point to the subsidiary function of authority in the Church, but does so indirectly. The Council discusses the charismatic element in the apostolate of the members of the People of God and the hierarchic element in the organization of that apostolate. The freedom which is necessary for laymen to give effective witness is only as complete as the freedom of the bishop to shepherd his flock and to make an honest judgment of the gifts of his people. The right of the bishop to exercise his jurisdiction without unnecessary intervention has, as one of its basic reasons, the right of the individual to pursue his sanctification and participate in the mission of the Church. This right is born of an office which is shared by the laity.[109]

The Holy Spirit, through the sacraments and the service of the ministry, helps the faithful to carry out their apostolate. He gives gifts as he wishes, and, because these gifts have been bestowed, the faithful have the right and duty to use them. They are to be used in freedom and cooperation with pastors, whose duty it is to judge the genuineness of the gifts, not "to extinguish the spirit" (1 Thess. 5:19), but "to test all things and hold on to that which is good" (1 Thess. 5:21).[110]

109. Decree *Apostolicam Actuositatem*, n. 2.
110. N. 3.

Lay people have the right to form and direct religious and charitable organizations.[111] The function of ecclesiastical authority is to procure unity and cooperation for the common good.[112] The hierarchy should encourage, instruct, coordinate and unify.[113] This should be the function of any higher authority in preservation of the autonomy and freedom of individuals and communities.

(h) The Constitution on the Church in the Modern World

Only in freedom can man direct himself toward goodness. Authentic freedom is the sign of the image of God in man. God has willed that man be controlled by his own decisions, seek his Creator spontaneously and come freely to perfection through loyalty to him. Man's dignity demands that he act according to a knowing and free choice that is personally motivated, not from blind impulse or external pressure.[114]

Man's social nature makes it evident that the progress of the human person and the advance of society itself hinge on one another. For the beginning, the subject, and the goal of all social institutions is and must be the human person, which for its part and by its very nature stands completely in need of social life.[115]

... the social order and its development must invariably work to the benefit of the human person if the dis-

111. N. 19.
112. N. 23.
113. N. 24.
114. Const. *Gaudium et Spes,* n. 19.
115. *Ibid.,* n. 25.

position of affairs is to be subordinate to the personal realm and not contrariwise, as the Lord indicated when he said that the Sabbath was made for man, and not man for the Sabbath.[116]

At the conclusion of the Constitution on the Church and the Modern World it is said that since the mission of the Church is to shed on the whole world the radiance of the Gospel message, this requires that those within the Church foster mutual esteem, reverence and harmony through the full recognition of lawful diversity. Thus all those who make up the People of God, both the pastors and the faithful, should engage in a fruitful dialogue. The bonds which unite the faithful are stronger than anything which divides them. Let there be unity in what is necessary, freedom in what is unsettled, and charity in all things.[117]

Since dialogue implies honest communication and charity encompasses the well-being of all, we must now come to the practical conclusions of our study.

CONCLUSION

In this fifth great cultural transition through which the Church is passing a new kind of ecclesiastical order is being born. The monarchical and jurisdictional polity of the Catholic Church will cede to a more sacramental understanding of the nature and mission of the Church. In this

116. *Ibid.,* n. 26.
117. *Ibid.,* n. 92.

understanding the principles of freedom and subsidiarity will assume paramount importance. The elements of an outmoded social and canonical ideology will be discarded to make possible the conditions of experimentation and variety in which a plurality of Church orders can be tested in a renewed and reuinted Christianity.

The bishops who attended the Synod in Rome in the fall of 1967 discussed at length the reform of canon law and the principles this reform should reflect. The reform of canon law, they said, must be guided by the principle of subsidiarity according to the mind of the Second Vatican Council. From what has been clarified in the elaboration of this study it seems manifest that this will require immediate theoretical and structural transformation. It is not unreasonable to suggest, therefore, that the practical implementation of this mandate include the following considerations:

1. The reform of canon law must not be accomplished by a small group of canonists of the old tradition. The commission should be opened to a truly representative membership and decisions should be made only after the widest possible consultation.

2. The universal law of the Church should be restricted to the statement of general constitutional norms. The specification of particular discipline should be left to the local ritual and national churches.

3. The Vatican should no longer conceive of itself as a member of the international society of nations and should renounce its political involvements. This will mean an extensive revision of the system of permanent papal representation. *Ad hoc* situations that

cannot be met by national hierarchies can still be served by special legations of the Holy See.

4. In each episcopal conference the elected president should assume the role of liaison between the Holy See and the particular church. He and his staff can apprise the pope and the particular church of needs and duties.

5. The following congregations of the Roman Curia should become centers of international cooperation, rather than control:

   a. The Congregation for Religious and Secular Institutes

   b. The Congregation for the Teaching of the Faith

   c. The Congregation for the Sacraments

   d. The Congregation for Catholic Education

   e. The Congregation for the Evangelization of the Nations

6. The following congregations of the Roman Curia should serve as offices of information and registry:

   a. The Congregation for Bishops

   b. The Congregation for Rites

   c. The Congregation for the Clergy

7. The Secretariate of State should become an agency through which the pope may engage in international cooperation with men of good will and the coordination of interchurch activities. The three other secretariates, of Christian Unity, for Believers and Unbelievers, should serve as agencies of the entire Church for their specified purposes.

8. The Congregation for the Oriental Churches and the Sacred Council for the Public Affairs of the Church should be dropped.

9. The courts of the Holy See should be unified and available primarily for appeal. They should be staffed by canonists and theologians of international competence and reputation.

10. The administration of the Holy See and its finances should be consolidated and full and honest disclosure of the disposition of all monies given to the faithful of the Church.

11. The central administrative offices of the Church should be staffed by competent representatives of the whole Church, lay and clerical.

12. Only in major causes should the Holy See exercise immediate jurisdiction in the pastoral care of the faithful outside the diocese of Rome. The central administration of the Church should not be engaged in granting dispensations to individuals or individual communities.

13. The honors, trappings, style and expressions of the *imperium* of the past should be dropped from the life of the Church.

14. Individual cases involving declarations of the nullity of marriage or dispensation from the marriage bond should be decided by local Ordinaries.

15. Resignation from the priestly ministry or the religious life should be standardized, dignified and done

within the local church itself, either in the pastoral care of the local Ordinary or the conference of bishops.

16. Bishops should be elected by the clergy and people of the particular community they will serve. Various methods of election can be devised to provide a proper system of checks and balances. The pope should approve the elected candidate, or disprove of him for serious reasons, but not directly appoint bishops.

17. Bishops should be elected for a term not to exceed ten years.

18. Bishops should not be translated from diocese to diocese, except in rare cases of extraordinary necessity.

19. Bishops and leaders in the Church generally should conceive of their ministry as primarily preaching, administering the sacraments and providing spiritual encouragement and guidance. Their life style should fit these qualifications.

20. Provincial, regional and national councils should meet regularly to decide with the deliberation of bishops, clergy and laity the major concerns of discipline, morals and unity.

21. There should be in each community of the Church open and participatory management of goods and resources by competent members of the community, lay and clerical.

22. The discipline and expectations of the ministry should be decided by national councils, with the fullest cooperation of the bishops, clergy and laity.

23. The conditions of ministry must be revised to place the clergy and laity in a participatory relationship of free choice and service with the bishops.

24. The institute of incardination should be changed from the present arrangement, to allow freedom of movement and initiative to the clergy. Though the bishop is entrusted with supervising the preaching word and the administration of the sacraments, he should not be able to exercise absolute control over the personal lives of ecclesiastical ministers.

25. The individual faithful should be given a meaningful choice in the appointment of pastors. This could be made in individual parishes, or in the pastoral councils of the dioceses.

26. The right of free association in the Church should be accorded to all. This is primarily a problem among religious today and among the laity. They should both be helped to form and belong to communities of their choice.

27. Inter- or supra-diocesan organizations and religious institutes should be coordinated by the offices of the national church administration.

28. Questions regarding liturgical law and practice should be decided by the conferences of bishops, with the consultation of the clergy and laity.

29. Provision should be made for full, free and open processes of justice to meet equitably and charitably problems of conflict and grievance.

30. Catholic universities and institutions of a charitable, religious or educational nature sponsored by the Church on a national level should be accorded the right of exemption from the authority of local ordinaries and serve directly under the authority of the national conference of bishops.

31. The prior censorship of books and publications should be dropped.

32. Ecclesiastical penalties should be greatly simplified and reserved only for cases of very serious dereliction. All automatic penalties *(latae sententiae)* should be dropped.

33. Women should be assured full participation and equality in the life of the Church.

34. Each diocese should have an active senate of priests and a pastoral council to enable all the faithful to participate in the life of the Church.

35. Conferences and dialogue should be initiated with other Christian men and women on Church order and ways and means of ecclesiastical administration to ease tensions and promote Christian unity.

POSITION PAPER

from the Symposium
which was directed to the Episcopal Synod

As people of God, clergy and laity, concerned that the Church accomplish its mission in the modern world, we wish to express our gratitude to Pope Paul VI for establishing the Synod of Bishops as an expression of collegiality rooted in the Gospels, in tradition and developed by the Second Vatican Council. The initiative of the pope has given all men increasing hope for the continued growth and orderly renewal of the Church.

When Pope Paul established the Synod, he said that it, like all human institutions, "can be still more perfected with the passage of time" (*Apostolica Sollicitudo,* n. 1). In our judgment the time has come to give the Synod of Bishops a more permanent form so that the collegial nature of the Church may be more adequately realized and more effectively accomplished.

The doctrine of collegiality expressed in the Constitution on the Church (n. 22) teaches that bishops who are united to the pope and to their fellow bishops in hierarchical communion constitute a collegial body possessing supreme power in governing the Church. Such power is exercised not only when the college is united in an ecumenical council such as Vatican II, but it also may be exercised through other forms of appropriate collegial action such as an episcopal synod. But an episcopal synod should have the bishops in full collaboration with the pope in view of their collegial prerogatives, not merely as advisers or consultors as the present Synod of Bishops is constituted.

THEOLOGICAL CONSIDERATIONS

The Church is necessarily collegial in its structure and government because it is collegial in its nature and in its biblical origins.

Collegiality is, in its first and deepest meaning, a matter of *community*. The Church is a *communio* brought together and sustained by the Holy Spirit. The Church, as community, comes into being in its most visible form when it gathers for the celebration of the Eucharist, at the level of the local assembly. But this local church is not merely an administrative unit within a larger corporate entity; it is a living cell containing the whole mystery of the one Body of Christ. Within these local churches, there has always existed a close bond among bishops, presbyters and deacons, and the community as a whole, and this fraternal relationship is a principal basis for the apostolicity of each community.

There have also existed important links among the various local churches: bishop with bishop, and community with community. It is clear from very early liturgical testimony (e.g., the consecration of a bishop by several other bishops rather than by one alone), that the individual bishop could have his episcopacy in no other way than in communion with the other bishops. The Church is a *communio ecclesiarum,* a fraternity of local churches brought together by the Spirit into a single body. The history of the Catholic Church, in large measure, is the record of balancing one value against the other, of preserving the integrity of the local church (apostolicity) without diminishing the unity of the Church universal (catholicity).

The mission of the Church, whether of proclaiming the Word of God, of celebrating the sacraments, or of ministering to the needs of mankind in the world for the sake of the Kingdom of God, presupposes and requires both order and structure, not only as a sign of internal unity but also for a more coherent and effective exercise of this mission. The unity of the Church and the fruitfulness of its mission is assured interiorly by the presence of the Spirit, and exteriorly by the presence of the college of bishops within the Church, and by the pope as the principle of unity within the college.

The pope, however, never acts as a purely private person when he acts as head of the Church. He is always head of the college and a member thereof. The primacy of the pope is a primacy within rather than over against the episcopal college. The Church is governed by a college in such wise that the pope is not the mere instrument of the college, while the college is not merely his executive organ. Indeed, the Catholic Church does not recognize the pope to be its absolute monarch, nor the bishops as the mere delegates of the pope. The supreme and full power for governing the Church, in view of its higher mission for the sake of the Kingdom of God, has been conferred upon the whole college. This power is exercised in different modes and forms, but it is radically one.

It was clearly not the intent of the First Vatican Council to propose a doctrine of the papacy that might be prejudicial to the rights and responsibilities of the bishops. This judgment is verified by the joint Declaration of the German Hierarchy in 1875. Herein it is asserted that the council did not teach that episcopal jurisdiction is absorbed into papal jurisdiction or that the pope in principle has taken the place of every individual bishop. Significantly, Pope Pius IX approved this statement of the German bishops as expressing "the true meaning of the Vatican decrees" and preventing the faithful from "forming a false idea of them."

This interpretation is further strengthened by the documents of the Second Vatican Council. Without prejudice to the rights and prerogatives of the pope, "all the bishops in hierarchical communion share in the responsibility for the Universal Church" (Decree on the Bishops' Pastoral Office in the Church, n. 5), and are thereby "the subject of supreme and full power over the universal Church" (Dogmatic Constitution on the Church, n. 22).

The testimony of Vatican II faithfully reflects the converging insights of biblical, liturgical, canonical, and theological scholarship: the Church must be collegial in structure and government because it is collegial in its nature and origins, and history records numerous examples of collegial action in every age of the Church's life.

PRACTICAL RECOMMENDATIONS FOR THE SYNOD

In light of the foregoing we make the following recommendations:

1. That the ordinary Synod of Bishops as described in n. 5 of the *Motu Proprio Apostolica Sollicitudo* of Pope Paul VI, meet regularly according to its norms of proportionate representation. In view of the present crises facing the Church in this post-conciliar period we recommend that this regular meeting be on an annual or biannual basis.

2. That the pope personally participate as often as possible in the actual working sessions of the Synod in order that its collegial nature be more effectively realized.

3. That national conferences of bishops mutually collaborate with the Holy See in determining matters to be placed on the agenda for each Synod session.

4. That the permanent synod secretariat work in continuous collaboration with national conferences, with offices of the Roman Curia and with the newly formed International Commission of Theologians.

5. That the accepted conclusions of the Synod be implemented as matters of the Church's top priority.

6. That secrecy, since it often breeds mistrust, suspicion and lack of confidence be imposed only when absolutely necessary. The People of God, both clergy and laity, have a right to adequate information both as to matters on the agenda and the discussions of the Synod as well as the final decisions.

PRACTICAL RECOMMENDATIONS FOR THE RELATIONSHIP
BETWEEN THE HOLY SEE AND NATIONAL CONFERENCES

We recommend that relations between the Holy See and the national conferences be improved by implementing the following proposals:

1. Liaison between the pope and the national conferences should be maintained through the president of each conference who should report directly to the Holy Father on the condition of the particular church.

2. Matters of universal importance should be promulgated to the People of God through the Synod in order to insure proper consultation and effective implementation.

3. National conferences should answer the call of the Holy See by providing some of their own members and other competent personnel to further the internationalization of the Roman Curia.

4. Since bishops through the Holy Spirit are pastors and true, authentic teachers of the faith, reservation of decision-making to central authority can be justified only by the needs of the Universal Church. Even such apparently necessary reservations should be modified if two-thirds of the bishops of a national conference request it because of pressing local conditions.

5. With the pastoral needs of today's church urgently calling for a fuller use of modern means of communication, it is imperative that the Holy See in conjunction with national conferences work out programs which would include evaluating current trends, counseling decision-

makers as well as providing accurate information inside and outside the Church.

THE APPLICATION OF SUBSIDIARITY:

A RESTORATION OF RESPONSIBILITIES

It is of highest importance that the Synod of Bishops adopt principles of administrative reform which effect a new division of labor and establish new levels of responsibility. The dedicated contribution of the Roman See to the unity and catholicity of the Universal Church and the integrity of faith must be gladly acknowledged. At the same time, the needs of persons in all areas of the Church today call for new efforts of pastoral care and guidance. The enormous growth and complexity of the Church, as well as regional and cultural variety, require effective implementation of the principles of subsidiarity, collegiality and co-responsibility in all orders of the faithful, so that the mission of Christ among men may be fulfilled.

Among the principles of reform none is more urgent than the restoration to the particular churches of their ancient freedom to adapt the discipline of the Christian life and ministry to the needs of their own people. To do this with confidence, alacrity, and an adequate sense of accountability to the legitimate needs and aspirations of the faithful entrusted to them, the leadership of the particular churches must be able to take full responsibility for the direct pastoral care of persons and groups. Such restoration will lift a weight of detail from the Roman See, insure freedom and justice to the particular communities within the Church, and assist Christians to realize their present initiatives and expectations of witness and service.

The following areas of decision are listed as examples of the types of competency that should no longer be exercised on a universal level but rather through the episcopal conferences in the particular churches:

1. The procedures for selecting bishops. The role of the Holy See should be one of confirmation or approval, not direct appointment.
2. The institution of provincial, regional, and national councils.
3. The discipline of the clergy and the general organization of the priestly life and ministry.
4. The ways and institutions of participation by the laity in decision-making.
5. Procedures and norms to be followed in the resolution of marriage cases and cases wherein persons seek leave to change their status in the Church, and generally all decisions bearing upon the rights and obligations of persons as individuals.
6. Judicial processes and procedural law for criminal and contentious causes. These should correspond to the traditions and sense of fairness of the people of the particular church. Nevertheless, the right of the faithful to ultimate appeal to the Roman See and its tribunals ought to be safeguarded.
7. Decisions affecting the liturgical, devotional, and ascetical practices of the faithful.
8. Questions bearing upon the apostolic activities of supradiocesan institutions.
9. The administration of ecclesiastical goods and properties.

PARTICIPANTS

Rev. William W. Bassett
School of Canon Law
Catholic University of America
Washington, D.C.

Most Rev. Alexander Carter, D.D.
Bishop of Sault Ste. Marie
Canada

Rev. James A. Coriden
School of Theology
Catholic University of America
Washington, D.C.

Dr. Robert E. Cushman
Dean, Divinity School
Duke University
North Carolina

Rev. Avery Dulles, S.J.
Woodstock College
Maryland

Prof. Fred H. Goldner
Graduate School of
Business Administration
Columbia University

Rev. John E. Lynch, C.S.P.
Department of History and
School of Canon Law
Catholic University of America
Washington, D.C.

Rev. Thomas J. Lynch
Executive Coordinator
Canon Law Society of America
Hartford, Connecticut

Rev. Richard P. McBrien
Pope John XXIII Seminary
Weston, Massachusetts

Rev. Robert E. McNally, S.J.
Department of Theology
Fordham University
Bronx, New York

Rev. Harry McSorley, C.S.P.
St. Paul's College
Washington, D.C.

Rev. Adam J. Maida, President
Canon Law Society of America
Pittsburgh, Pennsylvania

Rev. Francis Maurovich
Editor, *The Catholic Voice*
Oakland, California

Rt. Rev. Msgr. John S. Quinn
St. Andrew's Church
Chicago, Illinois

Dr. Kenneth L. Schmitz
School of Philosophy
Catholic University of America
Washington, D.C.

REFERENCES TO EPISCOPAL CONFERENCES
IN CONCILIAR AND OTHER RELATED
DOCUMENTS

Compiled by William K. Leahy

I. CONSTITUTION ON THE SACRED LITURGY

1. *General norm for the regulation of the Liturgy* (art. 22, n. 3): "In virtue of power conceded by the law, the regulation of the liturgy within certain defined limits (e.g., as defined throughout this Constitution in the Instruction for the implementation of the Constitution on the Sacred Liturgy and in other acts of the Post-Conciliar Commission for the liturgy) belongs also (i.e., besides to the Apostolic See and the local bishop, cf., art. 22, n. 1) to various kinds of competent territorial bodies of bishops legitimately established." Note: sections within parentheses are not part of the citation from the Constitution.

2. *The use of the vernacular in the Liturgy* (art. 36, n. 3): "These norms being observed (i.e., art. 36, nos. 1 & 2 on the retention of Latin in the Latin rite and the extended use of the vernacular in certain parts of the Liturgy), it is for the competent territorial ecclesiastical authority mentioned in art. 22, n. 2 (cf., 1 above) to decide whether, and to what extent, the vernacular language is to be used; their decrees are to be approved, that is, confirmed, by the Apostolic See. And, whenever it seems to be called for, this authority is to consult with bishops of neighboring regions which have the same language."

3. *Vernacular texts* (art. 36, n. 4): "Translations from the Latin text into the mother tongue intended for use in the liturgy must be approved by the competent territorial ecclesiastical authority mentioned above."

4. *Adaptations of the Liturgy*: (art. 39): "Within the limits set by the typical editions of the liturgical books, it shall be for the competent territorial ecclesiastical authority mentioned in art. 22, n. 2 (cf., 1 above) to specify adaptations, especially in the case of the administration of the sacraments, the sacramentals, processions, liturgical language, sacred music, and the arts, but according to the fundamental norms laid down in this Constitution."

5. *Further adaptations* (art. 40, n. 1): "In some places and circumstances, however, an even more radical adaptation of the liturgy is needed, and this entails greater difficulties. Wherefore: 1) The competent territorial ecclesiastical authority mentioned in art. 22, no. 2 (cf., 1 above), must, in this matter, carefully and prudently consider which elements from the traditions and culture of individual peoples might appropriately be admitted into divine worship. Adaptations which are judged to be useful or necessary should then be submitted to the Apostolic See, by whose consent they may be introduced."

6. *Preliminary Experiments* (art. 40, n. 2): 2) To ensure that adaptations may be made with all the circumspection which they demand, the Apostolic See will grant power to this same territorial ecclesiastical authority to permit and to direct, as the case requires, the necessary preliminary experiments over a determined period of the time among certain groups suited for the purpose."

7. *Liturgical Commission and Institute for Pastoral Liturgy* (art. 44): "It is desirable that the competent territorial ecclesiastical authority mentioned in art. 22, n. 2 (cf., 1 above) set up a liturgical commission, to be assisted by experts in liturgical science, sacred music, art, and pastoral practice. So far as possible the commission should be aided by some kind of Institute for Pastoral Liturgy, consisting of persons who are eminent in these matters, and including laymen as circumstances suggest. Under the direction of the above-mentioned territorial ecclesiastical authority the commission is to regulate pastoral-liturgical action throughout the territory, and to promote studies and necessary experiments whenever there is question of adaptations to be proposed to the Apostolic See."

8. *Vernacular in the Mass* (art. 54, 1st. and 3rd. par.): "In Masses which are celebrated with the people, a suitable place may be allotted to their mother tongue. This is to apply in the first place to the readings and "the common prayer," but also, as local conditions may warrant, to those parts which pertain to the people, according to the norm laid down in art. 36 (cf., 2 and 3 above) of this Constitution . . . . And wherever a more extended use of the mother tongue within the Mass appears desirable, the regulation laid down in art. 40 (cf., 5 and 6 above) of this Constitution is to be observed.

9. *Concelebration* (art. 57, no. 1, b): ". . . it has seemed good to the Council to extend permission for concelebration to the following cases: 1 . . . b) at Masses during . . . bishops' conferences . . ."

10. *Use of Vernacular in Administration of the Sacraments and Sacramentals, and New Rituals* (art. 63): "Because of the use of the mother tongue in the administration of the sacraments and sacramentals can often

be of considerable help to the people, this use is to be extended according to the following norms: a) The vernacular language may be used in administering the sacraments and sacramentals, according to the norm of art 36 (cf., 2 and 3 above); b) In harmony with the new edition of the Roman Ritual, particular rituals shall be prepared without delay by the competent territorial ecclesiastical authority mentioned in art. 22, n. 2 (cf., 1 above) of this Constitution. These rituals, which are to be adapted, also as regards the language employed, to the needs of the different regions, are to be reviewed by the Apostolic See and then introduced into the regions for which they have been prepared. But in drawing up these rituals or particular collections of rites, the instructions prefixed to the individual rites in the Roman Ritual, whether they be pastoral and rubrical or whether they have special social import, shall not be omitted."

11. *The Marriage Rite* (art. 77, 2nd. and 3rd. par.): ". . . If any regions are wont to use other praiseworthy customs and ceremonies when cele-brating the sacrament of matrimony, the Sacred Synod earnestly desires that these by all means be retained. Moreover, the competent territorial ecclesiastical authority mentioned in art. 22, n. 2 (cf., 1 above) of this Constitution is free to draw up its own rite suited to the usages of place and people, according to the provision of art. 63 (cf. 10 above). But the rite must always conform to the law that the priest assisting at the marriage must ask for and obtain the consent of the contracting parties."

12. *Vernacular Version of the Divine Office* (art. 101, n. 1): ". . . The vernacular version (of the Divine Office), however, must be one that is drawn up according to the provision of art. 36 (cf., 2 and 3 above)."

13. *Adaptations of the Liturgical Year* (art. 107): "The Liturgical Year is to be revised . . . . But if certain adaptations are considered neces-sary on account of local conditions, they are to be made in accordance with the provisions of arts. 39 and 40 (cf., 4-6 above)."

14. *The Practice of Penance* (art. 110, 1st. par.): ". . . The practice of penance should be fostered in ways that are possible in our own times and in different regions, and according to the circumstances of the faithful; it should be encouraged by the authorities mentioned in art. 22 (cf., above)."

15. *Language for Sacred Music* (art. 113, 2nd. par.):"As regards the language to be used (in sacred music), the provisions of art. 36 (cf., 2 and 3 above) are to be observed; for the Mass, art. 54 (cf., 8 above); for the sacraments, art. 63 (cf., 10 above); for the divine office, art. 101 (cf., 12 above)."

16. *Musical Instruments in the Liturgy* (art. 120, 2nd. par.): "But other instruments (besides the pipe organ — cf., 1st. par. of this art.) may be admitted for use in divine worship, with the knowledge and consent of the competent territorial authority, as laid down in arts. 22, no. 2 (cf., 1 above), 37, and 40 (cf., 5 and 6 above). This may be done, however, only on condition that the instruments are suitable, or can be made suitable, for sacred use, accord with the dignity of the temple, and truly contribute to the edification of the faithful."

17. *Adaptations of Sacred Furnishings* (art. 128, 2nd. par.): "According to the norm of art. 22 (cf., 1 above) of this Constitution, the territorial bodies of bishops are empowered to adapt such things (the placement and construction of sacred furnishings, etc.; cf., 1st. par. of this art.) to the needs and customs of their different regions; this applies especially to the materials and form of sacred furnishings and vestments."

Besides the above direct references to Episcopal Conferences in the Constitution on the Sacred Liturgy, the following might also have application to them on the national scale, although they can be understood as referring to bishops on the diocesan level as well.

18. *Special Devotions* (art. 13, 2nd. par.): "Devotions proper to individual Churches also have a special dignity if they are undertaken by mandate of the bishops according to customs or books lawfully approved."

19. *Transmissions of Sacred Rites* (art. 20): "Transmissions of the sacred rites by radio and television shall be done with discretion and dignity, under the leadership and direction of a suitable person appointed for this office by the bishops. This is especially important when the service to be broadcast is the Mass."

II. INSTRUCTION FOR THE PROPER IMPLEMENTATION OF THE CONSTITUTION ON THE SACRED LITURGY (Sacred Cong. of Rites, 26 Sept. 1964)

1. *Clarification of the Functions of the Bodies of Bishops* (art. 3): "... Therefore, the Commission, by mandate of the Supreme Pontiff, has prepared this Instruction, in which the functions of the bodies of bishops in liturgical matters are more clearly defined ..."

2. *Authority of and its Exercise by Episcopal Conferences* (art. 10): "Those matters which are entrusted to the competent territorial ecclesiastical authority in this Instruction may and should be put into effect by that authority alone through legitimate decrees. In individual cases, the time

and the circumstances in which these decrees will take effect shall be defined, always with a reasonable interval of time for the faithful to be instructed and prepared for their observance."

3. *Relationship to the Apostolic See* (art. 21 — cf., 1 above under the Constitution on the Sacred Liturgy): "It pertains to the Apostolic See . . . to approve, that is, confirm the acts and deliberations of the territorial authority; and to receive the proposals and petitions of the same territorial authority."

4. *Relationship to the Local Ordinary* (art. 22): "It pertains to the bishop to regulate the liturgy within the limits of his diocese, in accordance with the norms and spirit of . . . the decrees of . . . the competent territorial authority."

5. *Constitution of the Body of Bishops* (art. 23, a): "The various kinds of territorial bodies of bishops, to which the regulation of the liturgy pertains in virtue of art. 22, no. 2 of the Constitution (cf., 1 above under the Constitution of the Sacred Liturgy), must be understood to be, for the interim: a) either the body of all the bishops of a nation, in accordance with the norm of the apostolic letter SACRAM LITURGIAM, n. X . . ."

6. *Membership in the Episcopal Conference* (art. 24): "The following must be invited to the above-mentioned bodies (cf., 5 above): a) residential bishops; b) abbots and prelates nullius; c) vicars and prefects apostolic; d) apostolic administrators of dioceses who have been appointed permanently; e) all other local ordinaries except vicars general. Coadjutor and auxiliary bishops may be invited by the president, with the consent of the majority of those who take part in the body with deliberative vote."

7. *Convocation of the Body* (art. 25): "Unless the law provides otherwise for certain places in view of particular circumstances, the convocation of the body must be made: a) by the respective president, in the case of bodies already lawfully established; b) in other cases, by the archbishop or bishop who has the right of precedence in accordance with the norm of law."

8. *Procedure in the Conference* (art. 26): "The president, with the consent of the Fathers, determines the order to be followed in the examination of questions, and opens, transfers, prorogues, and closes the conference."

9. *Subjects of Deliberative Vote* (art. 27): "A deliberative vote belongs to all who are named in art. 24 (cf., 6 above), including coadjutor and auxiliary bishops, unless a different provision is expressly made in the document of convocation."

10. *Requirement of two-thirds majority* (art. 28): "For the lawful enactment of decrees, two-thirds of the votes, taken by secret ballot, are required."

11. *Procedure for Transmission of Acts to the Apostolic See* (art. 29): "The acts of the competent territorial authority which are to be transmitted to the Apostolic See for approval, that is, confirmation, should contain the following: a) the name of those who took part in the session; b) a report of matters taken up; c) the result of voting for the individual decrees. Two copies of these acts, signed by the president and the secretary of the body, and with the proper seal, shall be sent to the Commission for the Implementation of the Constitution on the Sacred Liturgy."

12. *Transmission of Acts Concerning the Use of the Vernacular* (art. 30): "When, however, it is a question of acts in which there are decrees concerning the use and extent of the vernacular language to be admitted in the liturgy, besides what is enumerated in art. 29 (cf., 11 above), in accordance with art. 36, n. 3, of the Constitution (cf., 2 above under the Constitution on the Sacred Liturgy) and the apostolic letter SACRAM LITURGIAM, n. IX, the acts should also contain: a) an indication of the individual parts of the liturgy which are to be said in the vernacular; b) two copies of the liturgical texts prepared in the vernacular, one copy of which will be returned to the body of bishops; c) a brief report concerning the criteria upon which the work of translation was based."

13. *Time of Promulgation of Decrees Needing Approval or Confirmation of the Apostolic See* (art. 31): "The decrees of the territorial authority which need the approval, that is, the confirmation of the Apostolic See, shall be promulgated and put into practice only when they have been approved, that is, confirmed by the Apostolic See."

14. *Avoiding distinctions of person* (art. 34): "The individual bishops, or, if it seems opportune, the regional or national conferences of bishops shall see to it that the prescription of the holy Council which forbids any favor to private persons or any favor on the basis of social distinctions, either in ceremonies or in external pomp (cf., art. 32 of the Constitution), shall be put into effect in their territories."

15. *Vernacular Translations of Liturgical Texts* (art. 40): "In vernacular translations of liturgical texts prepared in accordance with the norm of art. 36, n. 3 (cf., the Constitution — cf., 2 above under the Constitution on the Sacred Liturgy), it is fitting that the following be observed: a) The vernacular translations of liturgical texts shall be made from the Latin liturgical text. The version of the biblical pericopes, however, should conform to the Latin liturgical text, but with the possibility of revising

this translation, if deemed advisable in accordance with the original text or some other clearer translation. b) The preparation of the translation of liturgical texts should be entrusted, as a special concern, to the liturgical commission mentioned in art. 44 of the Constitution (cf., 7 above under the Constitution on the Sacred Liturgy) and in art. 44 of this Instruction. So far as possible, the institute of pastoral liturgy should assist the commission ... c) Whenever it is called for, there should be consultation concerning translations with the bishops of neighboring regions which have the same language. d) In nations which have several languages, different vernacular translations should be prepared for these languages and submitted to the special examination of the bishops concerned. e) Consideration should be given to the dignity of the books from which the liturgical text is read to the people in the vernacular language, so that the dignity of the book itself may move the faithful to a greater reverence for the word of God and for sacred things."

16. *Special Groups of Another Language* (art. 41): "In liturgical services which are celebrated in some places with people of another language, it is lawful with the consent of the local ordinary to use the vernacular language known to these faithful, especially in the case of groups of migrants, or of members of a personal parish, or similar instances. This shall be done in accordance with the extent of the use of the vernacular language and its translation as legitimately approved by a competent territorial ecclesiastical authority of the respective language."

17. *New Vernacular Melodies for Celebrant and Ministers* (art. 42): "New melodies for parts to be sung in the vernacular language by the celebrant and the ministers must be approved by the competent territorial ecclesiastical authority."

18. *Membership and Meeting of the Conference's Liturgical Commission* (art. 44): "The liturgical commission, which it is desirable that the territorial authority establish (cf., 7 above under the Constitution of the Liturgy) shall be chosen from among the bishops themselves, as far as possible. At least it shall consist of one or other bishop, with the addition of some priests expert in liturgical and pastoral matters, who are designated by name for this office. It is desirable that the members of this Commission be convened several times a year with the consultors of the Commission that they may deal with questions together."

19. *Duties of the Conference's Liturgical Commission* (art. 45): "The territorial authority may, as circumstances suggest, entrust the following to this Commission: a) studies and experiments to be promoted in accordance with the norm of art. 40, nos. 1 and 2 of the Constitution (cf., 5 and 6 under the Constitution on the Sacred Liturgy); b) practical

initiatives to be undertaken for the entire territory, by which the liturgy and the application of the Constitution on the Liturgy may be encouraged; c) studies and the preparation of aids which become necessary in virtue of the decrees of the plenary body of bishops; d) the office of regulating the pastoral-liturgical action in the entire nation, supervising the application of the decrees of the plenary body, and reporting concerning all these matters to the body; e) consultations to be undertaken frequently and common initiatives to be promoted with associations in the same region which are concerned with scripture, catechetics, pastoral care, music, and sacred art, and with every kind of religious association of the laity."

20. *The Lord's Prayer* (art. 48, g): ". . . in sung Masses the Lord's Prayer may be chanted by the people together with the celebrant in the Latin language, and if the territorial ecclesiastical authority shall so decree, also in the vernacular language, to melodies approved by the same authority."

21. *The Prayer of the Faithful* (art. 56, 3rd. par.): "In places where the common prayer or prayer of the faithful is not in use, the competent territorial authority may decree that it be done in the manner indicated above (cf., 1st. and 2nd. par. of this art.), with formulas approved for the interim by that authority."

22. *The Use of the Vernacular in Mass* (art. 57 — cf. 8 above under the Constitution on the Sacred Liturgy): "In Masses, whether sung or low, which are celebrated with the people, the competent territorial ecclesiastical authority may admit the vernacular language, the decrees having been approved, that is, confirmed, by the Apostolic See: a) especially in proclaiming the lessons, epistle, and gospel, as well as in the common prayer or prayer of the faithful; b) according to the circumstances of the place, also in the chants of the Ordinary of the Mass, namely, Kyrie, Gloria, Creed, Sanctus-Benedictus, and Agnus Dei, and in the antiphons at the Introit, Offertory, and Communion, as well as in the chants that occur between the lessons; c) moreover, in the acclamations, salutations, and dialogue formulas, together with the formulas as the communion of the faithful: *Ecce Agnus Dei, Domine, non sum dignus,* and *Corpus Christi,* and in the Lord's Prayer with its introduction and embolism. Missals for liturgical use, however, should contain the Latin text in addition to the vernacular translation."

23. *The Use of the Vernacular in the Sacraments and Sacramentals* (art. 61 — cf., 10 above under the Constitution on the Sacred Liturgy): "The competent territorial authority may admit the vernacular language, the decrees having been approved, that is, confirmed, by the Apostolic See: a) in the rites of baptism, confirmation, penance, anointing of the sick, and matrimony, including the essential forms, as well as in the

distribution of holy communion; b) in the conferral of orders: in the allocutions at the beginning of each ordination or consecration, as well as in the examination of the bishop-elect in episcopal consecration, and in the instructions; c) in the sacramentals; d) in funeral rites. Whenever a more extended use of the vernacular language appears desirable, the regulation of art. 40 of the Constitution (cf., 5 and 6 above under the Constitution on the Sacred Liturgy) is to be observed."

24. *Vernacular Text of Short Offices* (art. 82): "The translation of the text of a short office into the vernacular language for use as the public prayer of the Church must be approved by the competent territorial ecclesiastical authority, the decrees having been approved, that is, confirmed, by the Apostolic See."

III. DECREE ON THE MEDIA OF SOCIAL COMMUNICATION

Although Episcopal Conferences are nowhere expressly named in this decree, the following sections seem to call for joint action on the part of all the Bishops of the country:

1. *Special Day of Observance with regard to the Media of Social Communication* (art. 18): "Moreover, that the varied apostolates of the Church with respect to the media of social communication may be strengthened effectively, each year in every diocese of the world, by determination of the Bishops, there should be celebrated a day on which the faithful are instructed in their responsibilities in this regard. They should be invited to pray and contribute funds for this cause. Such funds are to be expended on the promotion, maintenance and development of institutes and undertakings of the Church in this field, according to the needs of the whole Catholic world."

2. *Establishment of National Offices* (art. 21): "Since an effective apostolate on a national scale calls for unity of planning and resources, this Sacred Synod decrees and orders that national offices for affairs of the press, films, radio and television be established everywhere and given every aid. It will be the special task of these offices to see to it that the consciences of the faithful are properly instructed with respect to these media. Likewise they should foster and guide whatever is done by Catholics in these fields. In each country the direction of such offices should be entrusted to a special committee of Bishops, or to a single delegated Bishop. Moreover, laymen who are experts in Catholic teaching and in these arts of techniques should have a role in these offices."

3. *International Cooperation* (art. 22): "Since the effectiveness of these media reaches beyond national boundaries and has an impact on

individual members of the whole human family, national offices should cooperate among themselves on an international plane. The offices spoken of in art. 21 (cf., 2 above) should assiduously work together with their own international Catholic associations. These Catholic international associations are legitimately approved by the Holy See alone and depend on it."

IV. CONSTITUTION ON THE CHURCH

1. *Collegiate Character of Episcopal Conferences* (art. 23, end of last par.): ". . . In like manner the Episcopal Conferences of today are in a position to render a manifold and fruitful assistance so that this collegiate feeling may be put into practical application."

2. *Permanent Diaconate* (art. 29, end of last par.): ". . . It pertains to the competent territorial conferences of Bishops, of one kind or another, with the approval of the Supreme Pontiff, to decide whether and where it is opportune for such (permanent) deacons to be established for the care of souls. With the consent of the Roman Pontiff, this diaconate can be conferred upon men of more mature age, even upon those living in the married state. It may also be conferred upon suitable young men, for whom, however, the law of celibacy must remain intact.

V. DECREE ON ECUMENISM

1. *Common Worship* (*Communicatio in sacris*) (art. 8, end of last par.): ". . . . The course to be adopted, with due regard to all the circumstances of time, place, and persons, is to be decided by local episcopal authority, unless otherwise provided for by the Bishops' Conference according to its statutes, or by the Holy See."

Although this is the only explicit reference to Bishops' Conferences in this decree, the following might also be understood to have relevance for Bishops' Conferences as well as for local Ordinaries:

2. *General Direction of Ecumenical Work* (art. 4, last par.): "This sacred Council is gratified to note that the participation by the Catholic faithful in ecumenical work is growing daily, and it commands this work to the Bishops everywhere in the world to be vigorously stimulated by them and guided with prudence."

VI. DECREE ON THE ORIENTAL CATHOLIC CHURCHES

Although no explicit reference to (Latin) Episcopal Conferences is made in this decree, the following might be understood as having some relevance to (Latin Rite) Episcopal Conferences, or rather to their Presidents or to persons (an individual or a committee) representing the President or the Conference:

1. *Relationships between various particular Churches in the same territory* (art. 4, at beginning): "... but the Heads (Hierarchs) of the various particular Churches with jurisdiction in the same territory will see to it that, by discussions in periodic conferences, a unity of action is promoted, and by united effort common interests are aided, in order that the good of religion may be the more readily advanced, and the discipline of the clergy more effectively preserved..."

This statement might have reference to meetings not only between Oriental Church authorities themselves, but also between Oriental and Latin rite authorities.

VII. DECREE ON THE PASTORAL OFFICE OF BISHOPS IN THE CHURCH

1. *Care of migrants, exiles and refugees, seafarers, air-travelers, gypsies, etc.* (art. 18, 2nd. par): "Episcopal Conferences, especially national ones, should pay special attention to the very pressing problems concerning the above-mentioned groups (i.e., migrants, exiles, refugees, seafarers, air-travelers, gypsies, etc. — cf., 1st par. of this art.). Through voluntary agreement and united efforts, they should look to and promote their spiritual care by means of suitable methods and institutions. They should also bear in mind the special rules either already laid down or to be laid down by the Apostolic See which can be wisely adapted to the circumstances of time, place, and persons."

2. *Boundaries of Dioceses* (art. 24): "In order to bring about the changes and alterations of dioceses as set forth in arts. 22-23 and leaving untouched the discipline of the Oriental Churches, it is desirable that the competent Episcopal Conferences examine these matters, each for its respective territory. If deemed opportune, they may employ a special episcopal commission for this purpose, but always taking into account the opinions of the bishops of the provinces or regions concerned. Finally, they are to propose their recommendations and desires to the Apostolic See."

3. _Relationships with Religious Communities_ (art. 35, end of no. 4 and no. 5): "4) ... Religious also are bound to observe all those things which councils or conferences of bishops shall legitimately prescribe for observance by all. 5) A well-ordered cooperation is to be encouraged between various religious communities and between them and the diocesan clergy. There should also be a very close coordination of all apostolic works and activities which especially depend upon a supernatural attitude of hearts and minds, rooted in and founded upon charity. The Apostolic See is competent to supervise this coordination for the universal Church; sacred Pastors are competent in their own respective dioceses: and patriarchal synods and episcopal conferences in their own territory. For those works of the apostolate which religious are to undertake, bishops or episcopal conferences, religious superiors or conferences of major religious superiors, should take action only after mutual consultations."

4. _Value of Episcopal Conferences_ (art. 37): "In these days especially bishops frequently are unable to fulfill their office effectively and fruitfully unless they develop a common effort involving constant growth in harmony and closeness of ties with other bishops. Episcopal Conferences — already established in many nations — have furnished outstanding proofs of a more fruitful apostolate. Therefore, this Sacred Synod considers it to be supremely fitting that everywhere bishops belonging to the same nation or region form an association which would meet at a fixed time. Thus, when the insights of prudence and experience have been shared and views exchanged, there will emerge a holy union of energies in the service of the common good of the Churches."

5. _Makeup, Constitution, Membership, Voting and Meetings of Episcopal Conferences_ (art. 38 — cf., 3, 5-10, above under the Instruction for the Proper Implementation of the Constitution on the Sacred Liturgy): "Wherefore, this sacred synod decrees the following concerning episcopal conferences:

1) An episcopal conference is, as it were, a council in which the bishops of a given nation or territory jointly exercise their pastoral office to promote the greater good which the Church offers mankind, especially through the forms and methods of the apostolate fittingly adapted to the circumstances of the age.

2) Members of the episcopal conference are all local Ordinaries of every rite — excluding vicar generals — and coadjutors, auxiliaries and other titular bishops who perform a special work entrusted to them by the Apostolic See or the episcopal conferences. Other titular bishops, legates of the Roman Pontiff, because of their exceptional office in the territory are not de jure members of the conference. Local Ordinaries and coadjutors

hold a deliberative vote. Auxiliaries and other bishops who have a right to attend the conference will hold either a deliberative or a consultative vote, as the statutes of the conference determine.

3) Each episcopal conference is to draft its own statutes for recognition by the Apostolic See. In these statutes, among other things, offices should be established which will aid in achieving its purpose more efficaciously, for example, a permanent board of bishops, episcopal commissions and a general secretariat.

4) Decisions of the episcopal conference, provided they have been approved legitimately and by the votes of at least two-thirds of the prelates who have a deliberative vote in the conference, and have been recognized by the Apostolic See, are to have juridically binding force only in those cases prescribed by the common law or determined by a special mandate of the Apostolic See, given either spontaneously or in response to a petition of the conference itself.

5) Wherever special circumstances require and with the approbation of the Apostolic See, bishops of many nations can establish a single conference.

Communications between episcopal conferences of different nations should be encouraged in order to promote and safeguard the common good.

6) It is highly recommended that the prelates of the Oriental Churches, promoting the discipline of their own churches in synods and efficaciously fostering works for the good of religion, should take into account also the common good of the whole territory where many churches of different rites exist. They should exchange views at inter-ritual meetings in keeping with norms to be given by the competent authority (cf., 1 above under the Decree on Oriental Catholic Churches).

6. *Boundaries of Provinces and Regions* (art. 41): "It is fitting that the competent episcopal conferences examine the question of boundaries of such provinces and the establishment of regions in keeping with the norms given with respect to diocesan boundaries in arts. 23-24 (cf. this Decree — cf., 2 above). They are then to submit their suggestions and desires to the Apostolic See."

7. *Inter-Diocesan Offices* (art. 42): "Since pastoral needs require more and more that some pastoral undertakings be directed and carried forward as joint projects, it is fitting that certain offices be created for the service of all or many dioceses of a determined region or nation. These offices can be filled by bishops. This Sacred Synod recommends that between the prelates or bishops serving in these offices and the diocesan bishops and the episcopal conferences, there exist always fraternal

association and harmonious cooperation in the expression of pastoral concern. These relationships should also be clearly defined by common law."

VIII.   MOTU PROPRIO "APOSTOLICA SOLLICITUDO" ON THE SYNOD OF BISHOPS (15 Sept. 1965)

1. *Membership of the General Assembly of the Synod of Bishops* (N. V., 1, b): "The general assembly of the Synod of Bishops includes, first of all and by its very constitution: 1 . . . b) Bishops elected by the individual National Episcopal Conferences, according to the norm laid down in No. VIII (of this Motu Proprio) . . ."

2. *Membership of the Extraordinary Assembly of the Synod of Bishops* (N. VI, 1, b): "The Extraordinary assembly of the Synod of Bishops includes: 1 . . . b) the Presidents of National Episcopal Conferences . . ."

3. *Membership of the Special Assembly of the Synod of Bishops* (N. VII): "The special assembly of the Synod of Bishops includes . . . those who act on behalf of the Episcopal Conferences of one or more nations . . . as laid down in Nos. V and VIII, as long as they pertain to the regions for which the Synod of Bishops has been convoked."

4. *Number of Bishops representing the Episcopal Conference on the Synod of Bishops* (N. VIII, d): "The Bishops who represent the individual Episcopal Conferences are elected in this way: . . . d) four from each National Episcopal Conference having more than 100 members . . ."

5. *Qualifications of those to be elected from Episcopal Conferences to take part in the Synod of Bishops* (N. IX): "In electing those to represent the Episcopal Conferences of one or more nations . . . account should be taken not only of their knowledge and prudence, which are general requisites, but also of their theoretical and practical familiarity with the subject matter which the Synod will treat."

IX.   DECREE ON THE ADAPTATION AND RENEWAL OF THE RELIGIOUS LIFE

1. *Relationship with Conferences of Major Superiors* (art. 23, at end): "This Synod favors conferences or councils of major superiors. . . . Suitable coordination and cooperation with episcopal conferences should be established with regard to the exercise of the apostolate."

X. DECREE ON PRIESTLY TRAINING

1. *General Norm and Direction* (art. 1 and note 2): "Since only general laws can be made for a such a wide variety of nations and regions, a special "program of priestly training" is to be undertaken by each country or rite. It must be set up by the episcopal conferences,[2] revised from time to time, and approved by the Apostolic See. In this way universal laws will be adapted to the particular circumstances of the times and localities so that the priestly training will always be in tune with the pastoral needs of those regions in which the ministry is to be exercised."

Note 2: "The entire priestly training, i.e., the running of the seminary, spiritual training, the curriculum of studies, the common life discipline of the students, and pastoral experimentations must be adapted to the various circumstances of the locale. This adaptation is to be carried out, as far as its main points are concerned, according to the general norms, by episcopal conferences for the secular clergy, and similarly by competent Superiors for the regular (or religious) clergy (cf., the General Statutes annexed to the Apostolic Constitution *Sedes Sapientiae*, art. 19)."

2. *Post-Seminary Training* (art. 22): "Since priestly training, because of the circumstances particularly of contemporary society, must be pursued and perfected even after the completion of the course of studies in seminaries, it will be the responsibility of episcopal conferences in individual nations to employ suitable means to this end. Such would be pastoral Institutes working together with suitably chosen parishes, meetings held at stated times, and appropriate projects whereby the younger clergy would be gradually introduced into the priestly life and apostolic activity, under its spiritual, intellectual, and pastoral aspects, and would be able, day by day, to renew and foster them more effectively."

Although the above are the only explicit references to episcopal conferences in this decree, the document does often speak of the activity of the "bishops" in regard to the specific areas of priestly training as outlined in the general norm above (cf., 1 above), and these passages, together with the following in particular, might readily have relevance for the bishops acting on the national as well as on the diocesan or provincial level:

3. *United Effort in Fostering Vocations* (art. 2, 2nd par.): "Bishops on the other hand are to encourage their flock to promote vocations and should be concerned with coordinating all forces in a united effort to this end. As father, moreover, they must assist without stint those whom they have judged to be called to the Lord's work." (Cf., also the 4th. and 5th. par. of this art.).

4. *Regional or National Seminaries* (art. 7, 1st. par. and note 12): "Where individual dioceses are unable to institute their own seminaries properly, seminaries for a number of dioceses or for an entire region or country are to be set up and developed . . . . These seminaries, if they are regional or national, are to be regulated according to directives set down by the bishops concerned [12] and approved by the Apostolic See." Note 12: "It is prescribed that in laying down the statutes for regional or national seminaries all the bishops concerned take part, thus superceding the directive of canon 1357, par. 4, of the Code of Canon Law."

5. *Introduction to the spiritual life and pastoral work, and extending the age of ordination* (art. 12): "In order that the spiritual training rest upon a more solid basis and that the students embrace their vocation with a fully deliberate choice, it will be the prerogative of the bishops to establish a fitting period of time for a more intense introduction to the spiritual life. It will also be their charge to determine the opportuneness of providing for a certain interruption in the studies or of establishing a suitable introduction to pastoral work, in order that they may more satisfactorily test the fitness of candidates for the priesthood. In accordance with the conditions of individual regions it will also be the bishops' responsibility to make a decision about extending the age beyond that demanded at present by common law for the reception of sacred orders, and of deliberating whether it be opportune to rule that students, at the end of their course in theology, exercise the order of deacon for a fitting period of time before being promoted to the priesthood." (Cf., also art. 21)

XI. DECLARATION ON CHRISTIAN EDUCATION

1. *General Norm of Application of Fundamental Principles* (Preface, end of last par.): ". . . Hence this Sacred Synod declares certain fundamental principles of Christian education, especially in schools. These principles will have to be developed at greater length by a special post-Conciliar Commission and applied by Episcopal Conferences to varying local situations."

Although the above is the only explicit reference to Episcopal Conferences in this Declaration, it calls for the application of the entire document by the Episcopal Conferences. Moreover, the following explicit reference to joint effort on the part of Bishops might have particular significance for the action of Episcopal Conferences:

2. *Care for students attending non-Catholic Universities* (art. 10 of Latin text, at beginning of last par.; last par. of n. 9 of English translation distributed to the U.S. Bishops by the Rome Council Office of N.C.W.C.):

"Since the destiny of society and of the Church itself is intimately linked with the progress of young people pursuing higher studies, the Pastors of the Church are to expand their energies not only on the spiritual life of students who attend Catholic universities, but, solicitous for the spiritual formation of all their children, they must see to it, after suitable consultations between Bishops, that even at universities that are not Catholic there should be associations and university centers under Catholic auspices in which priest, religious, and laity, carefully selected and prepared, should give abiding spiritual and intellectual assistance to the youth of the university . . . ."

XII. THE CONSTITUTION ON DIVINE REVELATION

Although no specific reference to Episcopal Conferences is made in this document, the following might have special relevance for the competency of such Conferences:

1. *Translations of Scripture* (art. 25, last two par.): "It devolves on sacred Bishops, 'who have the apostolic teaching,' to give the faithful entrusted to them suitable instruction in the right use of the divine books, especially the New Testament and above all the Gospels. This can be done through translations of the sacred texts, which are to be provided with the necessary and really adequate explanations so that the children of the Church may safely and profitably become conversant with the Sacred Scriptures and be penetrated with their spirit. Furthermore, editions of the Sacred Scriptures, provided with suitable footnotes, should be prepared also for the use of non-Christians and adapted to their situation. Both Pastors of souls and Christians generally should see to the wise distribution of these in one way or another."

XIII. DECREE ON THE APOSTOLATE OF THE LAITY

Although there are no references expressly relating to Episcopal Conferences in this document, the following guidelines are laid down with regard to the relationship between the lay apostolate and the hierarchy generally which might have particular references to Episcopal Conferences:

1. *Catholic Action* (art. 20, 1st par., d, next to last par.): ". . . the laity . . . grouped to themselves into various kinds of activities and societies which, while maintaining a closer union with the hierarchy, pursued and continue to pursue goals which are properly apostolic . . . . These societies were deservedly recommended and promoted by the popes and

many bishops, from whom they received the title of "Catholic Action," and were often described as the collaboration of the laity in the apostolate of the hierarchy. Whether these forms of the apostolate have the name of "Catholic Action" or some other title, they exercise an apostolate of great value for our times and consist in the combination and simultaneous possession of the following characteristics: ... d) whether they offer themselves spontaneously or are invited to action and direct cooperation with the apostolate of the hierarchy, the laity function under the higher direction of the hierarchy itself, and the latter can sanction this cooperation by an explicit mandate. Organizations in which, in the opinion of the hierarchy, the ensemble of these characteristics is realized, must be considered to be Catholic Action even though they take on various forms and titles because of the needs of different regions and peoples."

2. *Recommendation by the Hierarchy* (art. 21): "All associations of the apostolate must be given due appreciation. Those, however, which the hierarchy has praised or recommended as responsive to the needs of time and place, or have ordered to be established as particularly urgent, must be held in highest esteem by priests, religious, and laity, and promoted according to each one's ability ...."

3. *Relationships of the Lay Apostolate to the Hierarchy* (art. 23, 24): "Whether the Lay Apostolate is exercised by the faithful as individuals or as members of organizations it should be incorporated into the apostolate of the whole Church according to a right system of relationships. Indeed, union with those whom the Holy Spirit has assigned to rule his Church ... is an essential element of the Christian apostolate. No less necessary is cooperation among various projects of the apostolate which must be suitably directed by the hierarchy .... 24. The hierarchy should promote the apostolate of the laity ... direct the conduct of this apostolate to the common good of the Church, and attend to the preservation of doctrine and order. Indeed, the lay apostolate admits of different types of relationships with the hierarchy in accordance with the various forms and objects of this apostolate. For in the Church there are many apostolic undertakings which are established by the free choice of the laity and regulated by their prudent judgment. The mission of the Church can be better accomplished in certain circumstances by undertakings of this kind, and therefore they are frequently praised or recommended by the hierarchy. No project, however, may claim the name "Catholic" unless it has obtained the consent of the lawful Church authority. Certain forms of the apostolate of the laity are given explicit recognition by the hierarchy, though in various ways. Because of the demands of the common good of the Church, moreover, ecclesiastical authority can select and promote in a particular way some of the apostolic associations

and projects which have an immediately spiritual purpose, thereby assuming in them a special responsibility. Thus, making various dispositions of the apostolate according to circumstances, the hierarchy joins some particular form of it more closely with its own apostolic function. Yet the proper nature and distinctiveness of each apostolate must be preserved, and the laity must not be deprived of the possibility of acting on their own accord. In various Church documents this procedure of the hierarchy is called a mandate. Finally, the hierarchy entrusts to the laity certain functions which are more closely connected with pastoral duties, such as the teaching of Christian doctrine, certain liturgical actions, and the care of souls. By virtue of this mission, the laity are fully subject to higher ecclesiastical control in the performance of this work. As regards works and institutions in the temporal order, the role of the ecclesiastical hierarchy is to teach and authentically interpret the moral principles to be followed in temporal affairs. Furthermore, they have the right to judge, after careful consideration of all related matters and consultation with experts, whether or not such works and institutions conform to moral principles and the right to decide what is required for the protection and promotion of values of the supernatural order."

4. *Priests to promote particular forms of the Lay Apostolate* (art. 25, beg. of 2nd. par.): "Special care should be taken to select priests who are capable of promoting particular forms of the apostolate of the laity and are properly trained. Those who are engaged in this ministry represent the hierarchy in their pastoral activity by virtue of the mission they receive from the hierarchy. Always adhering faithfully to the spirit and teaching of the Church, they should promote proper relations between laity and hierarchy...."

5. *Diocesan and National Councils and Roman Secretariat for the Lay Apostolate* (art. 26): "In dioceses, insofar as possible, there should be councils which assist the apostolic work of the Church... these councils will be able to promote the mutual coordination of various lay associations and enterprises. Councils of this type should be established as far as possible also... in the national or international sphere. A special secretariat, moreover, should be established at the Holy See for the service and promotion of the lay apostolate. It can serve as... assisting the hierarchy and laity in their apostolic works with its advice. The various movements and projects of the apostolate of the laity throughout the world should also be represented in this secretariat."

XIV. DECREE ON THE MINISTRY AND LIFE OF PRIESTS

1. *Insurance and Support of Sick Priests* (art. 21, last par.): "Moreover, in nations where social security for the clergy is not yet aptly

established, let the Episcopal Conferences see to it that — in accord with
ecclesiastical and civil laws — there may be either diocesan institutes,
whether federated with one another or established for various dioceses
together, or territorial associations which under the vigilance of the
hierarchy would make sufficient and suitable provision for what is called
health insurance and the necessary support of priests who suffer from
sickness, invalid condition, or old age. Let priests share in this established
institute, prompted by a spirit of solidarity with their brothers to take part
in their tribulations while at the same time being freed from an anxious
concern for their own future so that they can cultivate evangelical
poverty more readily and give themselves fully to the salvation of souls.
Let those in charge of this act to bring together the institutes of various
nations in order that their strength be more firmly achieved and more
broadly based."

Although this is the only explicit reference to Episcopal Conferences
in this document, the following might have relevance to them if action
is to be taken on a national level:

2. *Pastoral Instruction after Ordination* (art. 19, next to last par. —
confer 5 above under the decree on priestly training): "... Moreover, let
bishops either individually or united in groups, see to it that all their
priests at established intervals, especially a few years after their ordination, may be able to frequent courses in which they will be given
the opportunity to acquire a fuller knowledge of pastoral methods and
theological science, both in order that they may strengthen their spiritual
life and mutually communicate their apostolic experiences with their
brothers . . . ."

3. *Equitable Remuneration for Priests* (art. 20, middle of 1st. par.):
". . . The bishops . . . should see to it — whether each individual for his
own diocese, or, more aptly, several together for their common territory —
that norms are established according to which suitable support is rightly
provided for those who do fulfill or have fulfilled a special office in the
service of the People of God. The remuneration received by each one,
in accord with his office and the conditions of time and place, should be
fundamentally the same for all in the same circumstances and befitting
his station. Moreover, those who have dedicated themselves to the service
of the priesthood, by reason of the remuneration they receive, should
not only be able to honorably provide for themselves but also themselves
be provided with some means of helping the needy. For the ministry to
the poor has always been held in great honor in the Church from its
beginnings. Furthermore, this remuneration should be such that it will
permit priests each year to take a suitable and sufficient vacation, something which indeed the bishops should see that their priests are able to
have."

4. *Diocesan and Regional Common Funds* (art. 21, middle of 1st. par.): ". . . Further it is hoped that insofar as is possible in individual dioceses or regions there be established a common fund enabling bishops to satisfy obligations to other deserving persons and meet the needs of various dioceses. This would also enable wealthier dioceses to help the poorer, that the need of the latter might be supplemented by the abundance of the former. These common funds, even though they should be principally made up of the offerings of the faithful, yet also should be provided for by other duly established sources."

XV. DECREE ON THE CHURCH'S MISSIONARY ACTIVITY

1. *Permanent Diaconate* (art. 16, last par.): "If it is considered useful by the Conferences of Bishops, the order of diaconate should be restored as a permanent state of life according to the rules laid down in the Council Constitution on the Church (cf., 2 above under the Constitution on the Church). Indeed, as regards those who perform the true functions of the diaconate, or preach the divine word as catechists, or rule the more isolated christian communities in the name of the pastor or bishop, or those who practice charity in social and charitable enterprises, it will indeed aid them to be strengthened by the imposition of hands handed down from the Apostles and to be more closely united to the altar. In this way their ministry will be more effectively fulfilled through the sacramental grace of the diaconate."

2. *Avoiding Over-Multiplication of Religious Congregations in the newer Churches* (art. 18, 3rd. par.): "In the newer Churches . . . the Conferences of Bishops shall see to it that congregations which have the identical apostolic aims shall not over-multiply to the detriment of both the religious life and the apostolate."

3. *Continuing Education of the Clergy* (art. 20, 5th. par. — cf., 2 above under the Decree on Priestly Training and 2 above under the Decree on Priestly Ministry and Life): "The Conference of Bishops shall see to it, that at specific times, courses on biblical, theological, spiritual and pastoral renewal are held so that their clergy may acquire a fuller knowledge of the sacred sciences and pastoral methods despite the variety of conditions and the changes of time."

4. *Fostering Dialogue with Various Groups* (art. 20, next to last par.): ". . . But since people everywhere are constantly becoming more group-minded, it certainly seems that the Conferences of Bishops should draw up joint plans for dialogue with each group . . . ."

5. *Adaptation according to Socio-Cultural Units* (art. 22, last par.): "It is therefore desired, and indeed, it is strongly recommended, that the Conferences of Bishops in each great socio-cultural geographical unit discuss this question together and agree upon one general plan to put this adaptation into effect."

6. *Specialists in Mission Science* (art. 26, end of last par.): "It is also strongly desired that the Regional Conferences of Bishops have plenty of these experts (in missionary needs and methods) available and put their knowledge and experience to good use in meeting the demands of their office. There should also be some who have a complete knowledge of mass-communications media, the importance of which must be given due consideration."

7. *Membership on the Board of Directors of the Propagation of the Faith* (art. 29, 6th. par.): "In the direction of this Dicasterium an active role with the right of deliberative vote shall be accorded selected representatives of all those who collaborate in mission work: bishops from around the world, after consultation with episcopal conferences . . . ."

8. *Collaboration in Mission Activity* (art. 31): "Episcopal Conferences should deliberate together the more important questions and urgent problems (of missionary activity), without however neglecting differences on the local level. To avoid wasting already insufficient personnel and funds and the multiplication of projects without necessity, it is recommended that they pool resources for undertakings which will serve the good of all. Such, for example, are seminaries, secondary and technical schools, and pastoral, catechetical, liturgical and social communications centers. This kind of cooperation, where practical, should also be established between different episcopal conferences." (Cf., 4 above under the Decree on the Pastoral Office of Bishops in the Church.)

9. *Norms of Relationship between Local Ordinaries and Mission Institutes in Mission Lands* (art. 32, next to last par.): "A new situation arises when the territorial commission (of a missionary institute) ceases. In that case conferences of Bishops and the institutes should by common agreement establish norms which will govern the relationship between the local ordinaries and the institutes. The Holy See will outline the general principles upon which regional or even particular agreements are to be based." (Cf., 3 above under the Decree on the Pastoral Office of Bishops in the Church.)

10. *Relationship between Conferences of Religious Institutes and Episcopal Conferences* (art. 33, 1st. par.): ". . . Highly advantageous, therefore, are conferences of religious men and unions of religious women in which all the institutes of the same nation or region take part. These

conferences shall try to find out what can be done through common effort and shall maintain a close relationship with episcopal conferences."

11. *Coordination of Cooperation in Mission Activity* (art. 38, 5th. par.): "So that the mission of the bishops can be exercised more effectively for the good of the whole Church, it is fitting that episcopal conferences supervise the arrangements which are made to secure orderly cooperation within their own region."

12. *Missionary Duties of Episcopal Conferences* (art. 38, last two par.): "In their conferences the bishops shall treat of releasing priests of the diocesan clergy for the work of preaching the Gospel to all peoples; of a fixed percentage of each diocesan budget which must be given each year for the missions (cf., 4 above under the Decree on the Pastoral Office of Bishops in the Church); of ways and means to assist directly in the government and organization of missions; of mission Institutes and seminaries of the diocesan clergy to help the missions, including, if necessary, the establishment of such; of the fostering of closer links between these institutes and the dioceses. The episcopal conferences likewise are responsible for initiating and fostering agencies to extend a fraternal welcome and provide proper pastoral care for those who for the sake of work or study immigrate from mission lands . . . ."

The following might have bearing as well on the work of episcopal conferences on a national level, although somewhat more indirectly:

13. *Training of Catechists* (art. 17, 3rd. par.): "Hence, as many diocesan and regional schools as possible are to be set up in order to train future catechists . . . ."

14. *Collaboration of the Laity in Missionary Activity* (art. 21, end of 3rd par., and art. 41, 1st. par.): "Indeed, wherever possible, lay people must be prepared for a more immediate collaboration with the hierarchy in performing special missions for the proclaiming of the Gospel and for communicating Christian doctrine in order to add vigor to the growing Church . . . 31. The laity shall cooperate in the Church's work of spreading the Gospel and as both witnesses and living instruments participate in her saving mission, especially if, recognized as called by God, they are enrolled by the bishops in this work."

CONTRIBUTORS

WILLIAM W. BASSETT, Associate Professor in the School of Canon Law, Catholic University of America, wrote *The Determination of Rite* (Rome: Gregorian University, 1967), edited *The Bond of Marriage* (Notre Dame University Press, 1968), and published articles in *The Jurist, Thought, American Ecclesiastical Review,* and *Cross Currents.*

PAUL M. BOYLE, C.P., Provincial Superior of the Passionist Fathers, is the President of the Conference of Major Superiors of Men. He is a past President of the Canon Law Society of America, and has consulted with many religious communities during their process of postconciliar renewal. He is the author of numerous articles on various aspects of Canon Law.

JAMES A. CORIDEN, Assistant Professor in the School of Theology, Catholic University of America, was the chairman of the symposium. He edited *We, The People of God . . . , A Study of Constitutional Government for the Church* (Huntington, Ind.: Our Sunday Visitor, 1968) and *The Case for Freedom: Human Rights in the Church* (Washington: Corpus, 1969), which were the proceedings of previous symposia. He has contributed articles to *American Ecclesiastical Review* and *Chicago Studies.*

FRANCIS DVORNIK, Professor Emeritus at Dumbarton Oaks, Trustees for Harvard University, is the author of several important works on Byzantine and Slavic history including, more recently, *The Slavs in European History and Civilization* (Rutgers University Press, 1966), *Early Christian and Byzantine Political Philosophy* (Washington: Dumbarton Oaks, 1966), and *Byzantine Missions Among the Slavs,* (Rutgers University Press, 1970).

301

JAMES J. HENNESEY, S.J., Associate Professor of Modern and American Religious History at Fordham University, wrote *The First Council of the Vatican: The American Experience* (New York: Herder & Herder, 1963). He has published over fifty articles on various aspects of American Church history.

WILLIAM K. LEAHY, a priest of the Archdiocese of Philadelphia, received an S.S.L. from the Pontifical Biblical Institute and an S.T.D. from the Angelicum University in Rome. He assisted the American bishops during the Second Vatican Council and later co-edited *Third Session Council Speeches of Vatican II* (Paulist Press, 1966).

JOHN E. LYNCH, C.S.P., Assistant Professor of History and Canon Law at Catholic University of America, has taught and written for several years in the earliest periods of Church history. He has published articles in *Franciscan Studies* and *The Jurist*.

RICHARD P. McBRIEN, Associate Professor of Theology at Boston College, is the author of *The Church in the Thought of Bishop John Robinson* (Philadelphia: Westminster Press, 1966), *Do We Need the Church?* (New York; Newman Press, 1970), and several articles in the area of ecclesiology.

FREDERICK R. McMANUS, Dean of the School of Canon Law at Catholic University of America and Director of the Secretariat of the Bishop's Committee on the Liturgy, has written numerous articles on problems of public worship and church order. He is the author of *Sacramental Liturgy* (New York: Herder & Herder, 1967).

ROBERT E. McNALLY, S.J., Professor of Church History at Fordham University, wrote *Reform of the Church* (New York: Herder & Herder, 1963) and *The Unreformed Church* (New York: Sheed & Ward, 1965), in addition to several other studies of the late medieval and Reformation periods.

GENERAL INDEX

Agde, Synod of (506) 49
Alanus 93
Albrecht of Hohenzollern 113ff.
Alexander II, Pope 83
Alexander III, Pope 87, 104, 105, 108
Alexander IV, Pope 93
Ambrose, St. 62
Ammann, Bishop Joachim 202f.
Anastasius II, Pope 67
Anselm of Lucca 101
Antioch, Council of (?341) 27f., 32, 224n.20
Apostolic delegate 181f.
Apostolica Sollicitudo 267, 271, 290
Apostolicam Actuositatem 257-8, 293-5
Arles, Synod of (314) 48, 51, 62, 224n.20
Ashtishat, Synod of (435) 42

Baltimore, III Plenary Council of (1884) 142, 145, 191

Benedict VIII, Pope 105
Benedict XV, Pope 148, 149
Bernard of Clairvaux 84
Bernard of Pavia 103
Bernold of Constance 86, 101
Bishops, appointment of 90-94, 223
Boniface, St. 73f.
Boniface VIII, Pope 94, 97, 220, 221
Burgos, Council of (1085) 85

Cajetan 117, 122f.
Callistus, Pope 61, 224n.20
Carroll, Archbishop John 143, 190
Carthage, III Synod of 43
causae majores 67f., 70, 76, 83
Celestine, Pope 52, 91
Celestine III, Pope 95, 106
Censures, papal reservation of 104-106
Chalcedon, Council of (451) 33, 42
Charlemagne 50

AUTHORS CITED

307